BUILDING
BELIEF

Constructing Faith
from the Ground Up

CHAD V. MEISTER

BakerBooks

Grand Rapids, Michigan

© 2006 by Chad V. Meister

Published by Baker Books
a division of Baker Publishing Group
P.O. Box 6287, Grand Rapids, MI 49516-6287
www.bakerbooks.com

Printed in the United States of America

Library of Congress Cataloging-in-Publication Data
Meister, Chad V., 1965–
    Building belief : constructing faith from the ground up / Chad V. Meister.
        p.   cm.
    Includes bibliographical references (p   ) and index.
    ISBN 10: 0-8010-6569-0 (pbk.)
    ISBN 978-0-8010-6569-9 (pbk.)
    1. Apologetics. I. Title.
BT1103.M45 2006
239—dc22   2006005989

BUILDING
BELIEF

God's best
to you!

[signature]

To my wife, Tammi,
whose friendship, love, prayer,
and support were fundamental in the
construction of my faith

Contents

Acknowledgments

I am very pleased to acknowledge a number of people for their help in the development of this project. Several philosophers and teachers have been instrumental in the formation of my Christian faith. Francis Schaeffer introduced to me the concept of a worldview and to the very enterprise of having reasons for faith. Norman Geisler got me interested in defending my faith, and his life and writings have been a real inspiration. Bill Craig and J. P. Moreland have been exemplars of Christian scholarship and living, and I greatly appreciate their friendship and encouragement. Through his teaching and writings, Dallas Willard has given me new lenses by which to see and understand the central message of Jesus. Lee Strobel and Mark Mittelberg have modeled for me how to communicate to real people and have given me opportunities I could have only imagined. Scott Chapman and the late Bob Passantino have been friends and fellow advocates for the faith for many years, and I appreciate their wisdom and example. I owe a great debt to all of these men, and this book reflects their continued impact on my life.

More than a few people helped in the development of the manuscript. I owe much to Jim Stump and Donald McLaughlin for reading through most of the text. Their careful eye for detail and their razor-sharp minds have made this a much better book than it would have been otherwise. My research assistants, Dave Cramer and David Wright, have been invaluable resources. My teaching cohort, Beth McLaughlin, has been a true friend and a source of spiritual encouragement. All my colleagues in the Division of Religion and Philosophy at Bethel College have been supportive, and I am blessed to be among them. I am especially thankful to Fred Long, Gene Carpenter, Tim Erdel, John Dendiu, and Rob Myers for carefully reading portions of the manuscript and offering helpful insights from their respective areas of expertise. I am grateful for the secretarial support of Barb Rodgers and Renee Kaufman, who diligently typed, scanned, and formatted documents. Bethel College graciously offered me a Summer Research Grant and release time funded by Bethel's Lilly Fund for Excellence (Lilly Endowment, Inc.), which enabled me to devote the time necessary to complete this book. I wish to thank Bob Hosack and Paul Brinkerhoff at Baker Books and Laura Weller for their encouragement and excellent editorial support. Also, I am indebted to countless students and seekers over the years, especially Margarette Firman, who worked through early forms of this material, challenging the arguments and counterarguments and engaging in the dialectic.

Finally, I am thankful for my wonderful wife and best friend, Tammi, to whom I dedicate this book. She was exceedingly patient through periods of my questioning and doubting early in our marriage, never sure where I would end up. And she was longsuffering through several years of work, buoying me through this and many other projects. She carefully read through each chapter of this book, some chapters multiple times, and offered numerous helpful insights. She is the love of my life and a wife and mother of which none greater can be conceived, to borrow a line from St. Anselm. Our sons, Justin and Joshua, are the delight of our lives, and I appreciate their willingness to sacrifice spending time with me more than they should have to do.

Introduction

All human beings by nature desire to know.

Aristotle

About ten years ago I headed up a ministry at Willow Creek Community Church called Defenders (now called Truthquest). One afternoon Lee Strobel, who was a teaching pastor there at the time, asked me if I would be interested in meeting a guy named Bill* who was a visitor at the church. According to Lee, Bill was an atheist, but he still wanted to talk about God. I agreed to meet, and Bill ended up coming over to my house for the evening. In preparation for our time together, I sketched out a diagram that was the culmination of several years of study and reflection as well as what I take to be a divine epiphany that afternoon. I call it the Apologetics Pyramid,[1] and this book consists of that same basic structure (see figure that follows) plus ten years of research and reflection on the topics of which it is composed. It is based on my personal journey from being a spiritually seeking engineer to becoming a convinced Christian philosopher, and it includes real-life stories involving me and people of other faiths and belief systems.

* Most of the personal names referenced and used in illustrations in this book have been changed.

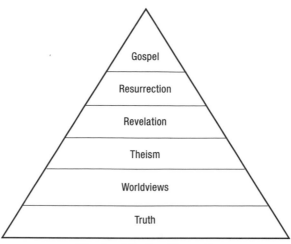

The Apologetics Pyramid

The Apologetics Pyramid

If you are like most people, you are probably troubled by the opposing cultural concepts of pluralism on the one hand and absolutism on the other. You may not be familiar with this terminology, but chances are the ideas they represent are of central importance to your way of thinking about the world in which we live. Let me explain.

The twentieth century demonstrated important and radical changes from previous generations in the way people thought and believed. There were social changes: we went from typical two-parent homes with the father being the breadwinner to single-parent homes with mothers advancing to high-level management positions at major corporations. There were moral changes: we went from the prohibition of alcohol to allowing abortion on demand and moving toward the legalization of gay marriage. And there were religious changes: we went from mandating prayer in public schools to disallowing religious symbols on virtually all government property. Along with this religious evolution, the past century was also characterized by the infusion of dozens of new religions and belief systems, including novel and non-Western religious teachings like yoga and transcendental meditation, which have now become mainstream.

Back in the "old days," it was easy to criticize and condemn other ways of thinking and acting because they were foreign and unfamiliar concepts. When my grandfather was young, Hinduism, Buddhism, and Islam, for example, were considered by most in the West to be barbaric and evil religions held by uneducated, malicious, and even wildly immoral people groups. But now that Hindus, Buddhists, Muslims, and adherents of many other religions have become a regular part of our culture, and even our next-door neighbors, we have found most of them to be not all that different from ourselves. They are generally kind, generous, friendly, and thoughtful people—not at all like previous generations described them. Furthermore, they are typically as educated about and devoted to their views as we are to ours, if not more so.

Here, then, is the rub. We have our views—moral, social, religious, or what have you—and they have their views. And many of our views are significantly different from many of their views. This is *pluralism*. In the past, people held to the idea that if two different views contradict one another, then one of them must be true and the other false. This is *absolutism*. How do we unite pluralism and absolutism? Pluralism in this sense is simply a fact: rich and diverse beliefs coexist with our own. So do we dogmatically hold to absolutism and believe that our views are right and all other views are wrong? Or do we ditch absolutism—a view many now believe to be narrow, arrogant, and excessively rigid—and agree that everyone has his or her own truth? "To each his own," as the slogan goes. In this new century, there are no more fundamental questions for us to reflect on and discuss than these.

As the title of this book suggests, I maintain that we can, and should, work on building belief in our spiritual lives. I also think that a journey of this sort never ends. We will never have everything all figured out; the questions of life are just too big and the answers too complex for our finite minds to fully comprehend them all. This realization should create an attitude of humility within us as we begin this arduous but exciting quest. Nonetheless, I believe we can find truth and can be certain about many things, including some of these most fundamental issues in life.

My own spiritual journey began about two decades ago. I was working as a field engineer for Hewlett Packard and had only recently become a Christian. My conversion was one based primarily on my awareness of what seemed to be meaninglessness of life without God and my ultimate need for him. But my faith did not, at that time, have any significant, well thought out foundation. To put it differently, I didn't have what I considered to be any solid evidence for why I believed what I believed. I simply had not explored that aspect of faith.

Within six months of beginning the Hewlett Packard job, I discovered that I was working with a Hindu, a Mormon, a Wiccan (Wiccans are "white witches"—a term that designates witches who do not use magic to harm others), a New Age devotee, and a member of the religion founded by Herbert Armstrong, the Worldwide Church of God. None of them believed what I believed, and all of them held strongly to their own convictions. In our conversations these co-workers—some overtly and others unwittingly—were systematically undermining my new Christian faith. To top it off, one of my close friends who had been a Christian for many years was studying with the Jehovah's Witnesses, and he too, without being aware of it, was destroying my beliefs with the questions he was raising.

I became so frustrated and confused that I decided to shelve my Christianity and study these different religions to find out if one of them was really true. I wasn't sure if I could ever discover the answer to this question, but I decided to try anyway. It didn't really matter to me which one was true, but, to paraphrase the early Christian theologian Augustine, I wanted to seek truth wherever it may lead. In the pages that follow, then, we will be systematically working up the Apologetics Pyramid in our attempt to build belief. We will begin with *truth* in chapter 1, and through real-life stories, examples, and evidences, we will continue our journey until we reach the peak of the pyramid. I've sketched below a general overview of where we're headed.

Truth (Chapter 1)

Francis Schaeffer, one of the most important Christian thinkers of the twentieth century, pointed out years ago that a crucial starting point in dialoguing with others is to begin on common ground—to begin where everyone can agree. This common ground, he argued (and I will argue further in chapter 1), begins with the most fundamental law of logic and reality, the law of noncontradiction. It is common because it doesn't matter what a person's cultural or religious background; once it is carefully analyzed, it seems that we should all agree to its being universally true.

Beginning on common ground is important, because once a person sees the universality and ultimate rational undeniability of this basic law of thought and how it demonstrates that truth is absolute and not relative, the question of whether two contradictory claims can both be true is forever silenced. In other words, it proves, for example, that despite the fact that there are many different religious viewpoints, they cannot all be right given that they affirm contradictory claims. Either one of them is true and the others are false, or all of them are false and something else is true. For our postmodern age, this is an essential, though often denied, principle to be grasped. Establishing it is the first level of the Apologetics Pyramid.

I lay this approach out as a pyramid for two reasons. First, as a person moves up the various levels (and we will be doing so chapter by chapter), he or she is moving into an ever-narrower web of beliefs until reaching the peak. Second, just as with a pyramid, the bottom levels serve as the foundation for those above. As you move up a pyramid, each step should be solidly based on the previous one. So it is with this apologetics method. When you reach the peak, you have a secure structure below on which to stand, for you have constructed faith from the ground up.

The question of truth and logic, then, is foundational for everything that follows, and one should begin here. This is the focus of chapter 1. Once a person sees that truth is absolute and not relative, however, the next logical question is, what then is the truth? This is the right question. But the field of belief systems is too large to begin just anywhere. For example, studying all of the various religions themselves to establish which one may have more evidence than another would be a daunting and virtually endless task. There is, however, an easier way to advance in the quest.

Worldviews (Chapters 2–3)

As a number of scholars have demonstrated, by defining a worldview broadly enough, one can distill all possibilities down into a very small number. I maintain that these worldviews are best expressed by dividing them into three categories: *theism* (the belief in God or the gods), *atheism* (the belief in no God or gods), and *pantheism* (the belief that everything is God). A worldview, so described, includes an all-encompassing perspective of reality. It is the grid through which all of life is viewed. In chapter 2 I describe these different worldviews and mention various religions that fit within them.

Having established that truth is absolute in chapter 1, and having categorized the worldviews in chapter 2, I argue in chapter 3 that since each of the three worldviews contradicts the other two, only one of these alternatives can be true. I demonstrate the implausibility of the atheistic and pantheistic worldviews; and by eliminating them, a number of belief systems are also removed as viable alternatives. As with each of the levels of the pyramid, I examine philosophical and empirical arguments and offer real-life experiences and discussions to demonstrate the strengths and weaknesses of each of the worldviews. By the end of chapter 3, we are left with theism. But rather than merely be *left* with theism as the only reasonable alternative, I employ three powerful arguments *for* the existence of God as we move up to the next level.

Theism (Chapters 4–6)

The first two arguments for the theistic worldview, the argument from design and the cosmological argument, go all the way back to the earliest Greek philosophers. But these arguments have taken on new forms in recent times. Recent work in cosmology, physics, and microbiology has created a resurgence of interest in the design argument, so much so that even contemporary atheist philosophers, biologists, and other scholars are having to deal with its compelling force. I expound on this argument for God as the first positive case for the existence of a creator in chapter 4.

The cosmological argument on which I focus stands head and shoulders above the standard textbook accounts of cosmological arguments. Only recently has it begun to receive the full attention it deserves, and I demonstrate its persuasive force in chapter 5.

Finally, as C. S. Lewis argued a half century ago, we live in a moral universe and this morality needs a moral lawgiver to explain its existence. This argument from morality, however, needs to be reformulated for a new era. Many people in our generation believe that morality is subjective and personal, the conventional creation of human beings, rather than objective and universal. For example, I have spoken with people who believe that what Hitler did in Nazi Germany was "fine for him." In chapter 6, then, I use new examples and arguments to support the claim of universal morals and values and then, building on these claims, argue that God is the Moral Lawgiver.

Revelation (Chapter 7)

Having demonstrated that theism is more reasonable to believe than the other two worldviews, the next question is, which of the theistic options is true? To settle this question, we will need to delve into archaeological discoveries, the analysis of ancient texts, and other historical evidences. This project is the focus of chapter 7.

Given the impressive abundance of evidence for the reliability and divine inspiration of the Old and New Testaments, I argue that the Christian faith clearly emerges as the most reasonable, and in fact true, theistic system of belief.

Resurrection (Chapter 8)

As we move up to the next level, I examine the evidence for the resurrection of Jesus of Nazareth. The historical testimony for this event is well attested, even granting the limited amount of evidence that many contemporary "liberal" and critical scholars allow. I present six historical truths that support the view that Jesus rose bodily from the dead. I also examine several naturalistic explanations for the resurrection. Without heavy-handed or loaded claims, I demonstrate that, all things considered, it is more reasonable to believe in Jesus's resurrection than not.

Gospel (Chapter 9)

Finally, in chapter 9, we reach the peak of the pyramid, where I examine the gospel that Jesus and the apostles taught. It is different from what many people believe it to be. It is truly *gospel*—that is, good news—and Jesus described it as a kingdom more valuable than buried treasure. His message promises life to the fullest, both now and into eternity.

Conclusion

Beginning, then, without presuppositions or religious bias, we systematically and rationally come to see that Christianity is true—that Jesus is the Messiah, the Savior of the human race. He invites all of us to join him in his wonderful kingdom.

I mentioned earlier a discussion I had one evening with an atheist named Bill. Our time together lasted well into the night, and many of the objections he raised that evening and later on are included in this book. He was an informed atheist but an open-minded one nonetheless. My hope is that wherever you are on your spiritual pilgrimage—whether atheist or devoted Christian or somewhere in between—you will *use* this book and not merely *read* it. Seeing that there are objective criteria that can be utilized along the path to constructing a reasoned faith is important. What I have here is only an introduction to that quest, so I have included a number of references at the end of each chapter for further study. These references include works that support the views argued for here as well as some of the best critiques of them in print. I encourage you to read many of them for yourself so that you will be an informed and objective truth-seeker.

Work through the arguments with an open mind, and as you finish the book, find out if you reach the same conclusion Bill did.

1

Your Truth and My Truth

Why Can't Everyone Be Right?

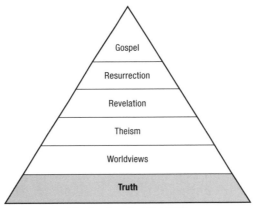

The Apologetics Pyramid

"An argument isn't just contradiction."
"Can be."
"No it can't. An argument is a connected series of statements intended to establish a proposition."
"No it isn't."
"Yes it is."

"Argument Clinic," from Monty Python's *Previous Record*

I recently had an extended conversation with a young woman named Danae who is a Wiccan, and I discovered that she, like most Wiccans, believes that there are no absolutes—no moral absolutes, no religious absolutes, no absolutes whatsoever. Danae argued that all absolutist claims are arrogant, narrow-minded, and unjust and should be condemned in a pluralistic society like ours. Of course this strong claim against absolutes is itself an absolutist claim, but she neither understood the inconsistency in absolutely denying absolutes nor cared whether her views were consistent. As I tried to point out her inconsistency, she gave an apathetic nod and noted that it didn't really matter anyway.

While this "who cares" attitude toward holding inconsistent beliefs is not the norm, it is a troubling trend that I have experienced in many discussions recently. It is troubling for a couple of reasons. First, it reflects an attitude that *truth* doesn't really matter. As I pushed the discussion a bit further with Danae and asked her why she didn't see a problem with holding a view that was inconsistent, she responded by saying that she has her views and I have my views, and why can't we be happy with that? She went on to ask why one of us has to be right and the other wrong. In the ensuing discussion, it seemed that she wasn't really interested in whether her views *were* right or wrong, but only in making sure that I didn't attempt to point out whether they were or not. It seems much nicer if we can just all be right.

An even more troubling problem with this laissez-faire attitude toward inconsistent beliefs is the idea that *there is no absolute truth anyway*. As one high school student recently mentioned to me, since there is no *real* truth, no Truth with a capital *T*, why hassle someone about his or her particular views? Why not just live and let live? Why not stay away from the old-fashioned attitude that "I'm right and you're wrong"?

This denial of absolute truth is common not only among those in the Wiccan religion, however. In a recent nationwide poll conducted by the Barna Research Group, only about 20 percent of all adults in the United States believe in absolute moral truth, a significant drop from the previous year, and the figure is almost as high when referring to religious absolutes.[1] The percentages drop even lower for younger adults.[2] Most people simply don't believe in absolutes anymore. Whether referring to morality, religion, or just about anything, more and more people in the West are becoming adherents of a view referred to as *relativism*—a denial of absolute and objective truths.

This notion that your views are true for you and my views are true for me often stems from a deeper philosophical belief that truth itself is relative, and nowhere is this belief more evident than in colleges and universities today. As political philosopher Allan Bloom notes in his best-selling book, *The Closing of the American Mind*, "There is one thing a professor can be absolutely certain of: almost every student entering the university believes, or says he believes, that truth is relative."[3]

If truth is relative, then of course it would be pompous to hold that I am right and you are wrong about matters of religion and morality (or anything else for that matter). But that is the question: Is truth relative? Are there no absolutes? For if truth is relative, then Danae is probably doing the right thing in chastising me for pointing out inconsistencies in other views. But if truth is not relative, if there really are absolute religious and moral truths, then attempting to find out what they are seems to be something we should not avoid but rather should pursue with all diligence and sincerity. After all, eternity may well be in the balance.

That is the question we will focus on in this chapter. Is truth relative and *determined* by what we believe, or are there absolute truths that can be *discovered* and rationally believed? Furthermore, if there are such absolute truths, how can we find out what they are? We will first examine these questions since they are fundamental to constructing a reasonable faith. Be prepared, though. These are not easy questions to deal with, and this first chapter is a bit tough going. Hard work here, however, will have tremendous benefits as we begin to build belief.[4]

What Is Truth?

Just before Jesus of Nazareth was delivered up to be crucified, Pontius Pilate asked him this seemingly simple and innocent question: "What is truth?" (John 18:38). The answer appears, at first glance, to be so obvious as to be not even worth mentioning. After all, we all know what "truth" is. Or do we? We use the word *true* countless times throughout our lives, so you would think we must know what it means. But upon further inspection, this question turns out to be a bit more difficult to answer than one might suppose.

The Correspondence View of Truth

Historically there has been a fairly consistent view of what truth is. The view even has a name—the *correspondence view* (or theory) of truth. As early as the fourth century BC, the great Greek philosopher Plato offered a description of the correspondence view in his book the *Sophist*.[5] As he describes it, the *true* claim is the one that states things the way they are, and the false claim is the one that states things differently from the way they are. In his book *Metaphysics*, Plato's student Aristotle offered a similar view. As he put it, "To say of what is that it is not, or of what is not that it is, is false, while to say of what is that it is, and of what is not that it is not, is true; so that he who says of anything that it is, or that it is not, will say either what is true or what is false."[6] This is a commonsense description of what *true* means, and most people up until the late nineteenth century agreed with it. Truth, then, was understood to be a kind of agreement with reality—a correspondence between what is stated and the facts about which the statement is concerned. This view of truth reflects our seemingly lucid notion that what is out there in the world is what makes a statement true or false.

To expound briefly on this view of truth, consider the following claim about our own planet:

> It is true that Earth is roughly 94 million miles from the sun on July 4, 2005.

What I mean by this claim is that the statement "Earth is roughly 94 million miles from the sun on July 4, 2005" corresponds with the fact that planet Earth is currently 94 million miles from the sun (on the day, July 4, 2005). If we were referring to Venus rather than Earth, then of course the statement would be not true. But, in fact, it is true—that is, the statement matches with reality. Reality—the facts of the world—make the claim true.

At one level the point is so simple that attempting to explain it makes it sound more confusing than it actually is. Even my son, when he was three years old, knew what I meant when I said that something was true. If, for example, I told him that it was true that the cookie was in the bottom cupboard, he knew that what I meant was that my statement matched with the fact. He went after the cookie in the bottom cupboard. Understanding what *truth* means is really not complicated at all. And the apparent simplicity of this understanding of truth has been one of the reasons for its constancy throughout history.

However, at the end of the nineteenth century, new views of truth began to unfold and this historic view underwent unprecedented scrutiny. A number of objections were raised against it, many of them quite technical, and new views of truth began to emerge.[7] For example, one central criticism had to do with statements involving claims that could not be empirically or scientifically verified. Consider this claim:

> It is true that the God of the Bible exists.

On the correspondence view of truth that we have been looking at, what is meant by this claim is that the statement "the God of the Bible exists" matches with reality—the God of the Bible is really there. But how could one ever prove such a claim from an empirical standpoint? We cannot see God in the heavens even with the powerful Hubble telescope! This claim about God seems to be of a different kind from the one about planet Earth noted above, and since this claim about God cannot be empirically verified, the argument goes, one could never really know if it is true or not.

This criticism of the correspondence view of truth was so significant that some scholars in the early twentieth century attempted to eliminate these kinds of religious claims altogether by arguing that they are meaningless. Talk about God is meaningless, they argued, since there is no way to verify a correspondence between statements and facts about God. However, this criticism turned out to be self-refuting since the claim that nothing is true unless it can be empirically verified cannot itself be empirically verified![8]

What should be done, then, with statements that include unverifiable claims like the one about God's existence? One approach was to develop new theories of truth—ones that could "make sense" of such claims rather than eliminate them from rational discourse.

The Coherence View of Truth

One of these new views of truth, often referred to as the *coherence view* (or theory), included the idea that truth is not a relation between statements and facts, as with the correspondence view, but rather it is a logical coherence among a set of beliefs. On this view, then, if one's beliefs are internally consistent with one another, they are true. Like mathematical or geometrical systems in which a statement is coherent when it can be logically derived from axioms and other more basic statements, so too on this view of truth our beliefs are true when they are logically consistent with our presuppositions and other beliefs we hold.

Consider, for example, the claim about God noted above:

It is true that the God of the Bible exists.

On the coherence view of truth, this claim would be true *for me* if it is logically consistent with other underlying and core beliefs I hold. But it would not be true *for you* if it is not logically consistent with other core beliefs you hold. So, on this view, it wouldn't be necessary to find out empirically if the claim matches reality or not; what is necessary are the logical relations among the various beliefs that people hold.

This view of truth has real benefits. For example, it seems to be very politically correct, since truth becomes relativized in such a way that I cannot say you are wrong merely on the basis of your view disagreeing with mine. We could both be right even though our views contradict one another. I can have my truth and you can have your truth. It also seems to entail an easier way of *discovering* what is true. Rather than finding out whether my view matches with reality or not (as the correspondence view requires), which can be a very daunting task, truth is simply what is consistent for me to believe given my other core beliefs. On the coherence view, then, there need not even be an objective "reality" in order to make truth claims. All that is required is logical consistency.

Adherents of the coherence view also note that we often do, in fact, *test* truth claims by noting their coherence with other beliefs. For example, contrary to my goddaughter's recent belief, I am not in the least bit tempted to think it is true that Winnie-the-Pooh is alive and currently on a great adventure with Piglet and Tigger. Why? Because such a view is not at all consistent with the rest of my beliefs, one of which is that fictional characters are just that—fictional.

However, as good as it may sound, the coherence view is unsatisfactory and ultimately untenable as a view of truth, and for several reasons. First, note that fairy tales and lies can be logically consistent. For example, A. A. Milne, the writer of the Pooh stories, may have a completely logical system in which the characters of his novels "live" and interact. Nevertheless, they are just stories. Pooh, Piglet, and Tigger never did, in fact, go on any great adventures, for they are merely fictitious characters. On the coherence theory, truth is synonymous with mere logical consistency, but something can be logically consistent and yet not match with reality. But surely matching with reality is what we mean when we use the word *true* of something. When my son asks me if the Pooh stories are really true (he does, in fact, ask such things), I don't respond by saying (or believing), "Yes, the stories are true, for they are logically consistent within themselves." Rather, I say, "No, they are not really true."

Furthermore, people sometimes make up lies that are completely consistent from a logical perspective yet don't match with reality. I can remember as a young boy making up a story to tell my grandparents about a missing dollar that I stole from a secret compartment in their refrigerator. It was a great story, and quite consistent. I was very proud of myself at the time for making it up. Unfortunately, it was a lie. But for the coherence theorist, such claims, since they are consistent, turn out to be true! Too bad I didn't know about this view of truth as a boy, or I could have avoided a lot of guilt. More seriously, it is obvious that such a view of truth is not what we mean when we use the word *true*. While logical consistency may well be a good *test* for truth, it cannot be what truth *actually is*. In other words, logical consistency may be a necessary condition for something's being true, but it is not a sufficient condition.

A second problem with the coherence view of truth is that it violates an inviolable law of logic—the law of noncontradiction. This is an incredibly important law to grasp, as we will see in the next few chapters, one even more fundamental than physical laws like the law of gravity? So as we work through this thorny and complex topic over the next few pages, hang in there to the end. The benefits of understanding it far outweigh the mental sweat generated in the process of grasping it. To comprehend the law of noncontradiction, then, and how it is inviolable, we will need to begin by using a few symbols and diagrams.

The law of noncontradiction* can be symbolized in this form:

$$A \neq \sim A$$

This formulation is sometimes expressed as "A cannot equal negative A." It can also be expressed as "If A is the case, it cannot be that notA (or the opposite of A) is the case." Or this way: "If A is true then notA cannot be true." The point here is simply that two contradictory claims cannot both be true—*true* in the way we really use the word (they cannot both be the case in the same way and at the same time).[9] Now the letter A may represent any claim or proposition. So, if we make the letter A represent the claim "The Eiffel Tower is located in Paris," then we can plug A into the formula, and it now reads, "If it is the case that the Eiffel Tower is located in Paris, then it cannot be the case that the Eiffel Tower is not located in Paris." Or, to put it more simply, the Eiffel Tower cannot both be in Paris and not be in Paris at the same time.

This seems straightforward enough. It also follows from this law that if it is the case that the Eiffel Tower is located in Paris *for me*, it cannot be the case that the Eiffel Tower is not located in Paris *for you* (or vice versa). You may believe that it is not located there, and you may even have logically consistent reasons for believing so. But since it really is located there (A), it doesn't matter how hard or sincerely a person believes it is not there (~A); either it is located in Paris or it is not, and as it turns out, it is.

As I already noted, the A in this formulation represents *any* claim or proposition. So you could also plug in religious claims as well. Let A represent "The Buddha offers the only path to a wonderful afterlife." Plugging this into our formula, we get "If it is the case that the Buddha offers the only path to a wonderful afterlife, then it cannot be the case that a non-Buddha offers the only path to a wonderful afterlife." In other words, if the Buddha offers the only path, there are no other paths! The Buddha cannot offer the only path *for me* while Muhammad or Jesus offers the only path *for you*. You cannot have it both ways. Someone is right and someone is wrong when such exclusive claims are made.

---

*In sybolizing the law of noncontradiction, the symbol "~" will be utilized, as it is commonly used in symbolic logic, to refer to the negation of that to which it is attached.

I was recently in a local coffee shop and overheard a conversation between two college students. One was a Christian and the other was a Zen Buddhist. The Christian was sharing the Good News with the Buddhist, and the Buddhist responded by asking why Christians are always saying that their view is right while everyone else's is wrong. "Why can't we just all be right?" he asked. "Why do you have to tell me I'm wrong?"

The Christian struggled a bit with a response, and I asked if I could join in the conversation. They both agreed, so I took a napkin and began to draw out the law of noncontradiction.[10] I then drew a box around it as in the diagram below.

$$A \neq {\sim}A$$

I asked the Buddhist if he had ever heard of this law, and he noted that he had. So I explained that given this law, if Christianity were true (if it were the case that Jesus offers the only way of salvation, as he claims in John 14:6), then it could not be true that there are other ways of salvation. He disagreed. He said that Christianity could be true *to me,* and Zen Buddhism could be true *to him.* So I said, "In other words, you believe the following:

$$A = {\sim}A$$

"Yes," he said. "It can be the case that Christianity is true (for you) and 'not Christianity' (Buddhism, that is) is true (for me)."

"But this is impossible," I quipped. "This violates the inviolable law of noncontradiction!"

"I don't believe in that law," he said. "It's simply false."

At this point I suggested that we call his view the "law of relativism," and I placed it directly above the law of noncontradiction, as shown below.

$A = {\sim}A$	Law of Relativism
$A \neq {\sim}A$	Law of Noncontradiction

I then asked him if he was saying that the law of relativism was true while the law of noncontradiction was false. "Yes," he said. "The law of noncontradiction is clearly false."

I then suggested that, for the sake of argument, we call the law of relativism A, and since the law of noncontradiction is clearly not the law of relativism, we call the law of noncontradiction ~A. So then we have the following:

A = ~A	Law of Relativism	→ A
A ≠ ~A	Law of Noncontradiction	→ ~A

Now the problem, of course, is that he was saying that A is the case, not ~A. But this *is* the law of noncontradiction! A ≠ ~A. In other words, he was using the law of noncontradiction in an attempt to refute the law of noncontradiction. So I drew his contradictory position on the napkin:

A = ~A	Law of Relativism	→ A
		≠
A ≠ ~A	Law of Noncontradiction	→ ~A

This is what philosophers call a self-stultifying claim. It is similar to the claim "I cannot write a word of English." Of course I just *did* write a word of English, so I refuted my own claim. It is impossible to deny the law of noncontradiction, since in the denial one is claiming that something is the case as opposed to its not being the case. That is to say, one is claiming that something is the case (A) rather than its not being the case (≠ ~A). One is thus using the law of noncontradiction in an attempt to deny the law of noncontradiction. Once this undeniable fact sinks in, the proverbial lightbulb flashes on and one sees that it is literally impossible to deny this law. It is an eternal truth that one simply cannot refute.[11]

So how does this relate to the views of truth noted above? Well, remember that the coherence view includes the possibility that two contradictory claims are both true. But this cannot be. Two contradictory claims cannot both be true—that is, true in the way we actually use the word. So the coherence view of truth is fallacious.

The Pragmatic View of Truth

Another attempt to get at the nature of truth is to define it neither as a relation between statements and facts (as with the correspondence view), nor as logical coherence among one's beliefs (as with the coherence view), but rather as what is useful or expedient to believe. This view, referred to as the *pragmatic view* (or theory) of truth, was first expressed this way: "The true is only the expedient in the way of our behaving, expedient in almost any fashion, and expedient in the long run and on the whole course."[12] Simply put, in the pragmatic view, what is true is what works for me. This view is even more radical in its relativism than the coherence view, since not even logical coherence is an essential element of it. What works for me—what is useful for me to believe—whether logically consistent or not, is what is true for me. And the same goes for everyone else. Thus, if it is useful for me to believe that I am the most qualified candidate for a particular job I am interviewing for (if such a belief helps me to interview well, for example), then it is true for me; I am the most qualified person for the job.

It is tough to take such a view of truth seriously, though, and while there are still a few significant holdouts, most scholars in the past decade or so have all but given up on it.[13] There are numerous problems with the view, but one of the most troubling difficulties is that a belief may work for me (such as the one noted above about an interview) and be clearly false. So, as with the coherence view, a "true" belief can turn out to be one that does not match with reality. While more sophisticated versions of the pragmatic view of truth have emerged, they all end in similar conundrums. They also all entail a denial of the law of noncontradiction. But, as we have seen, it is futile to deny that law. Truth is simply not a matter of pragmatics.

What is the correct view of truth, then? Interestingly, the only view of truth that does not violate the law of noncontradiction is the view with which we began—the correspondence view.[14] It is the only consistent view and the only one that corresponds with the way we actually use the word *true*. But what about the problem of correspondence noted above (the problem involving unverifiable claims, such as claims about God)?

28

Religious Truth: Absolute, Relative, or Personal?

On the correspondence view, to say something is true is to say that it corresponds with the facts. Typically, nowadays, there is no disagreement with this view when it comes to claims that can be empirically or scientifically verified. But while most people would agree that truth regarding empirical claims is not relative, many maintain that truth in religion is different. So, in an attempt to avoid the contradiction problem noted above, efforts have been made to place religious claims in a different category from objective, empirical truth claims.

Consider the following example. Most sane and educated people in the twenty-first century would agree that the earth is round and orbits the sun, and that this claim is an objective truth regardless of what culture the person is in who believes or disbelieves it. Furthermore, if someone, such as those in the Flat Earth Society, disagreed with this claim, we would say that they are simply wrong. We wouldn't say that it is true for them if it works for them, or that it is true for them if it coheres with the rest of their beliefs.

But when it comes to religion, things are often viewed differently. For when it comes to religious beliefs, many of these same people would claim that my religion is true for me and your religion is true for you even though our religions may contradict each other. The discussion I had with the Zen Buddhist at the coffee shop is a case in point. While he surely wouldn't hold a view such as that coffee exists (for me) and doesn't exist (for him), when it came to religion he viewed things differently. He *did* hold the view that God exists (for me) but does not exist (for him).

At first glance this bifurcation between the objective and religious may seem right. Many aspects of one's religion cannot be verified empirically, so, it is argued, my religious beliefs are just that—beliefs. Your view can be just as right as mine. But there is a serious problem here. The late philosopher Mortimer Adler captures the problem poignantly in the following parable:

A Buddhist Zen master who lives in Tokyo wishes to fly to Kyoto in a private plane. When he arrives at the airport, he is offered two planes: one that is faster but aeronautically questionable, and one that is slower but aeronautically sound. He is informed by the airport authorities that the faster plane violates some of the basic principles of aeronautical mechanics, and the slower plane does not.

The aeronautical or technological deficiencies of the faster plane represent underlying mistakes in physics. The Zen master, in his teaching, asks his disciples questions, the right answers to which require them to embrace contradictions. To do so is the path to wisdom about reality, which has contradictions at its core. But the Zen master does not waver from upholding this teaching about reality while, at the same time, he chooses the slower, aeronautically sounder and safer plane because it accords with a technology and physics that makes correct judgments about a physical world that abhors contradictions.

If there is scientific truth in technology and physics, then the unity of truth should require the Zen master to acknowledge that his choice of the slower but safer plane means that he repudiates his Zen doctrine about the wisdom of embracing contradictions.[15]

The problem here, of course, is that truth in religion is put into a different domain than truth in the rest of reality.

Religious Pluralism

The separation between religious truth claims and objective truth claims is attempted in different ways. For the religious pluralist, all of the religions are "true" in that they all offer different and valid paths to the same God/Ultimate Reality.[16] However, while all of the different paths are valid, the pluralist also asserts that each religion offers only a partial perspective. Consider the following Hindu parable:

> God is like a large elephant surrounded by several blind men. One man touches his tail and thinks it is a rope. Another touches his trunk and thinks it is a snake. Another touches his leg and thinks it is a tree. Yet another touches his side and thinks it is a wall. They all are experiencing the same elephant, but they are experiencing it in very different ways. The same goes for God and the various religions.

On this view, there is only one real truth about God/Ultimate Reality, and the different religions provide culturally filtered images of that truth. The pluralist view, then, is not relativistic, for it maintains that there is one objective truth. However, all of the religions are only "true" in the sense that they all have a sufficient enough grasp of the objective truth to provide salvation for their adherents.

While religious pluralism may provide a corrective to the often held imperialistic attitudes of certain religious devotees, there are also significant objections to it—objections that make it, in the end, unreasonable to hold. Consider briefly just two of them. First, while maintaining that in one sense all of the religions are true, pluralism is, in fact, claiming that they are all false! As noted above, central to religious pluralism is the view that all of the religions contain only partial perspectives of God. But, of course, the major world religions themselves are claiming much more than this; they are claiming that they are offering the *true* perspective of God. Pluralism is making the radically strong claim that none of them are correct. But before a person unreflectively buys into the pluralistic notion that all religions are wrong, it seems that he or she should have especially good evidence for believing it.[17] And, as will be argued in the following chapters, there is much evidence for the view that not all religions are wrong.

Second, and related to the first point, central to the pluralistic view is the idea that God, or Ultimate Reality, is actually unknowable, and that our religious perspectives are necessarily so culturally skewed that there is no way anyone could ever actually have the objective truth about him (her, it?). However, couldn't it be the case that if God really exists, and if he really is a personal being (as theists believe, anyway), he could make himself known to those who seek him? Would such a task be impossible for God? It seems clearly not.

Furthermore, how can a pluralist make the *objective* claim that we cannot have any objective knowledge about God/Ultimate Reality given our cultural filters? Are pluralists somehow so above their own enculturations that they can provide the rest of us with objective knowledge about these matters? That seems a rather arrogant and unjustified perspective.

Religion as Contextual/Personal Truth

One way that some religious scholars have attempted to avoid the various criticisms of pluralism is to maintain that truth in religion is not objective but contextual—that is, religion has various meanings, and those meanings need to be defined within the parameters of context. On this view, as the late Francis Schaeffer put it, religion gets placed in an "upper story" where contradictions are irrelevant.[18] Thus, religion should be understood to be neither true nor false, but it can *become true* as it informs the lives of those who believe it. Religion, on this account, is not objective but personal—that is, religious truth is not a correspondence with reality but rather an appropriation of religious beliefs in one's life. This is the "personalized truth" view of religion, and on this account the meaning of religious truth lies in persons and not in an objective reality. As one author puts it with respect to Christianity, "[It] is not true absolutely, impersonally, statically; rather, it can become true, if and as you or I appropriate it to ourselves and interiorize it, insofar as we live it out from day to day. It becomes true as we take it off the shelf and personalize it, in actual existence."[19]

Since we don't have a "God's-eye" view of religious matters, defenders of this view maintain that it is best not to make absolutist and universal claims to religious truth. Simply hold your beliefs, live them, and even share them with others if you want, but don't dare claim that they are objectively true.[20]

However, it is worth asking *what it is* that such defenders of religion are suggesting religious adherents should believe and share with others. Presumably it is their religion, but what is religion? While there is no simple answer to this question, one thing is certain: religious adherents hold religious commitments. And religious commitments, for most religions, are commitments to a supreme being—the "only true God"—or Ultimate Reality with a capital *R*. Furthermore, such commitments necessarily consist of beliefs and doctrines that are claims to *propositional truth*, and without those truth claims, describing at least to some extent whom or what one is putting his or her faith in, faith itself would not be possible. All major religions make truth claims, and commitment to them is an essential expression of the religion. Philosopher of religion Keith Yandell agrees: "Of course religions make claims—if they asserted nothing, there would be no religions. . . . It is in the very nature of a religion to offer an account of our situation, our problem, and its solution."[21]

The various religious traditions do contain claims to truth about reality, and these truth claims among the traditions contradict one another in significant ways. Consider the following examples:

1. The Advaita Vedanta form of Hinduism includes the claim that ultimate reality is Brahman—the impersonal and unchanging All. There exists no personal God who created or sustains the world, and salvation (*moksha*) is an esoteric experience attained by a person coming to the realization that he or she is in ignorance about reality.
2. For Theravada Buddhism, ultimate reality is made up of momentary, transitory states. All is in flux; nothing endures. Even individual persons, such as you and me, are a composite of fleeting and infinitely small bits of reality. Salvation for the Buddhist (nirvana) is the cessation of this fleeting self and the final release from all desire.
3. For Islam, ultimate reality is Allah—creator and sustainer of all that is. Salvation is found primarily through having the appropriate beliefs (*iman*) and following the correct practices (*amal*), typically defined by the five pillars of reciting the creed, praying, fasting, giving alms, and making the pilgrimage to Mecca.

Thus, even with this small sample of three world religions, we can see that they include radically different core beliefs, and these beliefs are no small matter for their adherents. To deny them is to be wrong, really wrong. Each of these religions, then, as with all of the major religions of the world, has a central core of beliefs that contradicts the other religions' core beliefs. Therefore, all religions simply cannot be correct.

Either one of them is true and the others false, or all of them are false. So, this view of religion as contextual isn't an accurate reflection of what religious adherents actually believe or what their core teachings essentially entail.

Religious Relativism

The religious relativist, on the other hand, takes the truth claims of the different religions more seriously and literally. For relativism—at least the more sophisticated version of religious relativism—the correctness of a religion is relative to the worldview of its adherents and under which it falls. One defender of this view puts it this way: "[A] relativist definitively holds that, corresponding to differences of world-view, there are mutually incompatible, yet individually adequate, sets of . . . relative truths. Thus for the Religious Relativist, unlike the Pluralist, truth itself is relative and plural."[22]

However, how the religious relativist attempts to maintain that truth in religion is relative is unclear. One way would be to hold to either a pragmatic or coherence view of truth. But, as we saw earlier, both of these views of truth are doomed. Another way may be to hold that the truth claims of the different religions are true in that they correspond to the basic concepts of the worldviews under which they fall. But this approach, too, is problematic. For on this view the truth claims would not "really" be true since they would only be corresponding to worldview concepts, not to objective reality. And since the differing worldview concepts contradict each other (e.g., the core concepts of theism contradict atheism, as we will see in chapters 2 and 3), they cannot each be true; one of them must be true and the others false. There are not many other options available for the relativist.

So the religious relativist is wrong; the different religions cannot all be true. While religious relativism appears to respect the various religions equally by maintaining that they all can be true, it rather devalues them by denying their objective claims. Such a relativistic view seems, as first glance, to elevate the religions to an equal plane—a plane where they all offer valid and true paths to the religious ultimate. But by denying their ultimate objectivity, the religions ironically end up being equally false, just as with religious pluralism. For what distinguishes the religions from one another is not only their varying practices and rituals but also their beliefs—beliefs that are held to be universally and objectively true by their teachers, gurus, adherents, and sacred texts. As theologian and cultural analyst John Stackhouse succinctly describes it, "Religion is fundamentally about truth: trying to figure out what is real and how best to represent it."[23]

Having determined that truth in religion is objective and absolute, the next question that naturally arises is, which one is true? We should be very cautious here, and humility should be the rule in such matters. It could be, for example, that Christianity is wrong about this or that claim, or maybe even wrong on the whole. But either it is or it is not. Either way, finding truth is part and parcel of the very enterprise of religion. The rest of this book is an exploration of this very question.

Summary

We have covered much ground in this chapter. First, we noted that there are three very different attempts to define truth: the correspondence, coherence, and pragmatic views. We saw that only one of these, the correspondence view, withstands scrutiny. Truth, then, is not relative to persons but is absolute—it is a correspondence between statements and reality. It follows that since all the religions make truth claims, and since they all contradict one another, they cannot all be true. As the law of noncontradiction demonstrates, either one of them is true and the others false or all of them are false and some other view, possibly atheism, is true.

Some have argued, however, that when it comes to religious truth, things are different. Religious truth is not absolute but is contextual or relative to a worldview. Nonetheless, we discovered that the contextual view is not an accurate reflection of what the world religions actually entail, and the relativized view of religion turns out to be incoherent. Whether talking about airplanes or Zen Buddhism, truth is truth, and it is absolute and objective. One simply cannot coherently deny the law of noncontradiction and absolute truth.

Some people take this absolutist view to be intolerant, narrow-minded, and bigoted. But *truth* is not bigoted. *People* can surely be bigots, whether they are Christians or atheists or Hindus or something else. I have seen both relativists and absolutists who are bigots. How we approach and communicate truth is what determines bigotry and narrow-mindedness. But truth is truth. It can be presented in a loving, kind, gracious, and humble manner, or it can be presented in an arrogant, defensive, and obnoxious way. Jesus and Gandhi typically gave their teachings in the humble and inoffensive manner of parables and stories. We would do well to emulate their practices.

Now that we have examined what truth itself is, we turn next to the question, what is *the* truth? This moves us up to the next level of the Apologetics Pyramid and is where chapter 2 begins.

Questions for Reflection

1. Can you clearly explain the law of noncontradiction to someone who is unfamiliar with it?
2. What is the relevance of the law of noncontradiction to the issue of religious diversity? To religious pluralism? To religious relativism?
3. What is the correspondence view of truth, and why is it relevant to discussions of religion?
4. Consider the following claims: "Cookie dough ice cream is the best." "No, chocolate ice cream is the best." If two different people are making these claims, it seems that they are both right. Cookie dough is the best for one person, and chocolate is the best for the other. Does this disprove the law of noncontradiction?
5. How would you respond to someone who told you that you were intolerant for believing that there is only one way of salvation?

For Further Reading in Defense of Absolute Truth

Beckwith, Francis, and Gregory Koukl. *Relativism: Feet Firmly Planted in Mid-air.* Grand Rapids: Baker, 1998. A solid response to various forms of relativism.

Copan, Paul. *True for You, but Not for Me.* Minneapolis: Bethany, 1998. A very readable guide for "deflating the slogans that keep Christians speechless."

Groothuis, Douglas. *Truth Decay: Defending Christianity against the Challenges of Postmodernism.* Downers Grove, IL: InterVarsity, 2000. A defense of the correspondence theory of truth and a response to elements of postmodernism.

Kirkham, Richard. *Theories of Truth: A Critical Introduction.* Cambridge, MA: MIT Press, 1992. A fairly advanced, technical work on the nature of truth as well as an evaluation of the different theories.

Netland, Harold. *Encountering Religious Pluralism: The Challenge to Christian Faith and Mission.* Downers Grove, IL: InterVarsity, 2001. The best work I am aware of defending religious exclusivism and opposing religious pluralism.

For Further Reading in Defense of Relativism and Pluralism

Hick, John. *An Interpretation of Religion: Human Responses to the Transcendent*. 2nd ed. New Haven: Yale University Press, 2004. The best philosophical defense of religious pluralism in print.

Krausz, Michael, ed. *Relativism: Interpretation and Confrontation*. Notre Dame, IN: University of Notre Dame Press, 1989. Contains a collection of articles, pro and con, on relativism.

Panikkar, Raimundo. *The Intrareligious Dialogue*. New York: Paulist Press, 1978. Panikkar is a Roman Catholic theologian who defends religious pluralism.

Runzo, Joseph. "God, Commitment, and Other Faiths," *Faith and Philosophy* 5 (October 1988): 343–64. The best defense of religious relativism of which I am aware.

Smith, Wilfred Cantwell. *The Meaning and End of Religion*. New York: Harper & Row, 1962. A classic on the meaning of religion.

Clashing Worldviews

The Three "Isms"

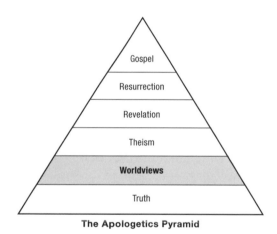

The Apologetics Pyramid

Religions are worldviews or metanarratives—inclusive posits concerning the ultimate nature of things.

Huston Smith

Nothing is more dangerous than a dogmatic world-view—nothing more constraining, more blinding to innovation, more destructive of openness to novelty.

Stephen J. Gould

We discovered in chapter 1 that truth is absolute, not relative. What this means is that if two objective claims contradict each other, they cannot both be true. Unlike previous generations who took this notion as a given, people in our postmodern culture no longer take it for granted; it must now be demonstrated. But once this concept is demonstrated—once it has been proven that two contradictory truth claims cannot both be true—the next question that logically arises is, what, then, is the truth?

A number of years ago I met two very bright young women, Lindsay and Margarette, at a church I was attending. After the service I was on the cleanup crew and ended up being the last person to leave the church. As I walked out into the parking lot, I saw them fussing with the lock on the door of their car. I walked up to see what they were doing and discovered that they had locked their keys inside. After a number of attempts to break into the vehicle without success, they asked me if I would give them a ride to their place to pick up a spare set of keys. I agreed, and on the way they told me that they were both agnostics—neither one of them believed that Christianity was true or even that God existed. They were visiting our church because someone had told them that it was very unique and worth the "experience." As we moved further into the conversation, I discovered that they both had graduated from a local Christian college—one at which I had taught—but had left as agnostics; one of them even called herself an atheist at the time.

I began to ask them a number of questions about their beliefs and doubts, and by the time we returned to the church parking lot, we had entered into what would turn out to be a long-lasting friendship. They asked me if we could continue this discussion, and I invited them over on the following Tuesday evening. My wife and I served them dinner, and we ended up having a fabulous discussion that lasted well into the evening. It went so well that we continued meeting on Tuesday evenings for about eighteen months!

What is relevant here is that after spending several months focusing on the law of noncontradiction, they finally agreed that truth was absolute and not relative. This had been a hard row to hoe, for they brought up every conceivable argument for relativism, and they were very good at coming up with ideas and examples. In the end, however, they both agreed that truth is absolute and that two contradictory beliefs cannot both be right.

After coming to this conclusion, the women then made this significant point: if two contradictory beliefs cannot both be true, we still are left with the question of what is true! And that is precisely where we are here at the beginning of chapter 2. It is here that many people have given up hope in their search for truth, for there are so many belief systems, so many religions and ideologies, that the quest for truth seems to be an impossible trek. Consider the religion of Hinduism, for example. With its 330 million deities and its vast complexity and diversity, it would take one a number of lifetimes (!) to have a full understanding of this one religion. And think of how many different religions there are. Thus, beginning with an exploration of the various religions and ideologies is a less than profitable venture.

Where, then, should we begin? The best way to begin a pilgrimage for truth, it seems, is to begin with the broadest categories possible, and the broadest categories would be what are often called worldviews.

What Is a Worldview?

Worldview is defined in a variety of ways. But simply put, a worldview is a collection of beliefs and ideas about the central issues of life. It is the lens through which we "see" all of reality. It is no mere theoretical concept advanced and held by professional philosophers and theologians. For no matter what one's profession is, from factory worker to university professor, everyone has a worldview, whether consciously chosen or not.[2] Studying worldviews, however, can be a complicated matter because there are just about as many kinds of them described in the literature as there are books written about the topic. Nonetheless, I think philosopher Ronald Nash has offered one of the most helpful and concise overviews in print. For while one could broaden or tighten the definition to include such diverse belief systems as communism, existentialism, polytheism, deism, and many more, Nash defines a worldview so as to include only three basic possibilities.

With some significant changes, I am going to follow Nash's lead here and describe the worldview landscape as including three plausible alternatives—theism, atheism, and pantheism.[3] If defined broadly enough, every religion, every belief system, and every ideology can be subsumed, or fit within, one of the three. Since each one of them contradicts the other two, and since these three are the only plausible possibilities, it is reasonable to believe that one is true and the other two are false. Also, since it is much easier to analyze and critique a worldview than a religion, this methodology will be more manageable than attempting a religion-by-religion analysis at this stage of the quest.

A worldview includes a variety of elements, but as Nash and others have noted, there are five fundamental issues that are widely considered to be a part of one.[4] Not only are these issues significant but, as we will see, even their sequence is important.[5] The five fundamentals and the questions on which they focus are as follows:

1. *Theology.* Is there a God, and if so, what is God like?
2. *Ontology.* What is ultimate reality?

3. *Epistemology.* How do we acquire knowledge?
4. *Axiology.* Where is the basis of morality and value to be found?
5. *Anthropology.* Who are we as human beings?

Each of the three worldviews includes an answer to these five questions. This is not to say that all persons have consistent belief systems in which they hold faithfully and consistently to each of the five. Rather, as we examine the history of ideas, we find these same three worldviews, with the same typical answers to these fundamental questions, offered over and over again. The meaning of a worldview should become clearer as we explore them in more depth in the following pages, and a chart which summarizes these points is provided at the end of the chapter.

Worldview #1: Theism

Theism, as I shall define it, is the belief in a personal God (or gods) who exists as a being separate from the world. I am broadening the definition a bit from the standard one to include polytheism (the belief in many gods) and deism (the belief in a creator God who is not involved in the world he created). So, by this definition, the main religions of Judaism, Christianity, and Islam, as well as those of the ancient Greeks and Romans, of the early American deists (such as Thomas Jefferson), and of contemporary Mormons, for example, would all be considered theistic. As we will note later, this expanded definition will help to simplify our search for truth, at least in these early stages.

The meaning of the theistic worldview is elucidated by examining its answers to the five basic worldview questions. First, then, we shall consider the question, Is there a God, and if so, what is God like? As I have already mentioned, for the theist, God (or the gods) exists and is separate from the world. Given the different theistic religions, who God is takes a variety of forms. For the major "monotheistic" religions of Judaism, Christianity, and Islam, there is only one God, and he is the eternal creator of the universe. He is generally understood to be omniscient (all-knowing), omnipotent (all-powerful), omnipresent (all-present), omnibenevolent (all-good), and many other "omnis" as well.

Furthermore, God is not typically understood to be physical on the theistic account, but rather is spiritual, or immaterial; that is, he is not made up of matter as are humans and animals and man-made objects. As we will see later on, there are significant and contradictory differences among these three theistic religions, and therefore they cannot all be right. But they agree that God is one, separate from the world, powerful, and personal.

Other theistic religions have held different views about the nature of God. For example, many ancient Greeks believed in the existence of a multitude of gods, and they typically had anthropomorphic (humanlike) characteristics. The Greek god Zeus, for example, was fairly powerful but had a body—one that he used for a variety of good and evil purposes. Zeus and the Greek pantheon were physically located as well, on Mount Olympus in Greece. They lacked all of the "omnis" and were, in a significant way, not much different from powerful human beings in their stature and actions. The Romans held similar views. Yet these Greeks and Romans, like adherents of most monotheistic religions, believed in and worshiped their deity (or deities) and denied the worldviews of atheism and pantheism that existed during these periods of antiquity as well.

The belief in many gods is a view held not only by the ancients, however, for even today there are those who believe that more than one god exists. Mormons, for example, while *worshiping* only one God, also believe that many deities exist, and even that we can become gods ourselves if we follow the appropriate practices and teachings. Deism is also on the rise in some quarters. However, since the three major monotheistic religions are by far the prevalent theistic religions in the modern world, emphasis here will be placed on them.[6]

But whether polytheists or monotheists, for most theists the answer to the second question—What is ultimate reality?—stems from the first, for ultimate reality is spiritual, immaterial, and personal. God is ultimate, and he is beyond the mere physical realm of existence. But contrary to the pantheistic view analyzed below, on the theistic account the universe does include a physical aspect as well. For example, for the theistic religions of Judaism, Christianity, and Islam, God is not a physical being at all but a spiritual one who transcends the created universe. The universe is fully real apart from him—it exists as a unification of time, space, matter, and energy. But whatever one's theistic bent, virtually all theists agree that reality is both physical and spiritual—both natural and supernatural.[7]

The typical theistic answer to the third question—How do we acquire knowledge?—is that knowledge is gained through the physical senses. How do I know that Wall Street is located in New York City? I have either seen it with my eyes (directly or indirectly) or heard about it with my ears. How do I know that the object in my hand is a fresh head of lettuce? I can see, taste, smell, or touch it. How do I know what is true about any domain of reality? Generally, as with Wall Street and the head of lettuce, my knowledge comes through one of my five sense organs.

However, theists also believe that it is possible to acquire knowledge through other means. God could very well communicate with one spiritually if he chose to. The term that is often used for such divine communication is *revelation*. In the Bible, for example, the apostle Paul claims that he is imparting knowledge "in words not taught by human wisdom but taught by the Spirit" (1 Cor. 2:13). Most theists agree that such direct communication is not generally audible or attained by any of the five senses. Rather, it comes through thoughts that enter the mind from the outside. The testimony of theists through the centuries is that God speaks about all manner of things to his followers—sometimes with very specific information.[8] At other times it is more vague, like a general sense of being loved by someone, or a strong feeling of guilt being imposed by another. Whatever the mode, while this may not be a common form of acquiring knowledge, nonetheless, it is still a way—a nonempirical way—that theists claim to acquire knowledge.[9]

The standard theistic response to the fourth question—Where is the basis of morality and value to be found?—is that *God* is the objective ground of morality and value. Right and wrong, good and evil, are based on the nature of the infinite, personal God who created the world and everything in it. While there are a number of different theistic approaches to explain how morality is grounded in God, one way or another it is believed to be so by most theists.[10] Much more will be said about this in chapters 3 and 6.

Regarding the fifth question—What does it mean to be human?—there are a variety of theistic responses. In general, though, the idea is that we are not on a par with God although we are on a "higher plane" than the rest of the animal kingdom, for we were created by God and made in his image.[11] We reflect this image in a number of ways, including having a spiritual dimension, being free agents, and having power to accomplish our intended goals and objectives. Whether we obtained these things quickly by God's direct act or they evolved over a long period of time, the central point is that God created human beings uniquely. Furthermore, this spiritual dimension of the self includes an immaterial soul that lives on after death, and it is this soul, the immaterial agent that is not bound up in the deterministic physical world, that has the ability or power to freely act and make moral decisions.

Historically, theism has dominated the ideological landscape. As a matter of fact, belief in God has been so widespread throughout the history of the human race that it seems as if, to put it in the words of the great Christian theist Blaise Pascal, there is a "God-shaped vacuum" in every person.[12] While some have argued that such widespread belief in God proves that he exists, this seems to me to be a rather weak argument. In recent times considerable numbers of thoughtful, well-educated people have held to one of the two other worldviews. So, in our quest for truth, it is worthwhile to do a careful analysis of them as well. We look next at atheism.

Worldview #2: Atheism

The second worldview we must analyze is *atheism*, the disbelief in God or the gods. Unlike agnosticism, which is a view (not a worldview) denying that we can have certain knowledge about the existence of God and ultimate reality, atheism is an outright denial of the existence of any deity.[13] As noted above, throughout the history of humanity, theism has been the predominant worldview, and the number of atheists has been rather small in contrast. However, the twentieth century demonstrated a significant increase in those who denied the existence of God and the supernatural.[14] Many practitioners and professors of science developed a naturalistic presumption in which science itself negates belief in the miraculous. Some even began to hold the view that for something to be true and rational to believe, it must be verifiable, at least in principle, by the scientific method. This view, sometimes referred to as *scientism*, has virtually dominated the academic environment in the West since the mid-twentieth century.[15] It is not surprising, then, that most of the atheists of the Western world are university educated.

The second question, having to do with ultimate reality, flows naturally from the first for the atheist. As the late astronomer and producer of the *Cosmos* television series, Carl Sagan, put it, "The universe is all that ever was, is, or will be."[16] On this view, there is no supernatural domain or realm of existence beyond the physical universe. The standard model of explanation for the beginning of the universe is the big bang theory, in which, at some point in the finite past, all matter and energy were shrunk down to an infinitesimal point, often referred to as the initial singularity. From this finite beginning the universe exploded into existence in a massive cosmic blast, and it has continued to expand ever since. Currently, most atheistic cosmologists are reticent to explain where this singularity came from, if anywhere, or what caused the initial explosion. Nevertheless, there must have been a naturalistic cause for it since, on the atheistic account, a naturalistic cause is the only game in town.[17] (More on this in chapter 5.)

The third question answered by the atheistic worldview—How do we acquire knowledge?—again flows nicely from the previous one. Since the physical world is all that exists, any knowledge we have must be about it and it alone. The scientific method has proven quite effective in furthering our knowledge of the world. It has provided us with wonderful advances in medicine, architecture, transportation, communication, and a host of other domains. Its emphasis on verifiability, repeatability, and confirmation as opposed to superstition, dogma, and blind adherence to authority has no doubt been advantageous to the human race. Of course, according to the atheistic account, since there is no God or supernatural being to give us knowledge through any means other than the natural, we are limited to empirical kinds of knowledge. But for the atheist, this is no problem at all.[18]

Fourthly, morality and values for the atheist are generally not understood to be objectively true, but rather are inventions of the human race for its own perpetuation. They are rooted in the evolutionary development of *Homo sapiens*. The general view here is that human beings (or their genes) invented the idea of morality because it improved our chances of survival.

Other atheists, who are uncomfortable with such an illusory stance, argue that morality, while not derived from an objective source such as God, is nonetheless objective in some sense. Although this is a minority view among atheists, the atheist apologist Walter Sinnott-Armstrong argues that morality is objective after all.[19] He says that it is not based in a God, but neither is it simply invented by human beings. It just is. The plausibility of this explanation will be discussed in chapters 3 and 6.

Finally, the atheistic answer to the question of what human beings are should not be surprising. For the atheist, human beings are electromechanical machines—physical animals that evolved slowly and by chance over many aeons into what we are today: *Homo sapiens*. As world-renowned paleontologist George Gaylord Simpson put it, "Man is the result of a purposeless and natural process that did not have him in mind."[20] Zoologist Richard Dawkins adds this idea: "We are . . . robot vehicles blindly programmed to preserve the selfish molecules known as genes."[21] While not all atheists agree with Dawkins that our genes are *selfishly* programmed, the general consensus is that human beings are no more than evolved physical matter in motion, unities of small components genetically programmed to advance the species. We are, fundamentally, survival machines.

Furthermore, for the atheist there is no soul, or immaterial aspect, of a person. Since souls and spirits cannot be detected through scientific means, it is no more rational to believe in such things than to believe in fairy tales, ghosts, and goblins.[22] We live, die, and decompose. That is it.

Interestingly, and perhaps somewhat surprisingly, a number of religions fall under the worldview of atheism. For example, some types of Buddhism, such as Zen and versions of the Mahayana tradition, could be classified as atheistic. Several recent metaphysical religions and cults are also fundamentally atheistic. There is even a small atheistic movement within the Christian religion referred to as "Christian naturalism"! On this view, God is not a real being but rather a principle of love, virtue, and justice emulated by the religious and political radical Jesus of Nazareth.[23] Most religions, however, are either theistic or, as we will see next, pantheistic.

Worldview #3: Pantheism

Pantheism is the third and final worldview. For some of us in the West, this view of things seems a bit strange, even surreal. But we must not let unfamiliarity hinder an attitude of open-mindedness in our quest for truth. I have heard many students of religion mock the beliefs of others because of their apparent "strangeness," only to discover later that their beliefs, too, were mocked by those unfamiliar with them. Millions, if not billions, of people have embraced some form of pantheism over the centuries, and the number is on the rise. As one scholar has recently suggested, "There are probably more (grassroot) pantheists than Protestants, or theists in general."[24] While this is probably an overstatement, given its broad appeal and popularity, primarily in the East but even now in the West, it is important that we strive with all diligence for a careful examination of this perspective of reality.

First, then, what is the pantheistic view of God? Note that there is not a *single* form of pantheism; rather, there are philosophical as well as religious versions of it. For example, one of the most ardent defenders of pantheism was Baruch Spinoza, a Jewish philosopher who lived AD 1632–1677. In his book *Ethics*, published in 1675, he defended pantheism from a philosophical perspective. His position was not so much religious as it was theoretical in that through an elaborate sequence of arguments he deduced that only one substance (essential nature or reality) can exist. This substance, for Spinoza, can be referred to as either *God* or *Nature*; they are interchangeable since there is no real, ontological distinction between them. God is the world.[25]

Much earlier, the Greek philosopher Parmenides (ca. 515–450 BC) also argued for a pantheistic view of the world. Arguing from an abstract form of reasoning about what it means to be, or exist, Parmenides concluded that the world must be changeless, immovable, eternal, and one. While he admitted that we seem to experience the world as changing, mobile, and made up of a multitude of distinct and varied parts, this is all mere illusion. For contrary to the faulty information we receive from the senses, Parmenides and his follower Zeno maintained, pure, unadulterated reasoning leads to monistic pantheism.[26]

On the religious side, there exists quite a variety of pantheisms, both Eastern and Western. Even within the single religion of Hinduism, for example, there are different kinds of pantheistic thought. Thus, there is a kind of two-pronged pantheism, depicted as impersonal *Nirguna Brahman* on the one hand (the all-pervading, unapproachable Ultimate, which is beyond both being and thought), and the personal *Saguna Brahman*, who is represented by both male and female aspects on the other hand.[27]

But pantheism is not restricted to Hinduism. Within the religions of Taoism, Buddhism, and more recently the New Age movement, different strands of pantheistic thought exist. Some of these are probably more accurately placed within the theistic paradigm (e.g., *Saguna Brahman*, noted above), and thus would be better analyzed under the theistic worldview. But the type of pantheism I wish to focus on here is one that is clearly distinct from either theism or atheism. It is historically the central form of pantheism, and it takes different names, but the term often utilized for it is "absolute pantheism."[28]

Absolute pantheism, explicated and ardently defended by the medieval Hindu Shankara (ca. 788–820) and sometimes called Advaita Vedanta, is the view that reality is nondualistic or monistic. It is monistic in that there are no ultimate distinctions in the universe; all is changeless, all is one, and all is God (Brahman in Hinduism). This is difficult for many of our minds to grasp, as a number of Hindus acknowledge. Shankara himself admitted that Hindus often use various attributes, including personal ones, to describe this indescribable Brahman. But this is to follow the path of ignorance. For those following the path of true knowledge, no qualities can be attributed to God. One cannot even say that God is, for this would be to ascribe attributes to the indescribable.

Thus, for pantheists, theology and ontology merge. God is one with the universe. In answering the second question, then, ultimate reality is God—indistinguishable and ultimately indescribable. All distinctions turn out to be forms of *maya*—illusions of the self. In reality, everything is the same self, or rather the same "not-self," for God is also ultimately impersonal. Thus, animals, insects, plants, rocks, you, me—everything—is ultimately one and the same. Two recent authors, Norman Geisler and William Watkins, offer a helpful and concise summary of the pantheistic view of reality:

> A basic belief in any pantheistic system is that God or Reality is ultimately impersonal. Personality, consciousness, intellect, and so forth are characteristic of lower-level manifestations of God, but they are not to be identified with God. The One is beyond these things. The One is really It, not he. Further, It is absolutely simple, or one. It has no parts.[29]

But how do we know all of this? For the pantheist, acquiring knowledge follows a radically different path from the atheist and the theist, for there is no physical reality (including sensory organs) by which to know such things. For consistent, absolute pantheists, true knowledge is not acquired through rational enquiry but through meditation and other practices that are aimed at emptying the mind. Often yogic exercises and chanting are practiced for the purpose of altering consciousness and experiencing a unity with all that is. While this oneness tenaciously eludes our cognitive awareness, through these altered states one can move beyond the illusion of distinction to finally realize the oneness of the universe of which we all are a part.[30]

Not only is physical reality an illusion for pantheists, but also on their view, as for some atheists, objective good and evil (or right and wrong), too, turn out to be mere illusions. A Zen poem expresses the view well:

> The perfect Way [Tao] is without difficulty,
> Save that it avoids picking and choosing.
> Only when you stop liking and disliking
> Will all be clearly understood. . . .
> If you want to get the plain truth,
> Be not concerned with right and wrong.
> The conflict between right and wrong
> Is the sickness of the mind.[31]

Similarly, Mary Baker Eddy—pantheist and founder of Christian Science—proclaims that "evil is but an illusion, and it has no real basis. Evil is a false belief."[32] This denial of objective evil, and of right and wrong, follows logically from the answers to the first three fundamental issues of pantheism. For if God is the indescribable All, the ultimate reality of which everything consists, then all actions are really just illusions too. All is one, and since fundamentally there are no distinctions of thought and action, there are no distinctions of right and wrong either.

Finally, then, our last question for the pantheistic worldview has already been answered. Who are we as human beings? For the pantheist we are God! We are not physical beings, as the atheists maintain, nor are we physical and spiritual beings as theists maintain, but we are spiritual divinity; we are one with the universe. Unfortunately, we are under the spell of *maya* (universal illusion) if we don't realize our divine nature, and that is why the salvific goal of pantheistic Hinduism is a recognition of this truth and a release from the illusion we all experience. We need to move beyond our ignorant illusions and come to see and experience the God we really are. This is difficult, admit pantheists, but to see this truth is to finally escape the wheel of karma that has kept us on the cyclical path of reincarnation, or transmigration, for countless aeons.[33]

This is pantheism. The growth of this worldview in the West has been most evident in the New Age movement. Brought into popularity decades ago by actress and author Shirley MacLaine, it is now virtually as mainstream as Lutheranism or Catholicism. Ironically, New Age pantheism may even be more prevalent in popular Western culture today than the atheistic scientism mentioned above.[34] Atheism is on the decline, and spirituality, particularly pantheistic spirituality, is on the rise.

The chart below summarizes the three worldviews and their typical answers to the five fundamental questions.

Fundamental Issue	Theism	Atheism	Pantheism
Theology: Is there a God, and if so, what is God like?	God (or the gods) exists and is separate from the world. God is a spiritual, not a physical, being, and God is personal.	There is no God or gods. The concept of God is just a human mental construct.	All is God. There are no distinctions between God and non-God. God is impersonal and changeless.
Ontology: What is ultimate reality?	Ultimate reality is spiritual, but since the creation of the world, reality is now both physical and spiritual.	Ultimate reality is physical—the material universe is all there ever was, is, or will be.	Ultimate reality is spiritual and divine. All is one, and the apparent distinction between things is mere illusion.
Epistemology: How do we acquire knowledge?	Knowledge is derived primarily from the senses, but God can also inform us in other nonempirical ways as well.	Knowledge is derived only from the senses.	True knowledge is acquired through meditation. All empirical knowledge is illusory.
Axiology: Where is the basis of morality and value to be found?	Morality and value are grounded in God; they are objective and absolute.	Morality and value are human constructs. They emerged either through social agreement or evolutionary processes. Morality is relative.	Since all distinctions and actions are illusory, so is morality.
Anthropology: Who are we as human beings?	Humans beings are both physical and spiritual beings; they consist of body and soul.	Human beings are electro-mechanical machines—physical animals that evolved slowly and by chance.	Human beings are God, and they are monistically one. There are no distinctions.

Summary

In this chapter I argued that there are three basic worldviews—theism, atheism, and pantheism. Since they contradict one another at their core, they cannot all be true. One of them must be true and the other two false.

We then explored the nature of each of the three worldviews by focusing on five fundamental questions: (1) Is there a God, and if so, what is God like? (2) What is ultimate reality? (3) How do we acquire knowledge? (4) Where is the basis of morality and value to be found? (5) Who are we as human beings? Each of the three offers different and contradictory answers to these fundamental questions and thus they cannot all be correct.

We also noted that not everyone holds consistently to one of the three worldviews; some people pick and choose various elements to form their own view of reality—a kind of worldview medley. But to do so is generally to hold to inconsistencies. The three as defined are not only historically the main worldviews, but they also form a tight unity of thought from which the different religions emerge.

The task of the next chapter will be to discover which one of the worldviews is most plausible to believe. Since every religion and belief system falls within one of the three, this will also hasten our search for which religion (if any) is true.

Questions for Reflection

1. How would you describe the three worldviews in your own words?
2. Do you know any pantheists? Which religions are pantheistic?
3. Do you think most people hold consistently to their worldview? Do you?
4. Can a person objectively analyze his or her own worldview?
5. Why do people sometimes change worldviews? How is this possible?

For Further Reading on Worldviews

Nash, Ronald. *Worldviews in Conflict*. Grand Rapids: Zondervan, 1992. A clear, concise, and helpful analysis of the three basic worldviews described in this chapter.

Naugle, David. *Worldview: The History of a Concept*. Grand Rapids: Eerdmans, 2002. A sophisticated and insightful analysis of worldviews in general.

Sire, James. *Naming the Elephant: Worldview as a Concept*. Downers Grove, IL: InterVarsity, 2004. A very helpful guide to worldview thinking.

Smart, Ninian. *Worldviews: Cross-cultural Explorations of Human Beliefs*. 3rd ed. Englewood Cliffs, NJ: Prentice Hall, 1999. This work is a wide-ranging approach to the study of religion from a type of worldview perspective.

3

Theism, Atheism, and Pantheism

Which One Is True?

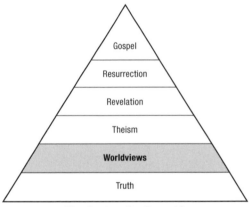

The Apologetics Pyramid

If . . . there are no grounds upon which one can argue that one civilization is superior to another, or that one moral code is loftier than another, or that one way of doing things is just better than another, then why learn about other cultures and philosophies and religions? If I go no further than to think that it's okay for you to do your thing and I to do mine, then where is the incentive to seriously consider whether I should adopt your thing and abandon mine?

John C. Stackhouse

There are general meta-criteria that can be applied across worldviews to assess [their] acceptability.

Joseph Runzo

In chapter 2 we examined the five fundamental beliefs of the three world-views. In this chapter we will evaluate them to see which one is most reasonable to believe. Our goal in this quest is not to find undeniable proof for all of our beliefs. For as philosophers have noted for centuries, it is virtually impossible to demonstrate almost anything with absolute and undeniable proof, with the possible exception of mathematical truths (and, I would add, logical laws such as the law of noncontradiction). The goal of this chapter is much more modest but no less important. It is to determine which worldview is most plausible—that is, which one is most reasonable to believe based on the evidence.[1] Once we determine the answer to this question, the field of inquiry narrows quite considerably and we move up another level on the Apologetics Pyramid.

Evaluating the Three Worldviews

A number of criteria could be utilized in evaluating a worldview, but two that seem especially effective and objective are *logic* and *livability*.[2] Here's why. First, as noted in chapter 1, one of the fundamental laws of logic, the law of noncontradiction, is rationally undeniable, and a contradiction is a necessary falsehood. Thus, a belief system would be necessarily false if, within its essential core of beliefs, it contained con-tradictions or incoherent elements. For example, as we will see shortly, atheists have argued for centuries that God *cannot* exist because several of the attributes ascribed to him entail contradictory and incoherent no-tions (e.g., how could evil exist if an omnibenevolent and all-powerful God exists?). If God's essential attributes are contradictory, then the atheist is right: God could not exist, and theism would be false.

Second, if a worldview is not truly livable, it should be rejected. If, for example, on the atheist account, right and wrong/good and evil are noth-ing more than conceptual illusions yet one cannot live without believing in moral absolutes, this would be a significant blow to the worldview. We will examine this argument shortly as well.

This existential, or "livability," element of a worldview is important, for if one's beliefs do not match one's life, this inconsistency reflects an obvious tension, at least, that a rational person would want to examine and correct. First, then, we will assess the worldview of theism by begin-ning with logic and the attributes of God.

Evaluating Theism

As with each of the worldviews, a number of challenges to theism could be raised in evaluating its plausibility. Serious and powerful arguments, as well as novice and feeble attempts, to disprove God's existence could be analyzed.[3] But rather than focusing on weak arguments and straw man fallacies, it is more beneficial to examine those objections to theism that are usually taken to be the strongest—those that have been most influential over the centuries. We will examine two of the most significant, one logical and the other existential.

Objection #1: The Problem of Evil and Suffering

The charge against theism based on evil and suffering is the most prominent challenge to the theistic worldview, and it goes back at least as far as the ancient philosopher Epicurus (341–271 BC). In summarizing Epicurus's argument, philosopher David Hume (1711–1776) formulated it this way: "Is [God] willing to prevent evil, but not able? Then he is impotent. Is he able, but not willing? Then he is malevolent. Is he both able and willing? Whence then is evil?"[4]

Added to this argument is the emotional force of evil and suffering. When a spouse develops cancer, for example, and suffers many agonizing years before death, the surviving spouse grieves over the horror of it all. Why would God allow this kind of pain and suffering? Or when a baby develops some debilitating disease and dies shortly after birth, the heartbroken parents often wonder how a beneficent God could allow such suffering of an innocent child. What is the point of it? Beyond the logic of argumentation, it just *feels* like this kind of suffering should not exist, especially if you are the one going through the tragedy or know well the one who is.

What is the theistic response to this argument? First, it should be noted that the problem of evil and suffering is not just a difficulty for the theist. The atheist and the pantheist also have to offer an accounting for its existence. This point is often overlooked, and as we will see below, it is a significant one.

Second, the historical theistic answer is that evil came from the free will of human beings (and angels, on some accounts). The great Christian theologian Augustine (AD 354–430), for example, wrote an entire book explaining how freedom of the will allows for the possibility of the free agent choosing evil over good.[5] He argued that it was a good thing for God to create humans with free will (after all, contemporary theists add, robots cannot be truly loved or offer love), but with this freedom came a real danger. Free creatures could decide to use this good gift for the wrong reasons, even malicious ones, and on the Christian, Jewish, and Islamic accounts, that is in fact what happened. Humankind decided to rebel against their Maker and turn away from him. This is the fall referred to in Christian literature over the centuries. Since it was not God but human beings who used their freedom to create evil, it is they who are responsible for it. This argument is known as the "free will defense."

Critics of theism often counter this response by noting that granting the free will defense against *moral* evil does not account for the *natural* evils that regularly occur. In other words, while free will may explain why someone murdered his business associate who was stealing from him, it does not explain why an earthquake killed dozens of children who were holed up in a school building in central Iran or why a helpless baby died of lymphoma.

These natural kinds of evils are more difficult to account for in a theistic universe, for certainly God could have stopped them. But the question is, might there perhaps be a reason why God did not stop them? This is where the atheistic argument against God, given the existence of evil, falls short. For according to the typical atheistic case against God, there is no inconsistency in God's existing and natural evils existing *if he has a good and sufficient reason for allowing them to exist*. While atheists often go on to argue that God has no good reason for allowing natural evils, an important question is how they know he has no such reason or reasons. If it is at least *logically* possible that God does have reasons for allowing natural evils, then their argument falls through. And it certainly seems to be logically possible that God could have his reasons for allowing moral and natural evils, even if we finite human beings cannot figure out what they are. For the atheist's argument to work, the atheist must prove that God could have *no reasons at all* for allowing natural evil, and this seems to be an impossible task. Thus, this argument against theism fails.[6]

Furthermore, sometimes we can at least have a good guess as to why God might allow natural evils. For example, a serious difficulty or even tragedy may be necessary to cause us to acknowledge God and our need for salvation. We often tend to ignore him and our own spiritual needs when life is going well, only to cry out to him when trials arise. Foxhole conversions are innumerable. God, in his mercy, may be reaching out to us through tragedy. Perhaps that is the only way he can get our attention. C. S. Lewis may be right when he says that "God whispers to us in our pleasures, speaks in our conscience, but shouts in our pains; [evil] is His megaphone to rouse a deaf world."[7]

Also, it should be noted that more often than not the real issue is not the intellectual or logical problem, but rather the emotional and psychological difficulties that arise during times of trouble. I can remember a discussion I had a number of years ago with a college student who quit believing in God because her father had recently died of cancer. As I spoke with her about this issue, I realized that she didn't need to hear a logical or rational answer; rather, she needed someone to listen to her pain and support her emotionally. This is the important role of the pastor, counselor, and friend, and this emotional component should be kept distinct from the logical argument as we assess the overall problem.

Clearly there are no easy answers for all of the natural or moral evils that exist. Therefore, another entire chapter will be devoted to examining this issue more carefully.[8] But our question here is this: Of the three worldviews, which one offers the best answer to this enduring enigma? As we examine the atheistic and pantheistic answers, you can decide for yourself which worldview makes the most sense.

Objection #2: Miracles and the Supernatural

The second challenge to theism is the notion that God, and many of the central beliefs of theism, are beyond the realm of empirical experience and so should not be believed as being factual and true. One cannot, for example, see God, even with the powerful Hubble telescope. Nor can one find a soul (another theistic belief) inside one's brain, even by utilizing the most advanced microscopes available. If one's epistemology (way of knowing) is such that the only truths are those that can be verified scientifically, then of course that would limit the number of truth claims that could be made about God. Therefore, atheists often argue that there are no possible scientific means for determining whether God exists. This is both a logical and an experiential argument for atheism in that it can be claimed that either (1) it is illogical to believe something as being true that cannot be factually verified, or (2) it is foolish to live life believing in unverifiable views about such fundamental issues.

I recall a discussion I had with an atheist in which he exclaimed, "If God really exists, why can't I see him? If he wants me to believe in him, why is he hiding from me and the rest of the human race? I can see other people, and I can see the stars, the sun, and even other galaxies, but I cannot see or hear any God. Believing in God is like believing in Santa Claus."

The same kind of challenge arises with miracles. Why should we believe that miracles really happen if they cannot be scientifically verified—if they are mere matters of faith? By definition miracles are, after all, violations of natural law; they are the exception to what normally happens in the world. But the reason natural laws are called *laws* is because they are what always happens; they can be scientifically proven. The occurrence of a miracle requires a direct violation of scientific law (that which has been established by overwhelming scientific evidence). Furthermore, it requires an immense amount of evidence for one to rationally believe that such a violation of law actually occurred. Skeptic David Hume describes the problem:

> A miracle is a violation of the laws of nature; and as a firm and unalterable experience has established these laws, the proof against a miracle, from the very nature of the fact, is as entire as any argument from experience can possibly be imagined. . . . The plain consequence is (and it is a general maxim worthy of our attention), "That no testimony is sufficient to establish a miracle, unless the testimony be of such a kind, that its falsehood would be more miraculous than the fact which it endeavors to establish."[9]

In support of this view against miracles, atheists often maintain that science *must* presuppose a position of atheism, or at least naturalism (the view that the natural world is all that can be known), for if science allowed for supernatural occurrences, there would be no further search for explanations in the world; scientific research would come to a halt.

On this view, which has come to be called *methodological naturalism*, no hypotheses that include the idea of supernatural occurrences can qualify as *scientific* hypotheses. Natural science, then, is just that: natural. Thus, supernatural or transcendent issues (like those about the origin of the universe or creation theories that postulate the emergence of living organisms *ex nihilo* [out of nothing]) remain outside the domain of natural science and so, too, outside the domain of facts and truth.[10]

But an important question to ask is this: How do we know *scientifically* that the properties of the cosmos are such that even if God exists, there can be no empirical consequences in nature of any actions taken by him, even in principle?[11] If there is a God, could he not interact with his creation in any way he chooses? Why should our method of research into what is true and real—the domain of scientific inquiry—include presuppositions that are contrary to our worldview and that eliminate, a priori, any possibility of supernatural activity in the world? If one of the leading thinkers of the late twentieth century has it right, belief in God is properly basic, just as is belief in an external world and the belief that I exist.[12] But regardless of whether this is true, one thing seems clear: whatever science tells us, it cannot, without an unjustified presumption of atheism, rule out God's existence or the possibility of miracles.[13]

More surprising is that there are empirical tests that can be utilized as evidence for belief in God and miracles, and the next several chapters are devoted to examining some of these evidences.[14] At this point, then, theism stands unscathed. Let's see how well atheism fares against the two tests of a worldview.

Evaluating Atheism

In evaluating atheism, we shall also look at both criteria mentioned at the beginning of the chapter—logic and livability—to assess its plausibility. We begin with logic.

Objection #1: The Logical Problem of Good

What follows are two stories—two true stories—that happened to me in recent years and express more vividly and clearly what I call the "logical problem of good" than any mere description of it could.

Moral Relativism

A few years ago I traveled to the French Quarter of New Orleans for an event that has been celebrated for several centuries. Ironically, Mardi Gras began as a religious festival in which devout followers of the Catholic faith would feast for a day ("Mardi Gras" means Fat Tuesday) before the long fast of Lent. Today, of course, it is a colossal seven-day party involving all manner of baseness and sordid activities. My purpose in going was not to revel in moral decadence (which is the reason some attend this bawdy event) but to talk about spiritual matters with anyone interested. After all, I figured, Mardi Gras did begin as a religious festival, so why not engage in the old religious activity of talking about God and other spiritual matters to anyone interested in discussing such things.

Other "spiritually" oriented folks were there as well: fortune-tellers, astrologers, spiritists, Wiccans, even black witches, devil worshipers, and self-proclaimed vampires. And a number of fellow Christians were there, many of them screaming into bullhorns disrespectful and odious expressions like "Queers, turn or burn in hell" and "Repent: God even loves people like you." But most of those attending were college students and various other Gen Xers who were interested in having a "good time."

In the midst of all this, my friends and I wanted to do something different; something new, or maybe something very old, to foster discussion. So we decided to utilize the ancient method of Socrates—asking questions. We painted a sign, one that reflected the liveliness and variety of color corresponding to the Mardi Gras experience, that asked in bold type: What Is Truth? The results were incredible. Crowds gathered around us to discuss that very question, and the discussion was often quite spirited. A few said there was no truth, and we asked them if that was true. Others claimed that you cannot know truth—that you cannot be certain of anything—and we asked them if they were certain about that. Still others chided that we were using Western "either/or" logic in believing in absolute truth, and we said that either we were or we weren't. It was like living a platonic dialogue.

In the end we had made a number of friends, fellow pilgrims who came to believe that truth really does exist, and who became interested in pursuing that truth wherever it may lead. One young man who became a friend didn't begin on the friendliest of terms, however. His name was Caden, and he approached me one sunny afternoon as I was heading into the French Quarter. Spotting me and my sign, he walked straight up to me and said with a smirk, "You're just a slave," and then began to walk away.

I responded by asking him what he meant by calling me a slave.

He said, "You're a Christian, aren't you?"

"Yes," I said.

"Well then, you are a slave to your belief in God and the Bible. Because whatever the Bible says is right, you must do, and whatever the Bible says is wrong, you must not do. So you are a slave to the Bible and the God it describes."

As we talked I discovered that he was a college student at a major university in Ohio, and he had picked up this "slave morality" notion from his atheistic philosophy professor. His professor had been teaching about the moral theory of the nineteenth-century philosopher Friedrich Nietzsche, who had developed a slave morality motif regarding the Christian faith.

I asked Caden what *his* view of morality was.

"I'm morally free," he said. "I can determine for myself what is right and what is wrong. And you should be free like me."

I responded, with a twinkle in my eye, by saying that what I would like to do is take my sign and clobber him with it!

He laughed and said "No, man. You can't do that. You've gotta have compassion."

"Compassion!" I exclaimed. "You're telling me that I have to have compassion? I thought I was morally free and could determine for myself what is right and what is wrong. But now you're telling me what I can and cannot do. So now I'm your slave?"

He looked perplexed and thought for a long minute. "I guess I haven't thought this through," he said. "Maybe there really are moral absolutes."

I knew that he knew that I knew he was nabbed. But I didn't press him. That's the wrong thing to do in situations like these. I changed the subject and began asking him about his classes at the university and about his time at Mardi Gras. We hit it off and became friends. He had recognized that there are moral absolutes, and for the time being at least, that was a significant aspect of his trek, as well as mine, up the path of truth.

Evolution and Morality

About a week after I returned from the Mardi Gras trip, I was shopping for a gift for my wife at a mall in Gurnee, Illinois, where I lived at the time. I had walked for what seemed like hours, and stopped in at the McDonald's restaurant in the food court. As I was waiting in line, the guy ahead of me ordered a large iced tea and about ten packets of sweetener. Shocked, I said to him, "That stuff will kill you!"

He looked at me, somewhat surprised, and asked me if I was a Jehovah's Witness. I replied that I wasn't but that I believed in God nonetheless.

"Really?" he asked. "What do you do?"

I told him that I was completing my Ph.D. in philosophy and was teaching philosophy at a local university.

He responded, "That's interesting. I've never met an educated person who believed in God."

I couldn't believe my ears. Was it possible that he hadn't met an educated person who believed in God? I asked him what he did for a career, and he shared with me that he was a medical doctor in the area. He could tell I was skeptical about both his being a doctor and not knowing any educated theists, so he gave me his business card and began talking about his position as an M.D. He was working at one of the hospitals in the northern suburbs of Chicago.

I began to ask him some questions about his worldview and how it applied to his medical profession. "Do you support abortion?" I asked.

"No," he said. "I think abortion is taking the life of an innocent person, and that is morally wrong."

"What about euthanasia? Do you support it?" I asked next.

"No," he replied again. "That, too, is the taking of innocent life. It is morally wrong, and I'm opposed to it as well."

Things were beginning to get interesting.

Wanting to get at the heart of the doctor's worldview, I asked him what the basis of right and wrong was for him.

He responded, "That's simple: evolution."

"Evolution!" I exclaimed. "How can evolution be the basis of morality when the pillars of evolutionary theory are chance, mutation, and natural selection? How do you arrive at such a strong pro-life stance—denouncing abortion, even of children who are physically and mentally challenged, and denouncing euthanasia, even for those who are terminally ill—by basing it on these survival-of-the-fittest Darwinian principles? Shouldn't you instead, to be consistent, hold to positions that will advance the species, whatever the 'cost' in terms of human life? How can you say that abortion and euthanasia are objectively wrong from evolutionary principles?"

He looked puzzled for a moment and then replied simply, "I guess I haven't thought about it that deeply before."

That deeply, I thought to myself. *That's not very deep at all!*

He then said, somewhat smugly, "I think I need to work through these problems at a more fundamental level."

He was probably right. After this point, we chatted about what it was like to be in the medical field in this litigious age. We then joked a bit about two strangers getting into philosophical and moral conversations in shopping malls, and he was off.

Examining the Logical Problem of Good

My purpose in sharing these experiences I had with Caden and the medical doctor is that they reflect a central logical problem with atheism. The problem here is not that atheists live immoral lives, nor is it that they could not believe in living a moral life. Many of them do believe in and live good moral lives. The question, however, is whether their worldview provides an adequate grounding for absolute morality. As we will see in chapter 6, clearly it does not.[15] If morality is a survival mechanism, then, as two atheistic ethicists admit, it is a mere illusion "fobbed off on us" by our genes.[16] It would thus be no more rational to believe in it than to believe in Santa Claus or in little green men on Mars. If, on the other hand, morality is not rooted in genetics but is just a social construct, as other atheists argue, then again it is not objective but subjective and relative.

Atheists cannot have their cake and eat it too. Philosopher Norman Geisler explains:

> To complain about unjustified evil in the world, one must also suppose an ultimate standard of justice beyond the world. In other words, if there is no absolute standard (i.e., a God who is or has an absolute moral standard), then in order to complain about unjustified evil in the world, one must "smuggle in" the concept of an absolute (such as is provided by theism) and assume that there is an ultimate, absolute standard of justice beyond this world.[17]

For if there is no objective morality, then the atheist cannot pretend that there really are such things as right and wrong, good and evil; she cannot consistently believe, for example, that abortion and euthanasia are morally evil. She cannot even believe that rape, torture, and the murder of innocent children are objectively, morally evil. She could maintain that she doesn't like such acts, or that she is offended by them and opposes them, but she cannot consistently affirm that they are really wrong.

But if there is objective morality, if some things are really right and good and others really wrong and evil, then it could not have been invented by a mere human being or even an entire culture. As will be argued in chapter 6, objective moral values require an objective moral value giver. The atheist, then, has no basis for holding to objective moral values.

The argument can be put simply in this logical form:

1. If objective moral values exist, then atheism must be false.
2. Objective moral values do exist.
3. Therefore, atheism must be false.

I call this the "problem of good." It is the flip side of the problem of evil, for in addition to requiring an accounting for evil and suffering, we also need to account for goods like objective moral values. Obviously one could consistently believe in atheism and deny that objective moral values exist. But it seems clear at this point that if one does believe in real, objective right and wrong (and who doesn't?), then he or she cannot do so with good reason within the atheistic worldview.

Objection #2: The Existential Problem of Good

Some atheists bite the bullet and affirm that there are no objective moral evils or goods. This, however, raises a second question: Can one consistently live with the view that morality is illusory or relative? The classic question I ask my college students is whether the statement "Torturing babies for fun is evil" is objectively true or merely an opinion. If someone held that torturing babies for fun is a good thing, would that too be simply an opinion? Even diehard relativists have a hard time denying that it would be morally abhorrent and really wrong to do such a thing.

Some moral principles, like this one and many others, are recognized in all cultures and in all times to be morally wrong. As C. S. Lewis demonstrates in *Mere Christianity*, all people recognize objective right and wrong whether they admit it or not. He puts it this way:

> The most remarkable thing is this. Whenever you find a man who says he does not believe in a real Right and Wrong, you will find the same man going back on this a moment later. He may break his promise to you, but if you try breaking one to him he will be complaining "It's not fair" before you can say Jack Robinson. A nation may say treaties do not matter; but

then, next minute, they spoil their case by saying that the particular treaty they want to break was an unfair one. But if treaties do not matter, and if there is no such thing as Right and Wrong . . . what is the difference between a fair treaty and an unfair one? Have they not let the cat out of the bag . . . ? It seems, then, that we are forced to believe in a real Right and Wrong.[18]

In other words, people can *say* that they do not believe in moral absolutes, but when it comes to living their lives, they are inconsistent, for they live as if they do. As a matter of fact, this point can actually be used as an argument for the existence of God! We will examine this issue in more detail later.

Because of this point and others, some atheists, such as the Christian evangelist-turned-atheist Charles Templeton, seem to realize that true atheism is not plausible given the world in which we live. Therefore, he and others have opted for a truncated version of atheism—one that actually fits better under the worldview category of pantheism. Templeton says:

> I believe that there is no supreme being with human attributes—no God in the biblical sense—but that all life is the result of timeless evolutionary forces, having reached its present transient state over millions of years. . . . I believe that there is what may best be described as a Life Force. . . . I believe that the Life Force is not a "being." It does not love nor can it be loved: it simply is.[19]

Atheists sometimes argue that all that is within the universe, even moral values, have emerged from this "Life Force," so there need not be a personal God to explain anything. But believing in a force that accounts for everything in the world but is also impersonal and all-pervading lands one in a worldview that is better described as pantheistic than atheistic. So let's examine pantheism next.

Evaluating Pantheism

Once again, pantheism (absolute pantheism) is the view that all of reality is God and all is one. Everything is divine, and there are no distinctions. It is the view of many Hindus and New Age adherents, for example, and while initially an Eastern view of the world, it is quickly moving to the West. In assessing this worldview, we shall once again utilize the two criteria of logic and livability, and we begin with a true story that occurred a number of years ago.

Objection #1: The Existential Problem of Right and Wrong

I had been meeting with Lindsay and Margarette (the two young women I mentioned in chapter 2) for several months, and after we had moved up the Apologetics Pyramid to the second level—the level of worldviews—Margarette proclaimed that she was now a pantheist! She had moved from being an atheist in college to an agnostic in graduate school, and now she was holding to pantheism. To this day I am not certain whether she really became a pantheist or was merely toying with me to see if I could prove this view wrong. Either way, she said that pantheism was a plausible worldview and one much better than theism.

I decided to test her position to determine its livability. My wife and I had been cooking dinner for the evening, and Margarette was sitting at the kitchen table. On the stove was a pan of boiling water, and just before I added the spaghetti noodles, a thought came to mind.[20] I said to her, "Margarette, with the pantheistic worldview everything is God, right?"

"Yes," she said, "everything is God and everything is one. There are no distinctions."

"But if there are no distinctions," I said, "then there is ultimately no right and wrong, no distinctions between cruelty and noncruelty, or between good and evil. Correct?"

"Yes," she confirmed, "there are no ultimate rights and wrongs, goods and evils."

But as she was saying this, I took the boiling water off the stove and held it over her head, pretending as though I would spill it on top of her. "Are you sure there are no rights and wrongs, no distinctions between good and evil, cruelty and noncruelty?" I asked.

Her sharp mind was racing. I could almost see the wheels spinning.

"Well," she said, "I guess maybe there is a distinction between these things!"

The point of this story, of course, is that we can say there are no distinctions between good and evil, that there are no rights and wrongs, that suffering is a mere illusion, and that cruelty is not morally distinct from noncruelty, but we don't really live that way. We live as if there truly are moral absolutes. Now this does not prove that there are, but it does demonstrate that those who hold to the atheistic worldview or the pantheistic worldview cannot *consistently* believe in real right and wrong. They must borrow what they hold to be true from theism!

Again, this does not prove theism, but the point is significant nonetheless. If one is to remain an atheist or a pantheist and avoid inconsistency, and thus incoherence, he or she must reject moral absolutes completely.

But I don't know of one person who actually lives with a total and absolute denial of right and wrong.

Objection #2: A Logical Problem of Pantheism

A second criticism of the pantheistic worldview is that it is intrinsically incoherent. The argument goes like this. On the pantheistic view, I am God and ultimately impersonal—I am the changeless All. Yet I am encouraged to discover this fact about myself. Through the practices of meditation and yoga, for example, I need to come to the realization that I am one with the Divine.[21] But there is a problem here that can be depicted in the following way. Pantheists believe that:

1. We are one with God.
2. God is the changeless All.
3. We (God) need to move beyond our ignorance and become enlightened by realizing our own divinity.

Clearly, statements 1, 2, and 3 are logically inconsistent. To *come to know* something is to *change* from a state of ignorance to a state of enlightenment, and I cannot be changeless and at the same time change in order to realize that I am changeless! This is incoherent at best.

Beyond this, there is the related problem that the impersonal Universe (which is me, remember) sure acts like it is personal! I am a person with thoughts and feelings, wants and desires, hopes and dreams, and so on. But for the pantheist all of this is mere illusion. Somehow the impersonal Universe has coughed up illusory and deceived persons (which are really nonpersons) like me, and I now need to get back to the impersonal self of which I am. But how can an impersonal me be deceived into believing that I am a personal being who needs to recognize my true, impersonal nature? What does it mean for something impersonal to be deceived anyway? These claims seem to me, at least, to make no sense whatsoever.

In response, some pantheists have suggested that we need to move beyond rational thought and rid ourselves of this mental, logical restriction. Zen masters even go so far as to have their students focus on contradictory ideas such as listening to the sound of one hand clapping or imagining what the color green tastes like.[22] These contradictory mental activities, they argue, free the mind from its rational trappings and open one up to a mystical awareness of one's unity with the cosmos. But, as was noted in chapter 1, to argue against reason is to use reason in an attempt to deny reason. It is to refute one's own position. There is simply no getting around it; if one is to be reasonable in his or her views, pantheism is not the view to hold.

On the other hand, if one attempts to avoid these contradictions by denying that he or she is God or by holding that God is personal rather than the impersonal, changeless All, then that person is by definition no longer a pantheist but has moved into the worldview of theism.[23] For better or worse, not too many options are available at the level of worldviews.

Summary

After clarifying each of the three worldviews in chapter 2, we evaluated them in this chapter by utilizing two objective criteria: logic and livability. We saw that based on these two criteria, both the atheistic and the pantheistic worldviews fall short. Since neither of them passes the tests, it is unreasonable to believe them to be true. So too with those religions and belief systems that fall within them, such as Christian Science, Hinduism, and New Age ideology (which are all pantheistic), and secular humanism, Mahayana and other atheistic forms of Buddhism, as well as atheism in general.

I am not saying that atheism and pantheism offer no contribution to the discussion of worldviews. Atheists have added significant input to the philosophical study of religious belief and even to the study of God. They have pointed out fallacious and inconsistent views of God and his nature that some theists have held, and they have pushed theists to clarify their worldview in a way that is logically consistent and clear.

Pantheists too have offered noteworthy insights in the field of religious study. They have focused on the immanence of God and the world, as opposed to the focus often made by theists of his transcendence. God is very much in the world and not merely "out there" as the deists used to argue. Also, as pantheists note, the world is a unified whole. While the pantheistic view of the world is so unified as to negate its true diversity, pantheists are correct to emphasize this unity in contrast to the atheistic position that tends to ignore it for fear of requiring a guiding, unifying hand in the creation.[24]

This brief analysis is not meant to replace your own hard study of the many arguments for and against the different worldviews. It is obviously short and incomplete. Nevertheless, the evaluation presented here raises profound and troubling problems for the atheistic and pantheistic worldviews. At this point, the evidence is clear: of the three worldviews, one stands head and shoulders above the other two in terms of rationality and livability. Thus, in our quest for truth, we are left with theism. But rather than merely be *left* with theism, the next three chapters examine three powerful arguments *for* the existence of God—both his existence (contrary to atheism) and his nature as a personal creator (contrary to pantheism). The field continues to narrow as we move up the Apologetics Pyramid.

Questions for Reflection

1. How would you explain the logical problem of good in your own words?
2. How would you respond to the notion that God/Ultimate Reality is beyond logic and critique?
3. Compare the various worldview answers to the problem of evil and suffering. Which one is most reasonable for you to believe? Why?
4. What are some difficulties with your own worldview that you need to spend time reflecting on?
5. Can you live consistently with your worldview? Are your beliefs consistent with your life?

For Further Reading in Support of the Theistic Worldview

Colson, Chuck, and Nancy Pearcey. *How Now Shall We Live?* Wheaton, IL: Tyndale, 1999. Colson's magnum opus, a thorough and articulate work on the Christian worldview. Highly recommended.

Geisler, Norman, and William Watkins. *Worlds Apart: A Handbook on Worldviews*. 2nd ed. Grand Rapids: Baker, 1989. A clearly written and insightful book on worldviews that offers arguments for and against what the authors describe as seven worldviews.

Schaeffer, Francis. *He Is There and He Is Not Silent*, vol. 1 of *The Complete Works of Francis A. Schaeffer*. 2nd ed. Westchester, IL: Crossway, 1982. The book that set me on the path to theism.

Sire, James. *The Universe Next Door*. 4th ed. Downers Grove, IL: InterVarsity, 2004. The classic work on worldviews.

For Further Reading in Support of the Atheistic Worldview

Dawkins, Richard. *The Selfish Gene*. New ed. New York: Oxford University Press, 1989. A *New York Times* best seller. Along with his *The Blind Watchmaker*, it was very influential in the late twentieth century.

Le Poidevin, Robin. *Arguing for Atheism: An Introduction to the Philosophy of Religion*. New York: Routledge, 1996. A concise, clear, and articulate work.

Martin, Michael. *Atheism: A Philosophical Justification*. Philadelphia: Temple University Press, 1990. Le Poidevin (*Arguing for Atheism*) and Martin both offer philosophically advanced defenses of atheism.

Russell, Bertrand. *Why I'm Not a Christian*. New York: Simon & Schuster, 1957. Very readable. Russell was one of the leading philosophers of the twentieth century and a staunch atheist.

For Further Reading in Support of the Pantheistic Worldview

Levine, Michael. *Pantheism: A Non-theistic Concept of Deity*. New York: Routledge, 1994. Despite the growing popularity of pantheism, as far as I know, this is the only recent book-length philosophical treatment of pantheism that is sympathetic to the worldview.

Radhakrishnan, Sarvepalli. *The Principal Upanishads*. New Delhi, India: Indus, 1994. The Upanishads are classic Hindu works and contain different descriptions of Vedic pantheism.

Radhakrishnan, Sarvepalli, and Charles A. Moore. *A Source Book in Indian Philosophy*. Princeton, NJ: Princeton University Press, 1957.

Spinoza, Baruch. *Ethics*. Edited by James Gutmann. New York: Hafner, 1949. The classic philosophical defense of pantheism.

4

The Fingerprints of God

On Finding Design throughout the "Just So" Universe

The Apologetics Pyramid

Whence arises all that order and beauty we see in the world?

Isaac Newton

The universe we observe has precisely the properties we should expect if there is, at bottom, no design, no purpose, no evil and no good, nothing but blind pitiless indifference.

Richard Dawkins

The equations of physics have in them incredible simplicity, elegance, and beauty. That in itself is sufficient to prove to me that there must be a God who is responsible for these laws and responsible for the universe.

Paul Davies

At this point in our quest, we have examined evidence against the three worldviews of pantheism, atheism, and theism. In chapter 3 I argued that of the three, theism is the most reasonable to believe; it withstands the central attacks against it better than either pantheism or atheism. In this chapter and the next two, we will explore three of the strongest evidences *for* theism.

One of these arguments for the existence of God that has been put forth historically is called the design, or teleological,* argument. We will be using the term *argument* in this chapter and those that follow to refer to a claim that is being made along with evidential support for that claim. The argument from design includes the claim that the universe was created by an intelligent designer.

While the argument is centuries old, the most substantial support for it in recent times comes from two different arenas, one having to do with the fundamental structure of the universe—what's called "fine tuning"—and the other having to do with irreducibly complex systems within living organisms—systems that seem to require an intelligent designer.

To account for the scientific discoveries from these two fields, there are three basic options from which to choose: chance, law, or intelligent design. With the first option, chance, the fine-tuning of the universe and what are (seemingly, at least) irreducibly complex biological systems happened as lucky accidents. The second option, law, includes the idea that the universe had to be just the way it is; from the natural laws that exist, our universe could not have been any different than it is, and so we should not be surprised at its apparently designed features. The third option, intelligent design, is the view that an intelligent designer provides the best explanation for our universe.

Before examining the design argument, it will be helpful first to expound briefly on the differences between several terms we will be using: *chance, law,* and *specified complexity*. There is no doubt that chance can generate rare events. For example, the chance of any particular person being struck by lightning is extremely small, yet a number of people are struck every year. But even though such unlikely events do occur, no one would claim that they are designed. (Hence, they are referred to as "accidents.") Chance generated these contingent occurrences. What chance cannot generate is specified complexity.

Mathematician and philosopher William Dembski offers an insightful example to explain the meaning of specified complexity:

* The Greek word *telos* means "end" or "goal," and the word *logos* means "word" or "reasoned account."

70

A single letter of the alphabet is specified without being complex (i.e., it conforms to an independently given pattern but is simple). A long sequence of random letters is complex without being specified (i.e., it requires a complicated instruction-set to characterize but conforms to no independently given pattern). A Shakespearean sonnet is both complex and specified.[1]

He continues:

The exact time sequence of radioactive emissions from a chunk of uranium will be contingent, complex, but not specified. . . . [L]aws can explain specification but not complexity. For instance, the formation of a salt crystal follows well-defined laws, produces an independently known repetitive pattern, and is therefore specified; but that pattern will also be simple, not complex.[2]

Laws can explain specification but not complexity. Chance can explain complexity but not specification. Specified complexity—complex and improbable patterns that are independent from the events they explain—is how one empirically detects intelligent design. For example, the scientific organization SETI (Search for Extraterrestrial Intelligence) utilizes digital filters to ignore radio waves that do not reflect what they take to be specified complexity. As researchers have recognized, there is a distinct difference between radio noise, random patterns, and specified complexity. So far, the latter has not been detected in the radio waves received from outer space. However, if specified complexity were to be detected, one could reasonably infer (alien) intelligent design.[3] In a similar way, if specified complexity can be detected within the basic structure of the universe itself, then this too should count as evidence of intelligent design.[4]

Taking into consideration this explanation of specified complexity, then, and the three options of chance, law, and intelligent design, an argument from design can be put in the following four-step configuration:

1. The fine-tuning of the universe either happened by chance, law, or intelligent design.
2. The existence of irreducibly complex systems within living organisms either happened by chance, law, or intelligent design.
3. Neither the fine-tuning of the universe nor the existence of irreducibly complex systems within living organisms happened by chance or law.
4. Therefore, both the fine-tuning of the universe and the existence of irreducibly complex systems within living organisms happened by intelligent design.

The form of this argument is logically valid, which simply means that if steps 1 through 3 are true, then conclusion 4 necessarily follows. Of course, an intelligent designer is precisely how theists have described God for centuries. The question before us, then, is whether steps 1 through 3 are true. The step in this argument that is challenged by atheists and skeptics of the design argument is 3, so the remainder of this chapter will be focused on a careful examination of it.

In our study of step 3 we will first focus on the claim that the fine-tuning of the universe could not have happened by chance or law.

A Finely Tuned Universe? The Evidence from Physics

Our universe is, obviously, one that allows living organisms to exist. But scientists have discovered in recent decades that a life-permitting universe such as ours is extremely unlikely. Over the past century scientists have discovered that fundamental laws of the cosmos, as well as dozens of basic constants of physics, if varied even slightly, would either radically inhibit the existence of all living organisms or render them completely impossible. If there were only one such law or constant, the existence of life without a designer would be quite surprising. But given the fact that there are dozens of them, the probability of their occurring by undirected natural causes is quite small.

Fundamental Laws and Constants of Physics

Even though our universe is vastly complex and diverse, it is characterized by a surprisingly small number of physical laws. As professor Walter Bradley has noted, there are five fundamental laws of nature, each of which can be described in simple mathematical form:[5]

- **Mechanics** (Hamilton's Equations)

$$\dot{\mathbf{p}} = -\frac{\partial H}{\partial q} \quad \dot{\mathbf{q}} = \frac{\partial H}{\partial q}$$

- **Electrodynamics** (Maxwell's Equations)

$$F^{\mu\nu} = \partial^{\mu}A^{\nu} - \partial^{\nu}A^{\mu}$$

$$\partial_{\mu}F^{\mu\nu} = j^{\nu}$$

- **Statistical Mechanics** (Boltzmann's Equations)

$$S = -k\Sigma\, P_i\, ln\, P_i$$

$$\frac{dS}{dt} \geq 0$$

- **Quantum Mechanics** (Schrödinger's Equation and Heisenberg's Uncertainty Principle)

$$i\hbar \mid \dot{\psi} > = H \mid \psi >$$

$$\Delta x \Delta p \geq \frac{\hbar}{2}$$

- **General Relativity** (Einstein's Equation)

$$G_{\mu\nu} = -8\pi\, GT_{\mu\nu}$$

For one who has never studied physics and abstract mathematics, these equations may not seem too impressive. But astrophysicist Paul Davies notes:

> Beauty in physics is a value judgment involving professional intuition and cannot readily be communicated to the layman, because it is expressed in a language that the layman has not learned, the language of mathematics. But to one who is conversant with that language, the beauty is as apparent as poetry.[6]

He continues:

> All the evidence so far indicates that many complex structures depend most delicately on the existing form of these laws. It is tempting to believe, therefore, that a complex universe will emerge only if the laws of physics are very close to what they are. . . . The laws, which enable the universe to come into being spontaneously, seem themselves to be the product of exceedingly ingenious design. If physics is the product of design, the universe must have a purpose, and the evidence of modern physics suggests strongly to me that the purpose includes us.[7]

As a former engineer myself, it is quite remarkable to me that these simple mathematical forms so beautifully express the basic makeup of the universe. What is even more amazing is that not only are there fundamental physical laws that in and of themselves point to intelligent design, but there are also dozens of constants in physics, which, if slightly altered, would make life in the universe highly improbable, if not completely impossible. Consider just the following few examples:[8]

1. *The gravitational constant.* According to Isaac Newton's law of universal gravitation, the attractive force between two bodies is proportional to the product of their masses and inversely proportional to the square of the distance between them: $F = G \times (m_1 \times m_2/r^2)$. The gravitational constant, G, determines the gravitation force between two masses and has been calculated to be 6.67×10^{-11} newton meters squared per kilogram squared ($N \times m^2 \times kg^{-2}$). If G were larger, stars would be too hot and would burn up quickly; if G were smaller, stars would remain so cool that nuclear fusion would never ignite. In either case, sustained life would be impossible.

2. *The velocity of light.* The speed of light, c, is calculated to be 186,282.4 miles per second. If it were faster, stars would be too luminous for life; if it were slower, stars would not be luminous enough for life.

3. *The strong nuclear force constant.* The strong nuclear force holds together quarks inside of protons and neutrons and also binds together protons and neutrons inside atomic nuclei. If it had been stronger or weaker by even a very small percentage, no life would have been possible anywhere in the universe.

4. *The relative masses of elementary particles.* The mass of an electron is 9.11×10^{-31} kg; the mass of a proton is 1.6726×10^{-27} kg, or about 1,836 times the mass of an electron; and the mass of a neutron is 1.6749×10^{-27} kg, only slightly more than a proton. If the combined mass of electrons and protons was not slightly less than that of the neutron, the two would unite to form neutrons, leaving the world devoid of electrons and protons. If the combined mass was more than the neutron, then neutrons would decay into protons and electrons, leaving the world devoid of neutrons. Neither scenario results in a life-sustaining universe.

5. *The cosmological constant.* Denoted by the Greek letter Λ, the cosmological constant is a parameter describing the energy density of empty space. It is depicted this way: $\Lambda = (8\pi G/3c^2)P$ (where π is pi, G is the gravitational constant, c is the speed of light in a vacuum, and P is the average density in the universe). As with the other constants, there is no particular reason why this number should be

what it is. As a matter of fact, most cosmological theories predict a huge number rather than the infinitesimal one we actually find. However, if it were not within one part in 10^{53} of its current values, the universe would have expanded so quickly that matter would have dispersed before galaxies and stars could have formed.

These are only five examples of about fifty such constants and conditions of physics that are currently known. Individually, they are often referred to as "happy accidents" or "anthropic coincidences." But taken together, they constitute what most now call "fine-tuning." The improbability of the convergence of all these parameters such that life could exist in the universe is so wildly astronomical that the most reasonable explanation for them seems to be intelligent design rather than either mere chance or the necessity of natural law.

Objections to Fine-Tuning in Physics

Not surprisingly, some disagree that intelligent design must be conjectured in order to account for the existence of life in the world. There are a number of objections to the design hypothesis, and following are three of the most prominent ones.

Objection #1: The Many-Universes Hypothesis

One of the more popular ways of explaining our finely tuned universe, while excluding an intelligent designer, is to suggest that there are, or were, a very large number of universes (perhaps an infinite number of them). Given this large number, some of them, at least, are bound to include life-permitting physical constants. While everyone agrees that most of them would include parameters that are life-*prohibiting*, if the number of universes is large enough, surely some of them would have the right parameters for life. Fortunately for us, our universe happens to be one that has just the right parameters. This can be taken as chance—odds are that with an infinite number of universes, some are going to have the right parameters for life. Or it could be taken as natural necessity—given an actual infinite number of universes, the physical laws of some of them necessarily will have the right parameters for life.

The two most discussed models for the many-universes hypothesis are the big bang oscillating models and the inflation models. With the big bang models, the universe is understood to come to exist through a "big bang," or cosmic explosion, from which it expands until gravity pulls it back together again. This will eventually lead to a "big crunch" in which the universe will collapse into infinite density from which another explosion will occur, creating yet another universe. Since this process could have happened from eternity past (argue defenders of these models), an infinite number of universes could have existed already. Once this is granted, it should not surprise us that at least one of them (e.g., our own) has life-permitting physical laws and constants. The big bang theory will be discussed at length in chapter 5, so we will move on to the next view.

Inflation models are also growing in popularity, and essentially they all include the view that a large number of universes currently exist, perhaps an infinite number of them, each formed in what is called an early inflation field. Some quantum fluctuations in these microscopic regions of early space expanded, or inflated, to cosmic proportions that then developed into the structured universes (such as our own) that currently exist. Since there are such large numbers of them, we should not be surprised that at least one of them—our own—has physical parameters that permit life.

Note first that in response to this objection there is currently no experimental evidence in support of the many-universes hypotheses. While there is some support in physics for inflationary cosmology, it is currently provisional and highly speculative. Science fiction writers are having a heyday with these new theories, but the scientific facts are wanting, to say the least.[9]

Second, as philosopher Robin Collins has argued, even if there are an infinite number of universes, they must be produced by some kind of a "many-universe generator." Such a device itself, however, must be finely tuned and is thus in need of an intelligent designer explanation.[10] For, as he notes, even a simple mechanism like a bread maker needs to be well designed to produce loaves of bread. How much more so a universe maker that produces finely tuned universes like our own.[11]

Finally, it should be noted that even if we eventually discover that there are an infinite number of universes (chances are slim here, since most physicists agree that there can be no scientific verification of the actual existence of even one other universe, even in principle), this still doesn't disprove theism. As a matter of fact, given the general understanding of God by most theologians, he is himself infinite, and so it would not be surprising if his universe reflects his own nature in this way.[12] However, it should also be kept in mind that this hypothesis, lacking in experimental verification as it currently is, is "tantamount to a recognition that the resources for chance and necessity in *this* universe are limited and insufficient to explain what we observe."[13]

Objection #2: The Anthropic Principle

There are different versions of what is called the anthropic principle (*anthropic* meaning "related to human beings"). The most fundamental and probably most widely held version of it is what physicists John Barrow and Frank Tipler call the Weak Anthropic Principle, or WAP. Here is the definition they offer:

> Weak Anthropic Principle (WAP): The observed values of all physical and cosmological quantities are not equally probable, but they take on values restricted by the requirement that there exist sites where carbon-based life can evolve and by the requirement that the Universe be old enough for it to already have done so.[14]

They also note a central feature that emerges from this principle:

> The basic features of the Universe, including such properties as its shape, size, age, and laws of change, must be *observed* to be of a type that allows the evolution of observers, for if intelligent life did not evolve in an otherwise possible universe, it is obvious that no one would be asking the reason for the observed size, shape, age, and so forth of the Universe.[15]

In other words, if the physical laws and constants of the universe were not *just so*, we would not be here to realize that fact. But, since we are here, we should not be surprised that the conditions are such that life exists here. Thus, there is no need to conjecture an intelligent designer of the universe.

This anthropic principle objection to the design argument, however, is misguided. Consider the following well-known illustration first offered by philosopher John Leslie.[16] Suppose you were brought before a firing squad of fifty or one hundred marksmen, all with powerful rifles aimed directly at you. The command is given to fire, and you hear the piercing sounds of the guns. But alas, after the smoke clears, you are still alive and unharmed. Every single sharpshooter missed!

What should you make of this situation? Is it reasonable to believe that you somehow experienced a lucky accident whereby every single shooter somehow missed the mark (namely, your heart), even though they are trained experts at hitting their target? Or is it more reasonable to believe that this was a setup—that for whatever reason, these shooters intended *not* to kill you? The answer seems quite obvious.[17]

The improbability of a life-permitting universe is much greater than these marksmen missing their target, and many astronomers, physicists, and others, including the well-renowned astrophysicist Paul Davies, are now persuaded that some kind of God exists because of these anthropic "coincidences."

Objection #3: Who Designed the Designer?

A third objection is that putting forward an intelligent designer as the explanation for the finely tuned universe simply moves the debate back one step, for we can then ask, "Who designed the Designer?" In his famous dialogue on religion, eighteenth-century philosopher and skeptic David Hume raises this objection:

> How shall we satisfy ourselves concerning the cause of that Being whom you suppose the Author of Nature . . . the Ideal World into which you trace the material? Have we not the same reason to trace that ideal world into another ideal world or new intelligent principle? But if we stop and go no farther, why go so far? Why not stop at the material world? How can we satisfy ourselves without going on *in infinitum*? And, after all, what satisfaction is there in that infinite progression? Let us remember the story of the Indian philosopher and his elephant.* It was never more applicable than to the present subject. If the present world rests upon some ideal world, this ideal world must rest upon some other, and so on without end. It were better, therefore, never to look beyond the present material world. By supposing it to contain the principle of its order within itself, we really assert it to be God; and the sooner we arrive at the Divine Being, so much the better. When you get one step beyond the mundane system, you only excite an inquisitive humor which it is impossible ever to satisfy.[18]

To briefly paraphrase his argument in the language of the contemporary debate, even if we can explain the apparent fine-tuning of the world as being the product of an intelligent designer, that designer must have a mind that is just as "finely tuned" (if not much more so) as the natural world. So the designer, too, must need an explanation, and the designer of the designer, and so on. This process of explanation could go on indefinitely, but it is unnecessary to do so. Why add hypotheses unnecessarily? Why not simply stop with the physical world?[19]

This objection, however, seems to miss the central point of the argument that our finely tuned universe is better explained via intelligence than it is by chance. Consider the following example. Suppose that during a deep-sea expedition, divers came upon what appeared to be an underwater city. It was nothing like they had ever seen before, but there were structures apparently designed to sustain oxygen-breathing creatures,

---

* The Indian philosopher said that the world was resting on the back of an elephant, and the elephant was resting on the back of a great tortoise, and the tortoise on the back of he knew not what.

including large rooms from which water could be pumped out, long tubes that could be used to pump in oxygen from above the water, and inlets and outlets that could be used for various transportation purposes.

In such a scenario, it would be more reasonable to believe that there were intelligent beings who created such a place than it would be to suppose that it came into existence through underwater evolutionary erosion and/or other chance naturalistic processes. We would not claim that there is no need to suggest intelligent design for the city since such intelligence itself may be in need of further explanation. The question of whether or not God's mind needs further explanation is an interesting one, but it has no bearing on this argument.[20]

We have seen, then, that intelligent design best explains our finely tuned universe. There is no natural law demanding that the physical constants of our universe be just so, and the probabilities of a life-permitting universe are too great to be explained by mere chance.

Is Life Designed? The Evidence from Biochemistry

A second aspect of the design argument that has been under much discussion in recent times involves new discoveries in biology and biochemistry. For the past century and a half, Darwin's theory of evolution has held sway as an explanation for the emergence, diversity, and complexity of all flora and fauna—all living organisms—that exist on planet Earth. Central to this Darwinian explanation are undirected natural forces plus time and chance. No doubt these factors are involved in nature. But recent scientific evidence indicates that they are clearly not the whole of it, despite what many people believe.

On the last day of my career in engineering, my colleagues at the firm for which I worked took me out for lunch. In the car on the way to the restaurant, I got into a discussion with two fellow engineers who did not believe that God exists. I asked them why they were atheists, and they both agreed that given evolution, there is no need to believe in God; the world can be completely explained scientifically.

We began discussing the theory of evolution, and I noted some of the objections to it as well as some of the recent evidences for intelligent design in the universe. After just a few scientific criticisms of the theory, one of the guys looked as if he had lost his best friend. I inquired what was wrong, and he replied, "My entire theology was based on the scientific evidence for evolution."

In other words, my friend's view about God's nonexistence was based on what he took to be a cut-and-dried case for naturalistic evolution. When he saw that there might be reason to doubt that case, his world was shaken. Even though our conversation was very cordial, he would not engage in the discussion any more that day. He was in a daze the rest of the afternoon, as his worldview had been completely rattled by recent and powerful scientific evidence for design in the world.

As we will see next, these evidences demonstrate that more is needed to explain the complexity and apparent design of life than naturalistic Darwinian processes. What, then, best explains what appears to be purpose, plan, and design in the very structure of living organisms?

Biochemical Design and Irreducible Complexity

One of the strongest pieces of evidence against the view that naturalistic evolution (involving random genetic mutation and the blind mechanism of natural selection) has created all of the living organisms that exist has to do with recent advances in biochemistry. Currently a unified band of scholars and scientists who believe they have a solid case for the intelligent design of living organisms are doing research in various fields of study, most notably biology and biochemistry. This group, often referred to as adherents of "intelligent design" (or ID), was spearheaded by Berkeley professor Phillip Johnson in the 1990s and has grown considerably since its inception.[21]

Today a leading voice in this charge is Michael Behe, a biochemist at Lehigh University. He has put forward what he calls "irreducible complexity" as a powerful challenge to naturalistic Darwinian ideology:

> By *irreducibly complex* I mean a single system composed of several well-matched, interacting parts that contribute to the basic function, wherein the removal of any one of the parts causes the system to effectively cease functioning. An irreducibly complex system cannot be produced directly (that is, by continuously improving the initial function, which continues to work by the same mechanism) by slight, successive modifications of a precursor system, because any precursor to an irreducibly complex system that is missing a part is by definition nonfunctional.[22]

It may be helpful in understanding Behe's argument to consider, as he does, the simple example of the standard mousetrap (see diagram that follows).

A typical mousetrap consists of the following parts: a hammer, a spring, a catch, a holding bar, and a platform or base to which all of the other parts are connected. Note that each of these parts is necessary for catching a mouse. If any of the parts that make up the trap are missing, it won't work as a mouse-catching device. It is irreducibly complex in that it cannot be reduced in any way and still function as a mousetrap.

Behe's mousetrap example

Behe's argument, then, in a nutshell, is that the biochemical world has a number of systems that consist of finely calibrated, interdependent parts that will not function without each of its components operating together. These systems, being irreducibly complex, cannot therefore be explained by the gradualism of evolutionary theory. A designer for them is a much better hypothesis.

A prime example of an irreducibly complex biochemical system is the bacterial flagellum.* In the early 1970s, certain bacteria were seen to move about via rotating their flagella, or whiplike tails, which whirl around at high rates of speed (the motor of the *E. coli* bacteria, for example, rotates at 270 revolutions per second while also getting feedback from the environment!). The structure of these kinds of bacteria includes what is similar to an outboard motor, and these "flagellar motors," as they are called, are very complicated devices. As the picture below indicates, a number of different components (forty in all) work together to cause the bacteria to move, including a hook, filament, stator, and rotor.[23]

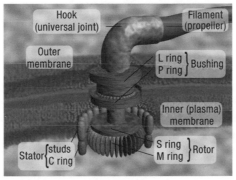

Flagellum

* The term *flagellum* is derived from Latin and means a whip or shoot.

What is so amazing here is that the forty parts of which this flagellar motor consists must be arranged just so. If any one of them is misplaced, the motor will not function at all. It is truly an irreducibly complex device. The question, then, is how such a system could develop gradually and naturalistically when each component is necessary for the device to function as a whole. Unless the mechanism works, natural selection would have no reason to preserve it.

Charles Darwin himself admitted that such evidence would be a problem: "If it could be demonstrated that any complex organ existed which could not possibly have been formed by numerous, successive, slight modifications, my theory would absolutely break down."[25] Given that natural selection could only go to work on the flagellar motor *after* it was fully developed, since functionally it basically comes complete or not at all, I think that, given this evidence, Darwin would have to admit that his theory is breaking down.[26]

Objections to Irreducible Complexity

Of course, not everyone agrees that there is evidence for intelligent design, biochemical or otherwise. A number of philosophers, biologists, and others have responded to arguments for irreducible complexity, and we will next explore two types of objections.

Objection #1: Evidence of Evolutionary Advancement

As this objection against intelligent design theory goes, a brief glance at any biology textbook will provide the novice science student with ample evidence that naturalistic evolution is empirically documented and scientifically verified. For example, given the hard evidence for natural selection—the naturalistic mechanism that accounts for the evolutionary development of living organisms—why even consider a design hypothesis? Isn't this a repeat of the old god-of-the-gaps view, in which God is brought into the equation whenever we are lacking a natural explanation? Doesn't this resemble the antediluvian view of some of the ancient Greeks and Romans, whereby thunder was attributed to the gods (such as Jupiter)? If we would simply remain hard-nosed scientists and stick with the facts, we wouldn't be led into wild-eyed theories about a supernatural being who tinkers with the universe. We are better off leaving stories about God to religion classes and Sunday school. At least that's how the story goes. But things aren't always as they first appear, and the evidence for naturalistic evolution isn't quite what many make it out to be.

Actually, there are two objections in the paragraph above, and they are often conflated: (1) evolution is a proven theory, and (2) science and religious belief are two different categories that should be kept separate. We will tackle the first one next and the second one under the section that follows titled "Can Real Science Include Design?".

The Problematic Meaning of the Term Evolution

In its classical form, the theory of evolution begins with the hypothesis that small, random, genetic changes in organisms (mutations or micromutations) on occasion offer positive survival value. The organisms that possess this positive value have an advantage over less fortunate ones in survival, reproduction, and the ability to pass these characteristics on to their offspring. The more fortunate organisms, consequently, survive and produce similar offspring, and the less fortunate ones simply die out. Over time these favorable characteristics spread throughout the population, causing it to change and advance. Thus, through small steps over great amounts of time, the theory goes, simple organisms developed from a soup of chemicals into more complex organisms that eventually branched out into all of the living organisms that exist today. All of this is typically understood in the meaning of the phrase "theory of evolution."

Sometimes, however, only one element of the theory is defined as evolution—an element that can be experimentally verified. For example, in a recent book on the topic, one of the most well-known evolutionists of our time offers this definition: "Evolution is the change in the properties of populations of organisms over time."[27] To support this meaning of the term, hard evidence is cited as observable, empirical proof of evolution. One common example of such proof that is found in many recent biology textbooks is the peppered moth case. This evidence is presented as follows.[28]

During the industrial revolution in Britain in the nineteenth century, the moth population near polluted cities turned dark, unlike the lighter color they were earlier in the same century. At the time it was unclear why the population had changed color. But then, in the 1950s, a British biologist named Bernard Kettlewell offered an explanation.

What Kettlewell suggested was that when trees turned black due to industrial smog, dark-colored moths in the population became predominant because predators had a difficult time finding them because they were blending in with the similarly colored trees. When the pollution cleared up and the trees became lighter again, the lighter-colored moths became predominant for the same reason. This became known as "industrial melanism," and it appeared to be a case of natural selection and thus proof for evolution.

Surprisingly, the peppered moth case has all but been discredited in recent times, despite the fact that it continues to be widely used as evidence for evolution.[29] But even granting its veracity, it still does not support "evolution" in the broad sense first described above. If true, it does substantiate the point that nature can select from small differences in a population. But no one denies this. The problem is that this "empirically verified fact" is then said to be hard evidence of *evolution*, when the term now means everything said above, including simpler organisms developing into more complex ones, rather than mere change for adaptation. Phillip Johnson puts the point concisely:

> Much confusion results from the fact that a single term—"evolution"—is used to designate processes that may have little or nothing in common. A shift in the relative number of dark and light moths in a population is called evolution, and so is the creative process that produced the cell, the multicellular organism, the eye, and the human mind. The semantic implication is that evolution is fundamentally a single process, and Darwinists enthusiastically exploit that implication as a substitute for scientific evidence.[30]

Other examples are cited as well. Darwin himself, about a century earlier, offered the variability of finches on the Galapagos Islands, most especially their beak variation, as hard evidence of evolution at work. What is being missed here in the presentation of this "hard" evidence of evolution, however, is the distinction between microevolution and macroevolution.

Microevolution and Macroevolution

Microevolution involves the minute, incremental changes that produce adaptations in species, and it is a substantiated theory. Macroevolution, on the other hand, is the view that the cumulative effects of those minute changes within a species have produced all of the variety of new species that exist today from earlier and less advanced ones. Macroevolution also involves the production of novel and advanced structures within the species—a notion that is seriously challenged by design theorists.

Virtually everyone agrees that evolution occurs if what is meant is *microevolution*. Selective breeding (whether with animals, plants, or bacteria) involves *change* within a species, and it is simply a fact that species do have a certain genetic plasticity. A quick glance at the plethora of dog breeds, for instance, bears this out. But the real question is whether or not this kind of change, undirected in the natural world, can create plants and pandas and people from simpler organisms through purely naturalistic, chance processes. Many scientists and scholars now claim that it cannot.[31]

Objection #2: Challenges to Claimed Examples of Irreducible Complexity

A second type of objection to biochemical design, and irreducible complexity specifically, involves challenges to the examples offered as being irreducibly complex. One of the primary challengers is biology researcher and professor Kenneth Miller. Miller offers the following concise criticism of the bacterial flagellum example and the attending mousetrap analogy:

> Ironically, Behe's own example, the mousetrap, shows what's wrong with the idea. Take away two parts (the catch and the metal bar), and you may not have a mousetrap but you do have a three-part machine that makes a fully functional tie clip or paper clip. Take away the spring, and you have a two-part key chain. The catch of some mousetraps could be used as a fishhook, and the wooden base as a paperweight. . . . The point, which science has long understood, is that bits and pieces of supposedly irreducibly complex machines may have different—but still useful—functions.[32]

He then applies this point to the bacterial flagellum example:

> Evolution produces complex biochemical machines by copying, modifying, and combining proteins previously used for other functions. Looking for examples? The system in Behe's essay will do just fine. He writes that in the absence of "almost any" of its parts, the bacterial flagellum "does not work." But guess what? A small group of proteins from the flagellum *does* work without the rest of the machine—it's used by many bacteria as a device for injecting poisons into other cells. Although the function performed by this small part when working alone is different, it nonetheless can be favored by natural selection.[33]

The criticism is clear. The flagellum is not a case of irreducible complexity since it does not need to be complete for natural selection to modify it until it eventually reached its current complex state. No designer is required.

Upon inspection of this criticism, however, it seems that Miller's point actually ends up supporting the design hypothesis. Here's why. While there could be individual functions of specific proteins before they form together to make a flagellum—just as there could be individual functions of some of the parts of a mousetrap—there is yet the problem of how all of the individual parts could form together into the vastly complex, machinelike flagellum. Paper clips, fishhooks, and key chains do not just magically join together to form a mousetrap. And the interrelations of the elementary proteins that make up the flagellar motor have surfaces that are much less suitably matched than the parts of a mousetrap, and there are also many more parts that need to be matched in the flagellum. So there is no Darwinian explanation for the assembly instructions that determined how the various parts would fit together.[34] Furthermore, only 10 percent of the flagellum's forty motor parts are found in other structures of the cell. Where the other thirty came from still requires explanation.[35]

So what we have here is not only a case of complexity, but specified complexity—complex and improbable patterns that are independent from the events they explain. As Paul Davies has noted, "Living organisms are mysterious not for their complexity per se, but for their tightly specified complexity."[36] Moreover, to date there has not been any Darwinian explanation put forth in a peer-reviewed scientific journal for how such irreducible systems could be produced through undirected scientific processes.

All of these factors combined make it much more plausible to believe that such systems arose from intelligent design than from either mere chance or natural law.

Can Real Science Include Design?

A significant objection to any design hypothesis in science is that natural science should presuppose a method that is naturalistic rather than supernaturalistic. Biochemist A. G. Cairns-Smith spells out a brief and concise synopsis of this point:

> It is a sterile stratagem to insert miracle to bridge the unknown. Soluble problems often seem to be baffling to begin with. Who would have thought a thousand years ago that the size of an atom or the age of the Earth would ever be discovered? . . . It is silly to say that because we cannot see a natural explanation for a phenomenon that we must look for a super-natural explanation.[37]

This view of how natural science should work, a view that has been dubbed "methodological naturalism," is a common ideology these days, not only among atheists but among a number of theists as well. On this view, scientific explanations should never get entangled in theological musings because the latter are untestable and therefore unscientific. A colleague who specializes in high-energy physics recently had this to say:

> The position taken by the majority of the scientific community is to assume that whatever gaps exist in our explanations of this physical world are due

to our not having yet found it. . . . Where I see evidence for God in science is not necessarily in the gaps of my understanding, but rather in what I do understand. I feel that it is important to pursue naturalistic explanations for what we observe. And to claim this excludes God is unwarranted bias.[38]

In my colleague's comments, he notes that the majority of the scientific community *assumes* that all gaps in our explanations are gaps because we have not yet discovered the naturalistic explanation for them. But why should we have this assumption? Why should we hold as a scientific presupposition that God never did anything in the creation process? If it is logically possible that God could have worked directly (and not only through secondary causes) in some of his creative acts, I do not see why the naturalistic assumption must be held. It is at least a logical possibility that God could have created some things directly and, if so, looking in the direction of a naturalistic answer only (without even allowing for a nonnaturalistic answer) is unwarranted bias.

Unlike many methodological naturalists, Cairns-Smith also adds these comments after his statement quoted above: "It is silly to say that because we cannot see a natural explanation for a phenomenon that we must look for a supernatural explanation. (*It is usually silly anyway.*) With so many past scientific puzzles now cleared up there have to be very clear reasons not to presume natural causes."[39] This is an important qualifier, and, in fact, I would argue that it actually eliminates him from truly holding to methodological naturalism. I think most thoughtful intelligent design theorists would agree. There should be "good reasons" for positing a nonnatural, or supernatural, cause as an explanation for an event in nature. But that is the point of most ID theorists—if there is good reason to consider intelligent design, let's not exclude it out of hand.[40]

Summary

I have argued in this chapter that it is more reasonable to believe that both the fine-tuning of the universe and the existence of irreducibly complex systems within living organisms happened by intelligent design rather than by chance or law. This is the crucial step in the new argument from design sketched out at the beginning of the chapter. Regarding fine-tuning, I have shown that the beauty and simplicity of the basic physical laws governing the universe, along with the cosmic constants that must be just so in order for life to exist in the universe, lend substantial support to an intelligent designer.

Regarding irreducible complexity, we have seen that there exist microscopic machines, such as the bacterial flagellar motor, that simply cannot be explained by naturalistic mechanisms or mere chance. Like the mousetrap, they are better explained by intelligent design. This is not to say that a theist cannot consistently believe in evolution. But as we saw, what this term means is of fundamental importance.

It is important to note here that reflecting on this argument from design is not merely a theoretical exercise that has no relevance to actual belief in God. One of the leading atheistic philosophers of the twentieth century, Antony Flew, has recently rejected atheism and now believes in God primarily because of this argument—one that he calls "a new and enormously powerful argument to design."[41] As science advances, the evidence for God just keeps mounting, and whether one studies the vast complexities of current scientific research or simply looks out across the world in which we live, it seems that the psalmist got it right: "The heavens declare the glory of God, the vault of heaven proclaims his handiwork. . . . No utterance at all, no speech, not a sound to be heard, but from the entire earth the design stands out, this message reaches the whole world" (Ps. 19:1–4 NJB).

Questions for Reflection

1. Explain in your own words the difference between chance, law, and intelligent design.
2. What do you consider to be the strongest argument for a designed universe? What about the strongest argument against a designed universe?
3. What is the difference between microevolution and macroevolution? Why is understanding this difference significant for the creation/intelligent design/evolution debate?
4. Explain how a mousetrap is an example of irreducible complexity. What are some similarities between the mousetrap example and the flagellar motor? What are some differences?
5. Can real science include intelligent design? Explain.

For Further Reading Supporting the Design Argument/against Naturalistic Evolution*

Behe, Michael. *Darwin's Black Box: The Biochemical Challenge to Evolution*. New York: Free Press, 1996.

* It must be noted that there is a clear distinction between intelligent design and scientific creationism. However, in the Further Reading sections, I am not separating the works on these lines.

Dembski, William A. *The Design Inference: Eliminating Chance through Small Probabilities*. Cambridge: Cambridge University Press, 1998. Using probability and information theory, Dembski argues persuasively for the design inference—a method for detecting intelligent causes. Fairly technical.

Johnson, Phillip E. *Darwin on Trial*. 2nd ed. Downers Grove, IL: InterVarsity, 1993. This book was the impetus for the intelligent design movement. It would be fruitful to read it along with Richard Dawkins's *The Blind Watchmaker*, listed below.

Leslie, John. *Universes*. New York: Routledge, 1989. Commonly understood to be the best book in print on the finely tuned universe.

Morris, Henry, ed. *Scientific Creationism*. El Cajon, CA: Master Books, 1985. The classic defense of "young earth" creationism. Clear and articulate.

Ratzsch, Del. *Science and Its Limits: The Natural Sciences in Christian Perspective*. 2nd ed. Downers Grove, IL: InterVarsity, 2000.

Strobel, Lee. *The Case for a Creator: A Journalist Investigates Scientific Evidence That Points toward God*. Grand Rapids: Zondervan, 2004. An award-winning book on intelligent design by a former skeptic.

Wells, Jonathan. *Icons of Evolution: Science or Myth?* Washington, DC: Regnery, 2000. An excellent work debunking many evolutionary icons by a well-respected scholar and biologist.

For Further Reading against the Design Argument/Supporting Naturalistic Evolution

Dawkins, Richard. *The Blind Watchmaker: Why the Evidence of Evolution Reveals a Universe without Design*. New York: W. W. Norton, 1987. Probably the most influential book defending naturalistic evolution. It would be fruitful to read this book along with Phillip Johnson's *Darwin on Trial*, listed above.

Eldredge, Niles. *The Triumph of Evolution and the Failure of Creationism*. New York: W. H. Freeman, 2000. An up-to-date defense of evolution against creationist accounts by a paleontologist and curator at the American Museum of Natural History.

Haught, John F. *God after Darwin: A Theology of Evolution*. Boulder, CO: Westview, 2000. A radical version of neo-Darwinian theory from a process theology perspective.

Miller, Kenneth R. *Finding Darwin's God: A Scientist's Search for Common Ground between God and Evolution*. New York: Harper Perennial, 2000. A defense of theistic evolution by a professor of biology.

Pennock, Robert T. *Tower of Babel: The Evidence against the New Creationism*. Cambridge, MA: MIT Press, 2000. A critique of the intelligent design theorists and their arguments.

Perakh, Mark. *Unintelligent Design*. Amherst, NY: Prometheus, 2003. A critique of intelligent design and scientific creationism.

Ruse, Michael. *Darwinism Defended*. Reading, MA: Addison-Wesley, 1982. A solid defense of Darwinism by a leading philosopher of biology.

Stenger, Victor J. *Has Science Found God? The Latest Results in the Search for Purpose in the Universe*. Amherst, NY: Prometheus, 2003. A critique of fine-tuning and other design evidences.

For Further Reading Pro and Con

Dembski, William A., and Michael Ruse, eds. *Debating Design: From Darwin to DNA*. Cambridge: Cambridge University Press, 2004. A fine collection of essays for and against intelligent design.

Pennock, Robert T., ed. *Intelligent Design Creationism and Its Critics: Philosophical, Theological, and Scientific Perspectives*. Cambridge, MA: MIT Press, 2001. Pro and con.

Manson, Neil A., ed. *God and Design: The Teleological Argument and Modern Science*. New York: Routledge, 2003. Pro and con.

5

In the Beginning . . . Bang!

Scientific and Philosophical Evidences for the Creation of the Universe

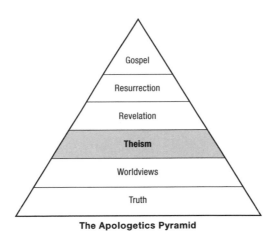

The Apologetics Pyramid

In the beginning God created the heavens and the earth.

Genesis 1:1 NIV

We go about our daily lives understanding almost nothing of the world. We give little thought to the machinery that generates the sunlight that makes life possible, to the gravity that glues us to an Earth that would otherwise send us spinning off into space, or to the atoms of which we are made and on whose stability we fundamentally depend. Except for children (who don't know enough not to ask the important questions), few of us spend much time wondering why nature is the way it is; where the cosmos came from, or whether it was always here; if time will one day flow backward and effects precede causes; or whether there are ultimate limits to what humans can know.

Carl Sagan

For many centuries philosophers and others have attempted to demonstrate that the universe was caused to exist by God. Such demonstrations come in a variety of forms and are referred to as *cosmological arguments*—the term *cosmological* being derived from the Greek words *cosmos* (world or universe) and *logos* (reason or rational account).[1] The different versions of the cosmological argument each focus on some characteristic or aspect of the universe from which it follows that the universe was caused to exist. For example, on one version of the argument, the universe is seen to be contingent (dependent on something else) rather than necessary (not dependent on something else), and therefore a necessary being must exist who then caused the contingent universe to come to be. This necessary being is then identified as God.[2]

While there may well be some merit to this contingency argument, there is another ancient form of the cosmological argument that seems by many, including myself, to be much more persuasive. Its most recent and avid defender, William Lane Craig, has called it the "kalam cosmological argument" (*kalam* is an Arabic term that simply means "speech," and it came to refer to an argument upholding a theological doctrine). In this chapter I will sketch out the argument, noting its strengths and providing responses to it by some of its most ardent foes.

The Kalam Cosmological Argument

In explaining and defending the kalam argument, Craig first sets up the following structure:

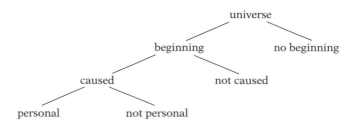

The dilemmas are obvious. Either the universe had a beginning or it didn't. If it did, either that beginning was caused or it wasn't. If it was caused, either the cause was personal or impersonal. Based on these dilemmas, the argument can first be put very simply in the following three-step logical form:

1. Whatever begins to exist must have a cause.
2. The universe began to exist.
3. Therefore, the universe must have a cause.

Given that what is meant by "universe" is time, space, matter, and physical energy (a generally accepted definition), it follows that this cause must itself be timeless, spaceless, and matterless and must be able to create the physical energy that exists in the universe. This cause, then, is identified as God. Whether this "God" is personal or not will be addressed later on in the chapter.

Note first that the argument above is logically valid. As noted in the previous chapter, validity simply means that if the claims of the argument are true, then the conclusion necessarily follows. If claims 1 and 2 are true, then conclusion 3 necessarily follows. So the question is, are the claims (or premises) true?

The step in the argument that has historically been most challenged by the antagonist is 2. However, as Craig and others have argued, there are philosophical arguments and scientific evidences that strongly support the view that the universe began to exist. Let's first examine several evidences for this claim, and toward the end of the chapter we will examine claim 1.

Scientific Evidences for the Beginning of the Universe

Second Law of Thermodynamics

One of the most established laws of science today is the second law of thermodynamics. Fundamental to the second law is what is called *entropy*, which is usually understood to be the measure of unavailable energy, or disorder, in a closed system. An example of entropy is the decrease of heat energy in a glowing ember. As the ember cools, the available energy in the wood dissipates as the heat disperses into the surrounding environment.

According to the second law, the amount of available energy in a closed thermodynamic system—a system within which no new mass or energy is placed—decreases over time. That is, the entropy *increases* over time.

If, as most agree, the universe is all there is in terms of matter and energy, and no new energy is being "fed into the system," the universe is such a closed thermodynamic system. So the entropy in the universe is increasing over time. To put it differently, the amount of available energy and order in the universe is *decreasing* over time. Therefore, the universe will eventually reach a state of thermodynamic equilibrium (in this case, such equilibrium would mean that the temperature would remain constant and change no longer). All of the hot stars, for example, will eventually cool off and remain stable at a constant temperature—no longer expending heat energy.

Paul Davies, a world-renowned theoretical physicist and popular science writer mentioned in the previous chapter, puts the point this way:

> Everywhere we look, in every corner of the cosmos, entropy is rising irreversibly and the vast stock of cosmic order is slowly but surely being depleted. The universe seems destined to continue crumbling, running down towards a state of thermodynamic equilibrium and maximum disorder, after which nothing further of interest will happen. Physicists call this depressing prospect "the heat death."[3]

So herein lies the rub for the person denying that the universe had a beginning: if the universe has always existed, why has it not already reached this state of thermodynamic equilibrium?

Consider the following analogy. Suppose that you walk into a room and see a cup of Starbucks coffee (my favorite brew) placed on the table before you. You wonder how long the coffee has been sitting there and so, while no one is watching, you take a sip. You discover that it is still fairly hot. Would you then conclude that the coffee had been sitting there in the cup for months, weeks, or even days? Of course not. Why not? Because of the second law of thermodynamics and entropy; the heat energy in the cup of coffee has not fully dissipated, so it could not have been sitting there for very long. Now, since the universe is still "hot," so to speak (note the hot star in our own solar system, for example, called the "sun"), it could not have existed forever or it too would have "cooled off" long ago (an infinite amount of time ago, to be precise). Conclusion: the universe could not have existed forever; it must have had a beginning.[4]

Not everyone is happy with this conclusion, of course. Some theorists, such as British physicist John Gribbin, have argued that the universe could escape this "heat death" through a cycle of expansion and contraction of the universe. In this "oscillating universe theory,"[5] after an expansion of the universe, gravity stops it and causes a contraction, and it collapses back into a singularity. To get a picture of this in your mind, imagine blowing up a balloon that has many tiny little dots all over it. The dots represent stars and galaxies. The balloon itself represents the universe. Blowing up the balloon represents the expansion of the universe, and letting the air out represents the contraction of the universe.

After the contraction and collapse, some (unknown) mechanism causes the universe to explode into a new universe and then to begin the expansion process once again. Since this cycle can continue on indefinitely as illustrated below (the radius is the distance across the universe), there is no need to posit a final heat death, and thus no need to posit a final end or even a beginning to the universe.

Radius of the Universe

However, the evidence against this model of the universe over the past forty years, and especially in the past decade, has been so strong that few continue to hold it today. Here are some of the reasons this theory has basically failed as an explanatory hypothesis:

1. The work of Stephen Hawking, Roger Penrose, and George Ellis demonstrated that the evidence strongly suggests that there was an *initial* cosmic singularity (an infinitely small point from which all the mass and energy of the universe exploded into existence) rather than a series of singularities.[6]
2. The entropy from each alleged oscillation cycle accumulates, thus causing successively larger oscillations, and therefore would result in an ever-increasing radius, traceable back to a first cycle.[7]
3. The density of the universe seems to be only about one-tenth the amount needed to halt its expansion.[8]
4. There is no known physical mechanism that could reverse a cosmic contraction.
5. Even if the universe were to collapse, a new bounce would not be possible given that it is so entropic; the oscillating theory could not be reconciled with the second law of thermodynamics.[9]

Besides the oscillating model, another conception that denied a beginning of the universe was introduced in 1948 by Hermann Bondi, Thomas Gold, and Fred Hoyle and is referred to as the "steady state model" (it is also sometimes referred to as the "continuous creation theory"). On this view, the universe has been expanding and will continue to expand indefinitely. New matter is constantly being generated to replace the receding galaxies (think again of the balloon example where the dots are moving away from each other), and so the overall density of the universe seems to remain the same, even though it is continually expanding.

However, in 1965, observational evidence given by Arno Penzias and Robert Wilson indicated that cosmic background radiation existed, left over from the big bang, which could not be accounted for given the steady state theory. That discovery, along with other observations that supported the view that the universe is changing, all but discredited this model. Today very few scientists still hold to it.[10]

Other models of the universe have been proposed over the last several decades, including the new "brane cosmology" theories that introduce multidimensions of the universe.[11] These models are currently considered protoscientific, and perhaps upcoming decades will offer new insights into their plausibility. At this time, however, the most well-established model of the universe—the one that continues to be corroborated by the scientific evidence—is the traditional big bang theory. Surprisingly to many, this model also provides scientific evidence for the beginning of the universe.

Big Bang Cosmology

For many centuries astronomers and scientists generally agreed that the universe was static—that it was stationary and not expanding in any significant sense. In the early 1900s, however, a number of very important scientific observations took place that changed the old paradigm. One of these observations was that of Vesto Slipher in 1914. He noted that a number of nebulae (a nebulae is a diffuse mass of interstellar gas or dust) were receding from the earth at very high rates of speed. Astronomers at the time didn't know what to make of this observational discovery, and its significance went all but unnoticed.

Then, in the 1920s, an astronomer by the name of Edwin Hubble, using a large, one-hundred-inch telescope, observed that the nebulae observed by Slipher were actually galaxies far beyond our own Milky Way galaxy and that they were, in fact, moving farther away at high velocities. Here is how Hubble demonstrated this recession of galaxies. He had been studying the light from distant galaxies, and he noted that the colors (colors understood to be wavelengths of light) emitted by these galaxies did not match the expected wavelengths. Instead, they were shifted to the far end of the red spectrum, and this "redshift" of light from galaxies increased in a direct ratio to how far away the galaxies were located. This observational redshift effect matched the theoretical views cosmologists had already suggested—that the universe was actually expanding.

Hubble's observational evidence along with the theoretical postulations have caused the vast majority of cosmologists today to agree that the universe originated in an infinitely dense singularity and that, from this initial beginning, space itself has expanded with the passage of time (see figure below). As theoretical physicist Stephen Hawking puts it, "Almost everyone now believes that the universe, and *time itself*, had a beginning at the Big Bang."[12]

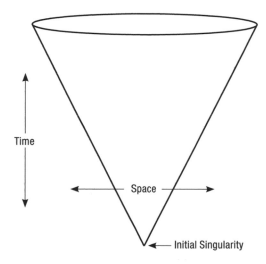

Time

Space

Initial Singularity

**Conical Representation of the Big Bang Model
of the Universe**

Philosophical Argument for the Beginning of the Universe

As mentioned earlier, there are also philosophical arguments for the idea that the universe had a beginning and was caused to exist by God. The ancient version of the kalam argument, noted above, did not, of course, have the scientific evidences just discussed. The earlier philosophers did, however, have philosophy and mathematics, which are still relevant to us today. While some people consider such arguments to be mere "armchair hypothesizing," I consider at least one of these philosophical arguments to be astonishingly compelling—so compelling, in fact, that I think it is even stronger than the scientific evidences available today.

We shall next explore what I take to be the stronger of these philosophical arguments for step 2 of the kalam argument, that the universe began to exist. I call it the "Crossing the Infinite Argument," and it, too, can be put in three steps:

1. The series of events in time that makes up the whole history of the universe is a collection formed by adding one member after another.
2. The collection formed by adding one member after another cannot be actually infinite.
3. Therefore, the series of events in time that makes up the whole history of the universe cannot be actually infinite.[13]

Since the series cannot be infinite, it must be finite. That is to say, the series of events in time must have a beginning.

Let's examine each of the steps of this argument, and by the end of this examination, the power of the argument should be evident. First, step 1 seems to be fairly clear-cut. The events that make up all of history are taken one after the other. They did not all happen at once, but were sequentially occurring as time moved forward.[14] Just as the events that occurred in my life from 8:00 a.m. to 8:00 p.m. today are a collection of events formed by successive addition (one added after another), so too are all of the events in my life and, indeed, all of the events in history.

Step 2 is the crucial claim. Before examining it, though, the phrase "actually infinite" needs to be explained. By definition, an actual infinite is a *completed* totality or set of things or events rather than an *indefinite* one. To better understand this concept, it is helpful to contrast an actual infinite with a potential infinite. A potential infinite is an incomplete set in that it continues on indefinitely but never reaches the point of being an actual infinite set. For example, I could begin counting now and continue on forever. But I would never get to the place where I could stop and say, "I've finally reached counting an actual infinite set of numbers."

A potential infinite, then, is indefinite in that it gains new members as it expands but never reaches an end. An actual infinite, on the other hand, is definite—it is a complete set; it has a fixed number of members in it.[15] The point of this argument, then, is that one could never reach an actual infinite by moving one member after another (that is, by successive addition), and so our universe could not be actually infinitely old; it must have had a beginning.

Here's how the argument works: if the universe never had a beginning, it would include an actual infinite set of events rather than a potential infinite, for here we are at the end of the set of events that makes up history to this point. It is, as such, a completed set. Furthermore, it would have come to this actual infinite point by successive addition, one member occurring after another. The problem, though, as will be argued next, is that an actual infinite set of events cannot be achieved by successive addition. So, the set of events that makes up history must be finite, and thus the universe must have a beginning.

So why can't an actual infinite set of events be achieved by successive addition? Why can't the temporal series of events that makes up the whole history of the universe be an actual infinite? Why couldn't the universe have existed forever?

Sub-argument #1 for Crossing the Infinite Argument

To demonstrate why it is impossible to cross over an actual infinite, we will look at two *sub-arguments* for this "Crossing the Infinite Argument." To grasp this first sub-argument, consider the following example. Suppose that you are visiting a restaurant in the hopes of having a scrumptious dinner. You ask the hostess how long the wait will be before you will be seated. She notes that there are five people ahead of you, and that the wait has been averaging about twenty minutes per person. So, you have about a one-and-a-half-hour wait before you will be seated.

Your spouse isn't too keen on waiting this long, but being a quick-thinking mathematician, you point out that if there were ten people ahead of you, as at the previous restaurant you visited, you would have to wait more than three hours; if there were twenty people ahead of you, you would have to wait more than six hours; if there were one hundred people ahead of you, you would have to wait more than thirty-three hours; and if there were an actual infinite number of people ahead of you, you never would get to eat at all. So, you exclaim, waiting one and a half hours isn't long at all compared to never eating!

While your spouse may not be impressed with your mathematical aptitude, you do have a valid point. If an infinite number of people were ahead of you, the issue would not be that it would take a very, very long time before you had the chance to enjoy the cuisine; you never would. Conversely, if you did finally eat, you would know that there must have been a finite number of people ahead of you. Here's why. On the road to infinity, there is always one more member that can be added. In reality, you never can get to the end of an infinite series, for there is no end—there is always one more member, since a series formed by successive addition is a potential infinite. You can never reach the point where you are finally at the end of such a series.

The same point applies to the argument above regarding the temporal series of events that makes up the history of the universe. If the universe were, in fact, infinitely old, to get to the present moment you would have had to cross an infinite number of successive moments from the infinite past to get here, since this moment is the last member of the temporal series. But as we have just seen, there is no possible way to do that, yet here we are at this present moment. The implication seems clear: the past cannot be an actual infinite but must have a definite beginning.

Sub-argument #2 for Crossing the Infinite Argument

A second but related problem with crossing the infinite is that if there were a *beginningless* starting point in the past (as some critics of the kalam argument have suggested), it would still be absurd to suppose that we ever could have reached the present moment. The problem here is not a matter of not having enough time, nor of infinitely adding one member after another as argued above. Rather, it is a metaphysical absurdity. Craig puts it this way:

> Indeed, the idea of a beginningless series ending in the present seems to be absurd. To give just one illustration: suppose we meet a man who claims to have been counting from eternity and is now finishing: . . . , -3, -2, -1, 0. We could ask, why did he not finish counting yesterday or the day before or the year before? By then an infinite time had already elapsed, so that he should already have finished by then. Thus, at no point in the infinite past could we ever find the man finishing his countdown, for by that point he should already be done! In fact, no matter how far back into the past we go, we can never find the man counting at all, for at any point we reach he will have already finished. But if at no point in the past do we find him counting, this contradicts the hypothesis that he has been counting from eternity. This illustrates the fact that the formation of an actual infinite by successive addition is equally impossible whether one proceeds to or from eternity.[16]

Given that the temporal series of events is finite, there must have been a beginning to it, and thus the universe must have had a beginning. Therefore, this philosophical argument based on the impossibility of crossing over an actual infinite supports step 2 of the kalam argument itself—the universe must have had a beginning.

Before moving on to demonstrate why such a beginning must have been caused by a personal God, we will first examine some of the objections to this argument.

Criticisms of the Philosophical Argument for the Beginning of the Universe

Several very fine atheistic philosophers have responded to this "Crossing the Infinite Argument" for step 2 of the kalam argument, and one of them is Nicholas Everitt. Perhaps, he suggests, there is *no* starting point at all to the temporal series; perhaps the series does not have an earliest member. No vicious regress emerges from such an assertion, he argues, for just as the future can go on forever, so too the past could go back forever. It is only in assuming a *beginning* to an infinite series that an objectionable problem is created. By denying a beginning, there is no problem left to solve.[17]

In response, we have just examined the problem with a beginningless past and seen that such a view is absurd. Beyond this, however, Everitt is missing the central point of the argument, it seems. The future and the past are significantly different. The past is a collection of events, added together, *that have already occurred.* The future, of course, has not yet happened. So the future can go on forever; it can continue on indefinitely. Beginning with this moment in time, time could continue on forever, but it would never reach a point at which an actual infinite amount of time elapsed. It would simply never get there. But we are here, at this moment in time with an actual number of events that have occurred before now. And so to say that we have reached an actual infinite at this end (looking from the past) is just as absurd as saying that sometime in the future we could reach an actual infinite point at that end.

Another objection that has been raised has to do with the ancient philosopher Zeno of Elea (ca. 495–430 BC). Zeno attempted to demonstrate the impossibility of all movement, as well as the idea that there is in reality no change from one state to another. While this may sound strange to our modern ears (let's not kid ourselves, this would sound strange to *any* ears), Zeno truly believed that our senses deceive us and that through reason we can discover that there is no actual movement in the world. He offered several paradoxes to make the point, and the one that is especially relevant to our argument is Achilles and the tortoise.

The argument goes something like this. Suppose Achilles and a tortoise are going to race each other. If the tortoise is given a head start, Achilles will never be able to catch up with him because he (Achilles) would have to first move from the starting point (SP0) to the point where the tortoise is currently located (TL1). But by the time Achilles reaches TL1, the tortoise will have moved on to TL2, and by the time Achilles reaches TL2, the tortoise will have moved on to TL3, and so on. While Achilles does continually narrow the gap, we can continue to divide up indefinitely the points that he would need to cross over. But Achilles will never be able to reach the tortoise because there is an *infinite* number of points for Achilles to traverse.

SP0_____ TL1 _____ TL2 _____ TL3 ____ . . .

Because of this and related paradoxes, Zeno concluded that all motion is impossible; it is merely an illusion of the mind. (Before we are too hard on Zeno for holding what seems to be a ridiculous idea that all motion is an illusion, consider that our senses tell us that this book in our hands is a static object. But we know from physics that it actually consists of mostly empty space along with very small particles swirling at extremely high rates of speed. Our senses do not always give us the most accurate information about the world.)

Contrary to Zeno, since most people would agree that movement is not, in fact, mere illusion, it has been argued that his paradoxes demonstrate that we do traverse the infinite all the time. In real life Achilles would *eventually* be able to catch the tortoise, so he *must* be able to cross over an actual infinite number of points. So, this argument goes, it is not impossible to cross over an actual infinite. And so it is not absurd to suppose that the universe consists of an actual infinite set of events that makes up history. Thus, it need not have a beginning.

What are we to make of Zeno's argument? One of the great philosophers in history was Aristotle (384–322 BC), and he proposed what I think is still the best solution to the problem.[18] Aristotle argued that we need to make a distinction between an actual infinite and a potential infinite (a distinction that was noted above). While one could *conceptually* continue to divide the points between Achilles and the tortoise indefinitely *in one's mind*, there is *in reality* not an actual infinite number of spatial distances, but only a potentially infinite number of them for him to cross over. We can mentally continue to slice up the racecourse as many times as we like, but no matter how many times we do so, there is still only a finite number of spatial distances to cross over. The infinity is only a potential one, not an actual one.

Thus, if one believes that it is possible for movement to occur, and for Achilles to eventually catch the tortoise (and doesn't it seem absurd to deny that he could?), then it seems reasonable to conclude that he doesn't have to get to the end of an actual infinite number of spatial distances along the way, endlessly reaching for the next one. Rather, no matter how we decide to cut up the racecourse into mental points and midpoints (ad infinitum and ad nauseam), Achilles has only to reach a finite set of spatial distances to finally catch the tortoise.[19]

We have examined the two strongest objections to the Crossing the Infinite Argument and found them to be inadequate refutations of it. Thus, the argument stands unscathed. It is impossible to cross over an actual infinite set of events, so the history of past events must be finite; the universe did have a beginning.

Does Whatever Begins to Exist Need a Cause?

The first step in the kalam argument, once again, is this: whatever begins to exist must have a cause. This step is not often denied, even by those who doubt or deny God's existence, for the simple reason that every physical event we know of that can be analyzed can be traced back to a prior cause (at least in theory).[20] The very enterprise of science includes the idea that events need causes. Imagine what science would be like if this principle were denied (imagine what medicine would be like, for example). Given the overwhelming evidence for the truth of this claim, it seems unreasonable to deny or even question it.[21]

A different kind of objection to this step in the kalam argument, however, is that if everything that exists needs a cause for its existence, doesn't God also need a cause for his existence? Note, however, that the claim is *not* that whatever *exists* needs a cause. Rather, the claim is that whatever *begins to exist* needs a cause. On the standard Christian, Jewish, and Islamic views, God did not *begin* to exist. He has always existed. He is the uncaused cause, so to ask who caused God is to ask an incoherent question.

Of course, one could object to this meaning of God, but the atheist or skeptic must at least grant that such a meaning is a coherent one; whether it is true or false is a different question. This is one of the major differences between the meanings of the terms *universe* and *God*. Everything that makes up the universe needs a prior cause—it is all contingent (most atheists and theists agree with this claim)—but God, by definition, is different in that he does not need a cause (the atheist and the theist can at least agree with this meaning of God while disagreeing about whether he really exists).[22]

Furthermore, if everything that makes up the universe needs a cause, then surely the universe itself needs a cause. Consider the following parable.[23] Suppose that two people are exploring an uncharted woods somewhere in North America; one of the explorers is an atheist and the other a theist. Suppose further that they come across a large spherical object—one the likes of which they have never seen before. The theist asks the atheist if he believes that this object came into existence without any cause whatsoever. "Of course not," says the atheist. "This object must have been caused to exist by something or someone."

As they continue on their journey, they find another, larger, spherical object. "What about this sphere," asks the theist. "Do you suppose that this thing came into being without a cause?"

"Of course not," exclaims the atheist. "Something must have caused this thing to come into existence as well."

They then come to a third sphere, much larger even than the second one. "What about this very large sphere. Did it pop into existence without any cause?" asks the theist.

"Certainly not!" exclaims the atheist. "It too must have been caused to exist."

"Well then," asks the theist, "what about the universe itself—the largest sphere of all? Was it caused to come into existence?"

"No," replies the atheist. "It popped into existence without any cause whatever."

In this scenario, who is being more rational? Who is being more consistent? The answer is obvious.

Was the Cause of the Beginning of the Universe a Personal God?

So far it has been argued that the universe began to exist and that it must have a cause for its existence. But the question remains: must the cause of the universe be a personal being, or could it have been caused by nonpersonal forces? Using our three-step approach once again, let's analyze the following argument.

1. If the universe began to exist, the cause of its existence must be a personal God.
2. The universe began to exist.
3. Therefore, the cause of the beginning of the universe must be a personal God.

We have already examined step 2, so that leaves us with step 1. Since the argument is logically valid, if step 1 is reasonable to believe (and we have already concluded that step 2 is reasonable to believe), then it follows that the conclusion is reasonable to believe as well. Let's examine step 1.

If all that exists is the universe, and if the universe is time, space, matter, and energy, then when the universe came into existence, all that existed must have come into existence from nothing and by nothing. But we have already noted that it is unreasonable to believe in something coming into existence without any cause whatsoever (at least the scientific evidence is against it).

But perhaps there is some other kind of impersonal cause of the beginning of the universe—some kind of force (or forces) beyond the known universe. Two things can be said about this claim. First, there is no evidence for it, scientific or otherwise; it is mere wishful thinking. Second, even if there were some kind of impersonal force outside of the universe, there is a deeper philosophical problem that must be addressed. Prior to the beginning of the universe, there was no time, space, matter, or energy, and thus no change from one state to another. If there were some kind of existing impersonal force, it would have existed in this timeless, changeless, spaceless state. But in such a state, how could a new event occur? Could it occur spontaneously? There would have to be a *prior* cause for it (if we could even make sense of "prior" in such a state). But that cause, too, would need a prior cause, and so back we go ad infinitum. Thus, there would need to be an actual infinite series of cause and effect that was traversed. But we have already seen that this is impossible.

Another possibility is a personal cause in which an agent freely chooses to act. This is the theistic answer: a personal God caused the universe to exist. On this view, such choices are not caused by a previous cause but are self-caused by the agent for reasons he (or she) alone chooses. Positing this kind of free will not only accounts for the cause of the existence of the universe but also for our own free, moral choices. To deny such free actions lands one in various kinds of moral conundrums (we will discuss this further in the next chapter), and thus it seems more reasonable to affirm such freedom than to deny it.[24]

A final possibility is that there is a cause outside of our universe that is personal but is not God. Perhaps it is some sort of alien or extradimensional creature. My wife is an accountant, and I vividly recall attending a number of annual after-tax-season dinners her company provided for their employees and spouses. They were five-star restaurant experiences, and every year I would end up in a discussion with someone over dinner about the existence of God. On one occasion I was having a discussion with one of the spouses who was a pilot for a major airline. We were deeply engrossed in a discussion about the kalam argument, and when we got to this final stage, he said that perhaps the cause of the universe was not God but rather an alien—someone like Q on *Star Trek*, a near-omnipotent, near-omniscient godlike being from a parallel universe.

Here was my response. "Let's call this extradimensional alien 'Bob.' Note that Bob is timeless, spaceless, and matterless, and while not having material energy it (he/she) was powerful enough to create all the energy in the universe—all the stars, planets, galaxies, quasars, and so on. You can call him Bob; I'll call him Yahweh. But that's what I mean by God!"

Summary

In this chapter I presented a set of alternatives regarding the universe: either it had a beginning or it didn't; either it was caused to exist or it wasn't; and either the cause was a personal God or it wasn't. I then argued that it is more plausible to believe that the universe had a beginning than to believe that it existed forever, that the universe was caused to exist, and that the best explanation for this cause is a personal God. In support of these positions, I offered scientific evidences and philosophical arguments.

First, I contended that according to one of the most established laws of science, the second law of thermodynamics, the amount of available energy in a closed system decreases over time. Given that the universe is such a system, and given that the amount of energy within it is finite (both are generally agreed upon by theistic and atheistic scientists alike), it could not have existed forever or it would have run down already. Responses to this argument were examined and found wanting.

The second reason I offered for why the universe must have had a beginning is the big bang theory. According to this theory, at some point in the finite past, the universe was shrunk down to nothing at all, and from this point of nothingness the universe—time, space, matter, and energy—exploded into existence. Other theories were mentioned and explored, including the oscillating universe model, and it was noted that the current scientific evidence still strongly supports the traditional big bang theory. While it could be a false theory, it is at this time the most reasonable one to believe.

Third, I presented a philosophical argument that I called the "Crossing the Infinite Argument." I showed that it is impossible to traverse an actual infinite set of things—to form an infinite collection of events by adding one member after another—and so the past temporal series of events that make up the history of the universe must be finite. In other words, the universe must have a beginning.

Finally, I argued that it is more reasonable to believe that the cause of the universe is a personal God rather than impersonal forces or aliens. Denying this lands one in logical, moral, and scientific difficulties. Whatever we call this timeless, spaceless, matterless, personal being, the qualities are the same ones used to describe the God of the major theistic religions.

As with the design argument presented in chapter 4, the kalam argument, too, is quite persuasive. A good friend of mine, Rob, became a theist through a study of this argument. He then went on to graduate school to study more about God. I encourage you to thoroughly examine the kalam argument, as well as the responses to it, and discover for yourself where the evidence points.

Questions for Reflection

1. What does the universe having a beginning have to do with the existence of God?

2. How would you explain, in your own words, the two scientific evidences for the beginning of the universe?
3. The philosophical argument for the beginning of the universe is quite abstract. Do you understand it? If so, how would you explain it to someone who is unfamiliar with it?
4. What do you make of the parable of the atheist and the theist in the uncharted woods? Who is being the most reasonable? Why?
5. Explain the argument for why the cause of the beginning of the universe was personal. What is wrong with supposing that such a personal cause was a being from a different galaxy or universe?

For Further Reading in Defense of Cosmological Arguments

Craig, William Lane. *The Kalam Cosmological Argument*. Eugene, OR: Wipf & Stock, 1979. The definitive work on the kalam argument.

Craig, William Lane, and Quentin Smith. *Theism, Atheism, and Big Bang Cosmology*. New York: Oxford University Press, 1993. Craig, a Christian theist, and Smith, an atheist, go head-to-head—chapter by chapter—defending their views. Technical, but an outstanding work.

Geisler, Norman, and Winfried Corduan. *Philosophy of Religion*. 2nd ed. Grand Rapids: Baker, 1988. Chapter 8 contains a list of many different kinds of cosmological arguments.

Ross, Hugh. *The Fingerprint of God*. 2nd ed. Orange, CA: Promise, 1991. A very helpful and readable work by a theistic astrophysicist.

For Further Reading against Cosmological Arguments

Craig, William Lane, and Quentin Smith. *Theism, Atheism, and Big Bang Cosmology*. New York: Oxford University Press, 1993. See above.

Everitt, Nicholas. *The Nonexistence of God*. New York: Routledge, 2004. This is a highly readable work. Chapter 4 focuses on cosmological arguments.

Le Poidevin, Robin. *Arguing for Atheism: An Introduction to the Philosophy of Religion*. New York: Routledge, 1996. An erudite, readable presentation by a leading philosopher. Note especially chapters 1 and 3.

Mackie, J. L. *The Miracle of Theism: Arguments for and against the Existence of God*. Oxford: Oxford University Press, 1982. Mackie was a well-known and well-respected atheist philosopher. Chapter 5 argues against cosmological arguments.

Rowe, William. *The Cosmological Argument*. New York: Fordham University Press, 1998.

Morality, Evil, and Religion

Are Right and Wrong Evidence for God?

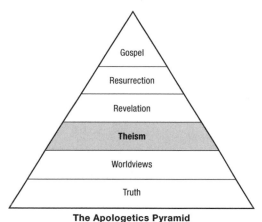

The Apologetics Pyramid

Everything is indeed permitted if God does not exist.

Jean-Paul Sartre

Anthropologists have ransacked the Melanesian Islands, the jungles of New Guinea, the steppes of Siberia, the deserts of Australia, the forests of central Africa, and have brought back with them countless examples of weird, extravagant, and fantastic "moral" customs with which to confound us. We learn that all kinds of horrible practices are, in this, that, or the other place, regarded as essential to virtue.

Walter T. Stace

I argued briefly in chapter 3 that since there are objective moral values, it is unreasonable to hold to the atheistic worldview. I also argued that given the good and evil that we really do experience in the world, the theistic answer is more reasonable to believe than the pantheistic answer that moral claims are illusory.

In this chapter we shall examine these issues more carefully, noting responses and counterarguments along the way. Given that historically the problem of evil and suffering has been the dominant objection to the existence of God, it certainly warrants further analysis and reflection.

The Argument for Objective Moral Values

I sketched out in chapter 3 what I called "the problem of good." In a nutshell, the problem is this: objective moral values exist in the world, values that are widely recognized as being true, and atheism is not able to account for their existence. So the problem is the atheist's. On the other hand, theism does provide an accounting for the existence of objective moral values. I will put the argument in positive form in this chapter:

1. If there are objective moral values, then God exists.
2. There are objective moral values.
3. Therefore, God exists.

The form of the argument is clearly valid, so the question that remains is whether steps 1 and 2 are true. Let's take them one at a time, beginning with step 2.

Examining Step 2: There Are Objective Moral Values

Is it true that there are objective moral values? What are objective moral values, anyway? By the term "objective moral values" I am referring to moral precepts or principles that are universally binding on all people at all times and places whether they actually recognize and follow them or not. We will call the view that there are objective moral values *moral objectivism*.

There are really only two basic options to choose from regarding moral values. Either the moral objectivist is right, and moral values are universally and objectively true, or the moral objectivist is wrong, and moral values are subjective opinions. We will call the view that there are no objective moral values *moral subjectivism*. For the moral subjectivist, moral actions are subjective, personally or culturally; they are not binding on all people at all times and places, for they are the inventions of someone, or some culture, at some particular time and some particular place.

Earlier I noted a couple of reasons why someone might believe that objective moral values do or do not exist. We will now take a closer look at these arguments as well as a few others.

The Universality of Moral Beliefs

A number of anthropologists and sociologists have claimed that universal moral norms are a myth. World-renowned anthropologist Ruth Benedict, for example, claims that the notions of right and wrong, normal and abnormal, are cultural inventions.[1] She cites examples of moral disparities, and downright contradictions, among the moral standards of different cultures and then concludes that due to this moral diversity, moral objectivism is false.

Consider the following argument against moral objectivism following her line of thought:[2]

1. The Greeks believed it was wrong to eat the dead, whereas the Callatians believed it was right to eat the dead.
2. Therefore, eating the dead is neither objectively right nor objectively wrong. It is merely a matter of opinion, which varies from culture to culture.

Here is another example:

1. The Eskimos see nothing wrong with infanticide, whereas other Americans believe infanticide is immoral.
2. Therefore, infanticide is neither objectively right nor objectively wrong. It is merely a matter of opinion, which varies from culture to culture.

Clearly there are social and moral incongruities among the differing cultures of world history. So how can there be a universal moral standard that exists for all cultures? Here is the insightful quote offered at the beginning of the chapter, but in full:

> Anthropologists have ransacked the Melanesian Islands, the jungles of New Guinea, the steppes of Siberia, the deserts of Australia, the forests of central Africa, and have brought back with them countless examples of weird, extravagant, and fantastic "moral" customs with which to confound us. We learn that all kinds of horrible practices are, in this, that, or the other place, regarded as essential to virtue. We find that there is nothing, or next

111

to nothing, which has always and everywhere been regarded as morally good by all men. Where, then, is our universal morality? Can we, in the face of all this evidence, deny that it is nothing but an empty dream?[3]

What are we to make of this line of reasoning? Clearly we have here an argument against *objective* moral values based on the variable moral customs of world cultures.

However, two points need to be made in response to this line of reasoning. First, the evidence indicates that Benedict and others didn't have quite all the facts necessary to make such a general moral assessment. Careful anthropological research indicates that, in fact, broad moral principles are held among virtually all cultures throughout recorded history—so much so that many now call Benedict's view "the anthropologist's heresy."[4] Here are some examples of moral commonality: the concept of murder is generally taken to be wrong and is distinguished from justifiable homicide; there are common interdictions against lying in specified contexts; and there are time-honored regulations of sexual behavior—including prohibitions against adultery.[5]

But there need not be a set of universally agreed upon moral precepts to make the point. Only one example is required to demonstrate the truth of moral objectivism. And as I noted in chapter 3, the following moral claim is, I think, one with which virtually all rational human beings would agree: "Torturing babies for fun is evil." Clearly we would want to say that in all societies, at all times—past or present—for all persons, torturing babies for fun is an evil activity. If this is true, it is strong evidence that there is at least one moral value that is objective, and thus that moral objectivism is true.

But this is not the whole of the matter. For even if it were not the case that there are an agreed upon set of moral values across cultures (not even *one*, like that just mentioned), it does not follow that such values do not exist. For it could well be that, for various reasons, people/cultures are ignorant of what the objective moral standard is. Just as cultures have disagreed about a number of other issues, from the size and shape of the earth to the role of the kidneys in human physiology, it doesn't follow from this that there is no absolute size and shape of the earth, or that the kidneys don't have a role in human physiology! This leads to our second set of arguments for and against objective moral values.

Proving Morality

Another line of reasoning that is commonly offered for not believing in objective moral values—one that we shall call the "lack-of-proof" argument—can be put this way:

1. If objective moral values exist, then we should be able to prove that some moral opinions are true and others are false.
2. But we cannot prove that some moral opinions are true and others are false.
3. Therefore, there are no objective moral values.[6]

At first blush, this argument may seem quite convincing. Suppose, for example, that you were in a discussion with another person about abortion. You claim that abortion is both legal and moral, and the person you are dialoguing with claims that abortion is legal but immoral. How are you to decide who is right? Unlike scientific claims, you cannot test such views in the lab.

Moreover, *all* moral matters are like this one in that they cannot be proven right or wrong by using any scientific criteria. So, argues the subjectivist, they are not factual matters after all. They are merely subjective opinions. The question before us, then, is which of these two views concerning the nature of morality is correct—objectivism or subjectivism? Which one is most plausible to believe? And, since we cannot use science, how would we offer a proof one way or the other?

To determine the answer to these questions, we must first remember to be consistent in our position, whatever it is. We cannot cheat, for example, by smuggling elements of objectivism into our subjectivism in order to satisfy certain psychological or emotional tensions. For example, a defender of subjective morality cannot consistently hold that morality is subjective opinion on the one hand and then defend gay rights as a moral imperative on the other hand by arguing that all people have the universal right to be treated fairly.

If morality is the *subjective invention* of an individual or community, it cannot then be the case that there is a universal moral mandate that all people should be treated with *objective moral dignity*. If morality is a relative set of beliefs, then it is inconsistent to assert universality to those beliefs. All we can consistently assert are our subjective feelings or tastes. Let's examine subjectivism a bit more carefully.

Moral Subjectivism as Personal Relativism

Moral subjectivism basically comes in two forms. First, the subjectivist can hold the view that morality is personal; each individual determines for himself or herself what is morally right and wrong. Obviously, if this is the case, then one could never consistently tell another person that his or her actions are morally wrong. But this leads to horrific conclusions. Consider the frightening words of murderer Ted Bundy to his victim:

113

Then I learned that all moral judgments are "value judgments," that all value judgments are subjective, and that none can be proved to be either "right" or "wrong." . . . I discovered that to become truly free, truly unfettered, I had to become truly uninhibited. And I quickly discovered that the greatest obstacle to my freedom, the greatest block and limitation to it, consists in the insupportable "value judgment" that I was bound to respect the rights of others. I asked myself, who were these "others"? Other human beings, with human rights? Why is it more wrong to kill a human animal than any other animal, a pig or a sheep or a steer? Is your life more to you than a hog's life to a hog? Why should I be willing to sacrifice my pleasure more for the one than for the other? Surely, you would not, in this age of scientific enlightenment, declare that God or nature has marked some pleasures as "moral" or "good" and others as "immoral" or "bad"? In any case, let me assure you, my dear young lady, that there is absolutely no comparison between the pleasure I might take in eating ham and the pleasure I anticipate in raping and murdering you. That is the honest conclusion to which my education has led me—after the most conscientious examination of my spontaneous and uninhibited self.[7]

Coming from the position of personal subjectivism, what could one say in response to Bundy's chilling remarks? On this view, there is no objective grounding to stand on by which one could "fight back," morally speaking. This is a radical, morally anarchistic view to hold, and therefore most thoughtful persons do not believe that each person determines for himself or herself what is right and good. For those reflective persons denying moral absolutism, then, there is another form of moral subjectivism that is more sophisticated and more commonly embraced: conventionalism.

Moral Subjectivism as Conventionalism

Second, a subjectivist could maintain that morality is not individual, but conventional—based on the subjective determinations of a culture. This is a more reasonable approach to ethics, it seems, than the personal relativism just discussed. It follows more consistently with the examples of the Greeks and Eskimos noted earlier and with the general notion that cultures sometimes have differing moral standards. But conventionalism, or cultural relativism (as it is sometimes called), also has implications that, in the end, seem just as unreasonable to believe as personal relativism. Consider the following responses to conventionalism.

1. *If right and wrong are cultural inventions, determined by culture, then it would always be wrong to speak out against them.* So, on this view, to speak out against slavery in Great Britain in the 1790s would have been a morally bad thing to do. But surely it was a good thing for William Wilberforce to want to abolish the slave trade and to defend this

viewpoint against the prevailing currents of his culture. Surely Martin Luther King Jr.'s eloquent position on racial equality in the United Sates is morally superior to the diatribes of members of the Ku Klux Klan about subjugating minorities. However, on the conventionalist's view, all moral reformers such as Wilberforce, King, or even Jesus and Gandhi, would be in the wrong—they would all be immoral by definition.

2. *The conventionalist cannot ever consistently speak out against another culture's activities—no matter what those activities are.* It would be morally wrong, for example, for the United States (or any other nation) to decry the activities of Adolph Hitler's regime, or to denounce the killing fields of Pol Pot's reign of terror, or to demand that terrorist governments, such as that currently in Iran, cease and desist the development of nuclear weapons. It would be wrong, on this view, for any nation to speak out against any other nation no matter how much it brutalizes its own innocent citizens.

But do we really believe these things? Do we really believe that it is wrong to oppose the Hitlers and the Pol Pots of the world? Do we really believe that slavery, opposition to women's suffrage, and terror networks are morally good for those persons or countries who practice them? Surely not. But if one is going to hold consistently to this kind of cultural moral relativism, then he or she cannot ever make moral assessments about *any* activities of any other culture.

3. *Perhaps worst of all, conventionalism collapses into personal relativism.* Here is the problem. We commonly speak of a culture's moral views or the moral norms of a particular society. But what, exactly, is a culture or a society? It seems that there are no clear-cut, unambiguous demarcations from one culture to another or one society to another. For example, suppose you live in the United States, are a member of the Southern Baptist Convention, and are an active member of NARAL Pro-Choice America.

If morality is determined by culture, from which of these "cultures" or "subcultures" are you to glean your moral views? On the issue of abortion, to use but a single moral example, American culture has deemed abortion legal, and a majority of its citizens consider it to be moral (at least in the early stages of pregnancy). However, the Southern Baptist Convention considers abortion to be immoral. But the NARAL community—the National Abortion Rights Action League—strongly supports the view that abortion is, or should be, the right of every woman—the moral, legal, personal right.

If one is a member of all of these groups, then which culture determines whether the moral issue is right or wrong? Is abortion both morally right and morally wrong at the same time? Clearly this is incoherent. A person has to personally decide which culture (or subculture) will determine for him or her whether abortion is morally right or wrong. So we are led back to a form of personal moral relativism.

Thus, conventionalism ends up involving personal preference. In the end this makes morality useless, for no one can say that what another person or group is doing is right or wrong (except according to their own moral viewpoint). Morality is thus reduced to mere personal aesthetic choice. This is, no doubt, an unacceptable conclusion for most rational human beings, given what we know to be true.[8]

Moral Absolutism

What we know to be true, if we carefully examine our moral intuitions, is that there are objective moral values. The selfless acts of love by a Catholic sister in the ghettos of Calcutta, for example, or the defense of minority groups who are being abused and discriminated against by apartheid-believing governments, are morally good actions. We rightly praise such people as Mother Teresa and Nelson Mandela for their work for humanity.

Not everyone agrees that we should trust our moral intuitions as giving us objective moral truth, however. A person espousing a strong form of *scientism*—the view that science is the paradigm of truth and rationality—would disparage such "moral intuitions" as being mere subjective opinions. But we need not take this criticism seriously, for scientism ends up being an incoherent account of knowledge since the very claim that science is the paradigm of truth and rationality cannot itself be demonstrated scientifically. Therefore, the position is self-defeating.[9]

There are many ways of obtaining objective truth, and while the scientific method can help us find truth in matters of physics, chemistry, and the like, it is an inappropriate method for finding truth in other domains such as mathematics and morality.

Whether we are referring to the atrocities of the Holocaust, the bloody massacres of the Khmer Rouge, or the brutality of an American child molester, to use some gruesome examples, these activities are objectively evil—they are, to put it bluntly, moral abominations. And the person whose moral faculties are functioning properly will know this to be the case. If someone disagrees that such actions are evil, their moral faculties are somehow obfuscated.

On the other hand, acts of mercy such as those demonstrated by the Missionaries of Charity or the workers in AIDS hospices are morally good actions. Any human being who is honestly reflecting on these matters would surely agree. Consider the chart below, and ask yourself which of the three views—objectivism, personal relativism, or conventionalism—best fits with the general beliefs people have across cultures.

General Beliefs Transculturally	Objectivist View (Moral Absolutism)	Subjectivist View #1 (Personal Relativism)	Subjectivist View #2 (Cultural Relativism or Conventionalism)
Human beings are intrinsically valuable.	Human beings have intrinsic value based on an objective God.	Each person determines his or her own moral value.	One's culture determines his or her moral value.
Some things are really evil, such as torturing babies for fun.	Evil exists; it is objectively real; torturing babies for fun is evil.	Evil is what each individual person decides it to be; torturing babies for fun is evil if I decide that it is.	Evil is what one's culture decides it to be; torturing babies for fun is evil if my culture decides that it is.
Some things are really good, such as providing food for starving children.	Goodness exists; it is objectively real; providing food for starving children is good.	Goodness is what each individual person decides it to be; providing food for starving children is good if I decide that it is.	Goodness is what one's culture decides it to be; providing food for starving children is good if my culture decides that it is.

It should be obvious as we look at these three moral beliefs people hold across temporal and cultural boundaries that moral absolutism best accounts for them. Neither personal relativism nor conventionalism suffices in providing an explanation for these universal beliefs.

Objection to Moral Absolutism

An important objection to the view that there are objective moral values is that there are often moral disagreements from society to society, as there certainly have been throughout history. As noted earlier, there are examples of transcultural moral commonality, such as prohibitions against murder, lying, and adultery.[10] But while granting that there are some moral precepts that are universally agreed upon, there are also a number of disagreements. So why are there moral discrepancies among the cultures of world history if objective moral values exist and if we have a moral faculty that is capable of being aware of them?

On the theistic, Christian perspective, there is an answer: transworld depravity.[11] Transworld depravity includes the idea that all human beings in the world end up using their free will to act against what is right and good, even against what they take to be true. It is a kind of moral malady that has infected the entire human race such that we not only often choose the wrong, but in some cases cannot even see the right. To use a helpful metaphor, our moral glasses are foggy, and moral issues are not always as lucid as we would like them to be. Not only is the fog there, but sometimes we even add to it and make things foggier.

The Bible says, "All have sinned and fall short of the glory of God" (Rom. 3:23 NIV). We don't have to go far to see the truth of this moral problem. For if we carefully examine our own motives, desires, and actions, we see that we don't always live up to our own moral beliefs and expectations. Thus, a world acting, occasionally at least, contrary to the universal moral code seems to square very well with the actual world in which we live. Our moral faculty is not always functioning properly, and it is in need of a divine renovation. So just because an individual, or even a culture, doesn't live according to a particular moral precept, it doesn't follow that the moral precept doesn't exist. Given transworld depravity, this is precisely what we should expect.

To summarize the general point of this section, then, it is more reasonable to believe that moral objectivism is true than that it is false. Several objections to subjectivism were offered, and while the "proof" for objectivism does not involve "scientific verification," it need not do so in order to be reasonably believed. The truth or falsity of some issues can be determined by means other than scientific ones.

There has been, however, a recent appeal to science in support of a type of universal morality by way of evolutionary biology. We will examine this claim next.

Evolutionary Ethics: Why It Won't Work

In the preface to his best-selling work, *The Selfish Gene*, Richard Dawkins comments, "We are survival machines—robot vehicles blindly programmed to preserve the selfish molecules known as genes."[12] In his view of things, our moral aspirations and beliefs are predetermined posits of our genetic machinery selfishly programmed to advance our gene pool.

Evolutionary ethicist and philosopher of science Michael Ruse, along with his colleague Edward Wilson, generally agree. They put it this way:

> Morality, or more strictly our belief in morality, is merely an adaptation put in place to further our reproductive ends. Hence the basis of ethics does not lie in God's will—or in the metaphorical roots of evolution or any other part of the framework of the Universe. In an important sense, ethics as we understand it is an illusion fobbed off on us by our genes to get us to cooperate. It is without external grounding. Ethics is produced by

118

evolution but is not justified by it because, like Macbeth's dagger, it serves a powerful purpose without existing in substance. . . . Unlike Macbeth's dagger, ethics is a *shared* illusion of the human race.[13]

However, there is no scientific (or other) evidence to suggest that morality is an illusory survival mechanism. To claim that natural selection is evidence simply begs the question. As I pointed out in chapter 3, we don't live as if moral values are mere adaptations. And the reason we don't live that way is because we know that there are objective moral values. We know many nonempirical claims. For example, we know that there are other minds (people we encounter every day are not droids that only appear to be rational persons), that there is an external world (we are not merely dreaming), and that there are certain necessary truths (2 + 2 = 4). So, too, we know that objective moral values exist.[14]

But there is another, perhaps more persuasive, reason for not believing in the evolutionary view of morality, nor for believing in naturalistic evolutionary theory as a whole. Surprisingly, the roots of the argument were first offered by Charles Darwin, who said: "With me the horrid doubt always arises whether the convictions of man's mind, which has been developed from the mind of the lower animals, are of any value or at all trustworthy. Would any one trust in the convictions of a monkey's mind, if there are any convictions in such a mind?"[15]

World-renowned scholar Alvin Plantinga demonstrates that this problem raised by Darwin, what he refers to as "Darwin's doubt," has a legitimate basis. The problem, as he notes, is that if naturalistic evolution is true, "then our cognitive faculties will have resulted from blind mechanisms like natural selection, working on such sources of genetic variation as random genetic mutation." But if this is the case, then "[e]volution is interested, not in true belief, but in survival or fitness. It is therefore unlikely that our cognitive faculties have the production of true belief as a proximate or any other function, and the probability of our faculties' being reliable (given naturalistic evolution) would be fairly low."[16] In other words, if naturalistic evolution really happened—if all that exists are naturalistic processes and no directing God is involved—then there is no good reason to believe that what we take to be true is true, even naturalistic evolution! The theory is, therefore, self-defeating. If you believe it, you have a high probability of being wrong.

This concludes the support for step 2 of the moral argument that there are objective moral values. Next, we will take a closer look at step 1: If there are objective moral values, then God exists.

Examining Step 1: If There Are Objective Moral Values, Then God Exists

We have seen above that there are very good reasons to believe that objective moral values do exist. But from this does it follow that God exists? Couldn't a person believe *both* that there are objective moral values and that God does not exist? Is the God-morality connection a necessary one? While some atheists, such as Jean-Paul Sartre, J. L. Mackie, and others, hold that morality cannot be objective without the existence of a God, others disagree.

One such person is atheist philosopher Walter Sinnott-Armstrong. He puts the point concisely:

> In fact, many atheists are happy to embrace objective moral values. I agree with them. Rape is morally wrong. So is discrimination against gays and lesbians. Even if somebody or some group *thinks* that these acts are not morally wrong, they still *are* morally wrong. . . . [However,] [t]his admission implies nothing about God, unless objective values depend on God. Why should we believe that they do?[17]

He also notes that many atheists, including himself, are nice people and that one need not be a theist to live a good, moral life.

The latter point is undoubtedly true. I personally know well several outspoken atheists, and they are very good, upstanding, moral individuals. They are just as moral, if not more so, than many theists I know. But it is important to see that being moral and having a reasonable basis or foundation for being moral are two very different issues. For example, I can wholeheartedly believe that the lights in the room will turn on after I flip the light switch without having any belief in, or understanding of, electricity. I can function well in society, going from place to place flipping light switches, never even entertaining the idea that electricity is involved in the process of causing the lights to turn on.

But the fact of the matter is that electricity *is* involved in the lights going on. If someone disbelieved in electricity, and even had large groups of followers who doubted its existence, that wouldn't mean a thing in terms of its actual nature, existence, and causal role in illumination. The fact is electricity grounds our explanation for the lights going on when the switch is turned on. It gives us a basis for our being "switch flippers."

So too with an infinite, personal God. One could deny his existence and still live a moral life.* But there would be no basis for such a life.

---

* However, it is relevant to note that such good and wonderful things as hospitals, hospices, and prison outreach have all arisen out of a theistic, Christian worldview. For

Either objective moral values came to be from an infinite, personal God or they emerged from the "accidental collocation of atoms."[18] Either they flow from the nature of a Being of infinite worth and value or they popped into existence haphazardly from mindless matter and energy. But if you begin with an impersonal universe, it is completely silent regarding moral matters.[19] The reason persons have value and dignity on the theistic worldview is that ultimate reality is itself personal, and human persons are created in the image of this personal Being.

The Problem of Horrendous Evils

We have seen that the existence of God offers a better explanation of good and evil than disbelief in God. But we must return again to the problem that was raised in chapter 3 regarding the existence of evil. Once again, the argument given by David Hume is this: "Is [God] willing to prevent evil, but not able? Then he is impotent. Is he able, but not willing? Then he is malevolent. Is he both able and willing? Whence then is evil?"[20]

A more recent defender of atheism, Walter Sinnott-Armstrong, reformulates this argument in a way that attempts to avoid responses to it offered by theists over the centuries:

1. If there were an all-powerful and all-good God, then there would not be any evil in the world unless that evil is logically necessary for an adequately compensating good.
2. There is lots of evil in the world.
3. Much of that evil is not logically necessary for any adequately compensating good.
4. Therefore, there is no God who is all-powerful and all-good.[21]

Simply put, if God is truly good and all-powerful, then how could there exist gratuitous, unnecessary evil and suffering in the world that he created? If he cannot destroy such evil, he is not all-powerful; and if he doesn't want to destroy it, he is not all-good. The only way evil and suffering could coexist with such a God is if goodness *necessitated* evil in some sense; in other words, if it were not gratuitous.

However, argue many atheists, goodness does not necessitate evil. Why would it? Even *theists* generally agree that God existed without any

---

more on this, see Vincent Carroll and David Shiflett, *Christianity on Trial* (San Francisco: Encounter Books, 2001) and David Sloan Wilson, *Darwin's Cathedral* (Chicago: University of Chicago Press, 2002). Ironically, the latter book is based on a nontheistic, evolutionary perspective.

evil prior to the creation of other beings. So, since goodness does not necessitate evil, and yet gratuitous evil exists, a good and all-powerful God cannot exist. The argument put this way is a significant challenge to theism. But the case gets even worse for the theist, for what about *horrendous evils*? What about those evil events that are incredibly horrific—ones that are terribly bad and seem to have no redeeming value whatsoever?

Consider the following grisly examples, some intentional, some accidental: raping women and cutting off their arms; cannibalizing one's offspring; producing child pornography; experiencing slow and torturous death by beating and starvation; accidentally running over and killing one's small child; having to choose, in front of your two children, which one will live and which one will be executed by a terrorist.[22] Can we account for the goodness of God given such seemingly unredemptive, gratuitous horrors? Is it rational to believe in God given their existence? A number of responses could be, and have been, offered to these kinds of evils. Here are a few of them that, taken collectively, constitute a strong response to the atheist's challenge.

1. *A first response that can be offered to the problem of horrendous evils is called the free will defense, or the free will theodicy.** I explained it briefly in chapter 3, but the clearest, most concise and cogent presentation of it that I am aware of is this:

> A world containing creatures who are significantly free (and freely perform more good than evil actions) is more valuable, all else being equal, than a world containing no free creatures at all. Now God can create free creatures, but He can't *cause* or *determine* them to do only what is right. For if He does so, then they aren't significantly free after all; they do not do what is right *freely*. To create creatures capable of *moral good*, therefore, He must create creatures capable of moral evil; and He can't give these creatures the freedom to perform evil and at the same time prevent them from doing so. As it turned out, sadly enough, some of the free creatures God created went wrong in the exercise of their freedom; this is the source of moral evil. The fact that free creatures sometimes go wrong, however, counts neither against God's omnipotence nor against His goodness; for He could have forestalled the occurrence of moral evil only by removing the possibility of moral good.[23]

A moral world is better than a world without morality (it is better than both no world at all and a world of only automatons), and a moral world by definition requires that free creatures exist—creatures who

---

* The word *theodicy* comes from two Greek terms—*theos*, "God," and *dikei*, "justice." A theodicy is a justification of the ways of God given all the evil and suffering that exists in the world.

can freely choose good or evil. As history has demonstrated, they ended up choosing evil.

2. *A second response is that there could be reasons for horrendous evils that God has not communicated to us.* A friend of mine recently lost a loved one in the prime of life, and he was having trouble making sense of it all. "Why would God let this happen to her?" he asked. "I can see no good that would come from her agonizing death, and I can see lots of good that would have come through her life if she would have lived for many more years. It just makes no sense."

Clearly this is an honest question regardless of one's theistic beliefs. In the midst of such grief, it can be difficult to consider that there might be an infinite perspective on events that we are unable to see, or perhaps even understand, given our limited viewpoint. If we do live on into eternity and are doing more there than floating on clouds and strumming harps, then perhaps the roles we will play in eternity are better served by our leaving this life at what seems like, from our temporal perspective, a premature, unfinished stage. One can only imagine what our life will be when we finally reach eternity.

3. *A third response is that the purpose in life may not be for us to be as happy as possible, but rather to come to know God and his kingdom.* Someone recently asked me why, if God really exists, he doesn't just appear on earth as a giant, one-hundred-foot-tall being so that people could see that he exists. Certainly God could do this and a whole lot more. But what purpose would that serve? It doesn't seem that God's main goal is to get us either to believe that he exists or to make us constantly happy (although a joy-filled life is waiting for the true Christian; see chapter 9 for more on this point).

From the earliest Jewish and Christian writings, it seems that God's primary desires are that we trust him, believe what he says, and follow him wherever he leads (note the many examples in the book of Genesis). However, it may take hardships of many kinds for us to be broken enough to swallow our pride and finally wake up and hear his voice. As Jesus inferentially notes many times in the Gospels, people may not have ears for hearing; they may have closed their ears to him and his message.

4. *A fourth response is that God can use the evil and suffering in our lives for our own greater good.* Several years ago I was giving a lecture on the topic of God and evil, and afterward a woman in her early forties came up to me with tears in her eyes. "Beth," we'll call her, told me that she wanted to share something with me, but it was too personal and traumatic for her to disclose verbally. So the next day she wrote me a letter telling her story, explaining how as a young child she had been sexually abused by her stepfather over a long period of time. Her question was, if God really exists and loved her, how could he let that happen to her?

123

In my reply I explained how God is big enough to take such horrendous experiences and use them for good purposes. The Bible itself makes this point in Romans 8:28. It's not that God wanted those things to happen, yet he can take them and use them in positive ways. "But how can he do that?" she asked. "Take your own case," I said. "I've known you for a long time, and you are an incredibly compassionate, encouraging, joy-filled person, more so than just about anyone I know. You care about others and can empathize with them in unique ways. It seems to me that God has taken the hurt and pain you've experienced and through them he's molded you into a wonderful person."

"It's kind of like baking a cake," I continued. "When you bake a cake from scratch, you use lots of different ingredients: raw eggs, baking soda, flour, salt, shortening, and sugar, among other things. Now suppose you decided to taste them all individually. With the exception of the sugar, they would be rather disgusting. But somehow, by mixing them all together and baking them, an amazing transformation takes place. So it can be with our lives and God. If we allow him, he can take our individual experiences—delightful, dreadful, and everything in between—and over time use them to transform us into people who are deep and rich in character."

It took her a while, but now she fully believes that God has done just that in her own life.

5. *A fifth and final response is that the goodness of God will, in the end, engulf all evils that have been experienced.* It could be that being eternally present in the face of God—what scholars in the medieval age called the beatific vision—could be so overwhelmingly and indescribably good that it melts away all experiences of evil in this life—even horrendous ones.

The fourteenth-century Christian mystic Julian of Norwich goes so far as to claim that God will, in the end, thank us for enduring all of the evil and suffering we faced in our earthly lives. She then says that our experience of this gratitude of God will bring us so much joy that it will be worth any pain we could have experienced throughout our lives.[24] Another medieval mystic, Saint Teresa, said something similar: "In light of heaven, the worst suffering on earth, a life full of the most atrocious tortures on earth, will be seen to be no more serious than one night in an inconvenient hotel."[25] They may well be right.

Summary

In this chapter I have argued that not only can there be no objective right and wrong without God, but, since there is objective right and wrong, it makes more sense to believe that God exists than that he doesn't. We examined each step of the argument from objective moral values: both that there are objective moral values and that if there are objective moral values, then God must exist.

We examined and found wanting several arguments against moral objectivism and for moral subjectivism. Neither personal relativism nor conventionalism corresponds with what we know to be true; only moral absolutism provides a satisfactory answer to our moral intuitions.

Also, I argued that such intuitions are a valid method for obtaining moral truth and that science is an inappropriate tool for obtaining such knowledge. One example of a scientific approach to finding a nonrelative ethic is evolutionary biology. But it, too, was seen to be deficient at best, incoherent at worst.

Given these arguments, as well as the lack of an adequate answer from both atheism and pantheism, discussed in chapter 3, it seems clear that not only does theism offer the best explanation of good and evil; it offers the only really believable one. And, given this good and evil, there must be an objective God to account for it.

Questions for Reflection

1. What is moral subjectivism? What is moral conventionalism? What is moral absolutism?
2. Review the words of Ted Bundy. What could an atheist say in response?
3. What is a central problem with evolutionary ethics, as argued in this chapter?
4. Ponder on the five responses offered above to the problem of horrendous evils. Do these answers satisfy you? Are there better answers?
5. Compare the theistic answers to the problem of evil and suffering with the answers offered by atheism and pantheism (you may need to review chapters 2 and 3). Which worldview has the most compelling solution? Why?

For Further Reading in Support of Moral Objectivism and the Moral Argument for God

Beckwith, Francis J., and Gregory Koukl. *Relativism: Feet Firmly Planted in Mid-air.* Grand Rapids: Baker, 1998. A readable yet solid critique of moral relativism and defense of moral absolutism.

Copan, Paul. "The Moral Argument," in Paul Copan and Paul K. Moser, eds., *The Rationality of Theism*. New York: Routledge, 2003. An excellent but somewhat scholarly piece. Copan is currently the leading proponent of the moral argument.

Geivett, R. Douglas. *Evil and the Evidence for* God. Philadelphia: Temple University Press, 1993. A rigorous defense of the free will theodicy.

Lewis, C. S. *Mere Christianity*. New York: MacMillan, 1952. The major defense of the moral argument in the twentieth century.

McCord Adams, Marilyn, and Robert Merrihew Adams, eds. *The Problem of Evil*. New York: Oxford University Press, 1990. A scholarly collection of essays from a variety of perspectives by leading philosophers both pro and con.

Pojman, Louis P. *Ethics: Discovering Right and Wrong*, 5th ed. Belmont, CA: Thompson Wadsworth, 2006. (Note especially chapters 2 and 3.) Concise, clear, and very helpful.

For Further Reading against Moral Objectivism and the Moral Argument for God

Ladd, John, ed. *Ethical Relativism*. Reprint, Lanham, MD: University Press of America, 2002. A collection of basic readings.

Le Poidevin, Robin. *Arguing for Atheism: An Introduction to the Philosophy of Religion*. New York: Routledge, 1996. This is a higher-level introductory textbook. In part 2 he argues quite powerfully against the moral argument.

Mackie, J. L. *Ethics: Inventing Right and Wrong*. New York: Penguin, 1976. A classic work defending ethical relativism and the error theory of ethics.

McCord Adams, Marilyn, and Robert Merrihew Adams, eds. *The Problem of Evil*. New York: Oxford University Press, 1990. A scholarly collection of essays from a variety of perspectives by leading philosophers both pro and con.

Nielsen, Kai. *Ethics without God*. Amherst, New York: Prometheus, 1990. Nielsen is currently one of the most recognized atheist philosophers and ethicists.

Ruse, Michael, ed. *Philosophy of Biology*. New York: Macmillan, 1989. Note the four chapters in the section titled "Evolution and Ethics."

7

Divine Revelation

Has God Spoken to Humanity?

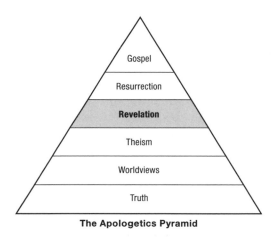

The Apologetics Pyramid

All human discoveries seem to be made only for the purpose of confirming more and more the Truths contained in the Sacred Scriptures.

Sir William Herschel

It is no doubt true that Revelation exhibits all the truths of Natural Religion, but it is no less true that reason must be employed to judge of that revelation; whether it comes from God. Both are great lights and we ought not to put out the one in order to use the other.

Thomas Reid

Having seen that the evidence strongly favors the theistic worldview (and it seems that if one is following the dictates of reason, he or she would conclude that it is more plausible to believe that God exists than that he doesn't), there are still significant questions to be answered, for there are different forms of theism. Historically, the three primary forms are Judaism, Christianity, and Islam. While an extensive analysis and comparison of these three is beyond the scope of this book, there is a concise and helpful method for approaching their veracity.

According to Christian belief and the teachings of the Bible, God's plan of salvation through history first involved his working through the Israelites, the group of people he chose to manifest the kingdom of God to the rest of the world. God raised up prophets along the way who both spoke and wrote down God's salvation plan (as recorded in the Old Testament), and this plan involved his sending a Messiah to save a lost world. This Messiah was Jesus of Nazareth.

However, the rejection of Jesus as the Messiah by many of the Jewish people caused God to shift his kingdom away from the unbelieving nation of Israel to a people who would live by its principles, whether they were Jews or Gentiles (Matt. 21:43). After Jesus's sacrificial death by crucifixion, God then raised up apostles and prophets to proclaim his offer of salvation to the world. The New Testament documents were written by some of these followers of Jesus as they were inspired by God to communicate what he wanted to convey to the human race (2 Tim. 3:16; 2 Peter 1:20–21). On this *Christian* account of things, then, the New Testament was a continuation and fulfillment of God's salvation strategy first elucidated centuries before and recorded in the books of the Old Testament.

Of course, not everyone agrees with this Christian account of things. Many Jews and Muslims, for example, while agreeing with the historical reality of much of the Old Testament and even its divine inspiration, do not agree that Jesus was the Messiah hoped for by the prophets of old. Nor do they agree with much of what the New Testament proclaims. Furthermore, there is now doubt among many historians and Bible critics alike concerning the reliability of these biblical documents—both the Old and the New Testament documents.

This chapter, therefore, focuses on three questions. First, are the biblical documents accurate accounts of what actually happened in the past, or should they not be trusted as reliable history? Second, is there good reason to believe that God has provided us with revelation from on high in the Bible? That is, has God communicated to human beings in a way that can be recognized as his word to us, or is this book a human invention? Finally, if God has provided such revelation, what does that say about the other theistic religions of Judaism and Islam? We begin our quest by focusing on the issue of the Bible's reliability.

The Reliability of the Bible

The Bible is a book that has been read, cherished, and revered by millions of people, believers and nonbelievers, for almost two thousand years. While many Christians consider the Bible to be *the* book offering the God-inspired way to the good life—that is, for understanding how to live morally in this life and how to achieve eternal life—many do not understand how the Bible came into existence or what evidence exists for believing that it is, in fact, divinely inspired. It is usually taken on blind faith to be "God's Word" to us.

But now that we have entered the twenty-first century, it is becoming more disconcerting to believe such things blindly, for there are others around us who have their own "holy books" that they claim have been divinely created as well. Whether it is the Bhagavad Gita of the Hindus, or the Qur'an of the Muslims, or the Book of Mormon for the Latter-day Saints, each of these religions claims that their sacred writings are just that—sacred—and as such are divinely inspired words graciously offered to us by God.

What reason is there to believe that the Bible is any different from these other religious works? What makes it special, if in fact it is?

Old Testament Reliability

No one knows for sure where or when writing first began, but we do have solid evidence that prior to 3000 BC the Egyptians wrote in hieroglyphics (pictorial symbols used to represent words or sounds) on the walls of temples and tombs.[1] Sometime after that, probably around 1700 BC, an alphabet was developed somewhere between Egypt and Mesopotamia, roughly the area of contemporary Iraq. The discovery of this ancient alphabet, from which all other alphabets derived, has a number of significant implications. One implication is that, contrary to some early critics of the Bible, writing was being done several hundred years before the time of Moses—the person whom Jews and Christians have historically understood to be the author of the first five books of the Bible.[2]

Many types of literature were produced during those early decades and centuries of the development of prose and poetry in the area of Mesopotamia. Thirty-nine books written over a span of several centuries by Jewish nomads were compiled roughly around 400 to 450 BC and came to be called the Old Testament (also called the "Hebrew Bible" in Judaism).[3] The books were cherished by the ancient Jews as being divinely inspired words of Yahweh—the God above all. Today many Jews and Christians still take this collection of diverse works to be holy writings. Given that they were compiled so long ago, however, how can we in our scientific age have any confidence that the documents are about actual history involving the persons, places, and events to which they refer? How can we be sure that they are trustworthy copies of what the original authors actually wrote down?[4]

We will examine several kinds of evidence in an attempt to answer these questions. This is not to say that if they are *reliable* documents then they are also divinely inspired. We will look at divine inspiration later. But for now we need to examine the evidence for historical reliability. To do this, we will consider three general tests for an ancient document's reliability: bibliographical, internal, and external evidence.[5]

Bibliographical Evidence

The bibliographical test for the reliability of an ancient manuscript refers to the textual transmission of the text from the original documents to the manuscript copies that currently exist. It includes determining how many copies we have of the originals, the ways in which they were copied, the quality of the copies, and how far removed the copies are in time from the originals. The central question to be answered is, since we don't have the originals, how reliable are the copies we do have, which are based on the earlier unavailable manuscripts? In terms of sheer numbers, we have far more New Testament copies of the originals than Old Testament copies. However, as we will see, the methods of copying these ancient works and the quality of the copies are quite impressive. To explore the bibliographical evidence, we will briefly examine two types of ancient Old Testament documents.

The Masoretic Texts. The earliest complete manuscript of the Old Testament that has been discovered dates from roughly AD 1009. Referred to as the Leningrad Codex (a codex is an ancient manuscript book), this edition of the Old Testament is a beautiful, ornate work that is currently located in the National Library of St. Petersburg (formerly Leningrad). This work is what is referred to as a Masoretic text—one of a number of such texts that were copied by Jewish scribes called Masoretes. Dating from about AD 600, the Masoretes worked tirelessly to ensure that the texts they had received from earlier scribes (who themselves had worked hard at scribal accuracy) were as accurate as possible. Scholar Neil Lightfoot notes the care that was taken by these scribes to ensure copying accuracy:

> They numbered the verses, words, and letters of each [Old Testament] book. They counted the number of times each letter was used in each book.

They noted verses that contained all the letters of the alphabet, or a certain number of them. They calculated the middle letter, the middle word, and the middle verse of the Pentateuch; the middle verse of the Psalms, the middle verse of the entire Bible, and so forth. In fact, they counted almost everything that could be counted.[6]

The Hebrew word for "scribe" is derived from a verb (*mesappēr*) that means to count, and the Masoretes were certainly counters. They not only knew that the Pentateuch contained 400,945 letters, but they knew the word in the middle (found in Lev. 10:16) and even the very letter in the middle (found in Lev. 11:42)![7] Such care and precision caused another scholar to say this about them: "They [along with the earlier Jewish scribes called Sopherim] gave the most diligent attention to accurate preservation of the Hebrew Scriptures that has ever been devoted to any ancient literature, secular or religious, in the history of human civilization."[8]

The copying care and accuracy of these scribes was so impressive and influential that the Hebrew text today is based on this early work and is frequently referred to as the "Masoretic Text." It was also so meticulously copied that a major archaeological discovery in the 1940s, which unearthed texts and fragments dating nearly nine hundred years earlier than this one, demonstrated that even though almost a millenium had passed, textual variants were extremely small. What is also significant is that these variances involved minor grammatical mishaps and spelling errors. No theological or historical changes were made in the Old Testament texts at all during that extended period of time.

The Dead Sea Scrolls. The discovery of scrolls at Qumran, near the northwest shore of the Dead Sea and roughly ten miles from Jericho, is probably the most significant archaeological discovery related to the Old Testament in close to a thousand years. Briefly, here's what happened. During the Roman-Jewish war of AD 66–70, the Jewish community that was dwelling at Qumran (the Essenes) hid many of their sacred scrolls in caves, probably to keep them from being destroyed by the Romans. These scrolls remained untouched until 1947 when a young Bedouin shepherd boy named Muhammad edh-Dhib wandered into the area where the caves were located in search of a lost goat from his flock. In his search he threw a rock up into the mouth of a cave situated in the cliffs and heard a breaking sound. The next day he took a friend and climbed up into the cave to see what had happened. They discovered several jars with leather scrolls in them—seven complete scrolls in all—wrapped in linen. The boys gave the scrolls to the Bedouin elders, who then sold them. Amazingly, the scrolls eventually ended up being owned by the Israeli authorities.

The Bedouins continued to search for more jars, as did professional archaeologists. Since that time, roughly forty thousand fragments have been discovered in eleven caves, and from them more than 190 biblical scrolls have been found. Some of these are complete or almost complete books, such as the book of Isaiah, and others are fragments. Based on carbon-14 tests, paleography, and archaeological research, these materials date from anywhere between 250 BC to AD 70, depending on the scroll.

All of this is quite fascinating, but what is really remarkable about these Dead Sea discoveries is that until these scrolls were found, the primary ancient work on which the Old Testament was based was the Masoretic text mentioned above. However, from the Dead Sea discoveries, copies were found that are approximately nine hundred years older. Not only were they much older, but they were surprisingly identical to the later Masoretic text. In fact, in a study comparing the Masoretic book of Isaiah with the Isaiah scroll discovered at Qumran, the works "proved to be word for word identical . . . in more than 95% of the text. The 5% variation consisted chiefly of slips of the pen and variation in spelling."[9] There were no historical or theological discrepancies between them even though they were separated by almost a millennium! The Masoretic scribes obviously had worked very carefully to ensure that the transmission of this Old Testament book was done accurately. From this and the other textual discoveries and comparisons, it can be confidently assumed that the scribes were just as careful copying the other Old Testament texts as well.[10]

The bibliographical evidence supports the view that the Old Testament texts we now have are an amazingly accurate representation of the original autographs. More care was taken by Jewish scribes to ensure an accurate transmission of the Old Testament than any other work in antiquity.

Internal Evidence

The internal test for the reliability of an ancient work refers to what the document claims about itself. Is it claiming to be actual history, for example, written by eyewitnesses? Or is it intentionally written as narrative, myth, or fable? We will deal with these questions specifically, but first I will expand the internal test to include the issue of textual unity, for many have claimed that the Old Testament is a set of disunified fictional tales that have been pieced together by later redactors (editors who brought together disparate writings and oral traditions).

The Unity of the Old Testament

The historicity of the Old Testament, especially the earlier stories such as those of the Hebrew patriarchs mentioned in the book of Genesis, have been doubted and denied by a number of scholars over the last few centuries. This doubt hit especially hard in the 1970s, most notably by biblical scholars Thomas Thompson and John Van Seters.[11] Thompson and Van Seters are often referred to as "biblical minimalists," especially by their critics. Biblical minimalists hold the view that the Bible is "made up of prose fiction, legends, folk tales, theological treatises, and novellas, and [is] thus devoid of history."[12] For many of the minimalists, all, or at least most, of the stories within it are mythical in nature and have no historical basis whatsoever. They generally also hold that the patriarchs of the Old Testament, including David and Solomon, never existed (or, if they did exist, their kingly reigns were highly embellished by the biblical authors), nor did the twelve tribes of Israel.

Furthermore, for the minimalists as well as for less radical critical scholars, the Pentateuch (i.e., the first five books of the Old Testament, Genesis through Deuteronomy) is not often taken to be a unitary work written by one author—Moses. Even though Mosaic authorship was almost unanimously held from the earliest times up through the seventeenth century, critical scholars argued that it was rather a combination of documents from different sources written much later than the time of Moses (if such a person even existed). From the beginning of the twentieth century until quite recently, the standard critical view of the matter was called the Wellhausen hypothesis (also referred to as the documentary or JEDP hypothesis), developed by the German historian Julius Wellhausen.[13]

According to Wellhausen, the Old Testament is an important historical work, but it should not be taken literally. He argued that a number of people wrote the Pentateuch, as well as the book of Joshua, and that these different authors could be divided into four camps, or narratives: **J**ahwist, **E**lohist, **D**euteronomist, and **P**riestly. He maintained that each of these narratives came from distinct source types during different time periods in Israelite history. He also suggested that they could be distinguished by the different language styles they used (most importantly the name applied to God) as well as the specific concerns they each focused on. Roughly, the sources can be divided up in the following manner:

J: The name of God, when written by this camp, was always YHWH, and is transliterated most recently as *Yahweh* (in the German it begins with *J* and was historically translated "Jehovah"). The J material is the oldest, and it came from Judah in the ninth century BC (roughly 850). This material is the simplest narrative style of the four, and it presents God in anthropomorphic (humanlike) terms. In this material, God usually deals with humans face-to-face.

E: The name of God, when written by this camp, was always Elohim (less intimate than Yahweh). The E material came from the eighth century BC. (J and E were later combined in the mid-seventh century.)

D: This camp wrote the book of Deuteronomy (as well as Joshua and some other later books). The D material came from the mid-sixth century BC, but it neglected the concerns of the priestly class.

P: The P material was written by a group of priestly writers. It came from the fifth century BC and addressed the concerns of the priests, the sacrificial system, and the transcendence of God.[14]

In this view of the development of the Pentateuch, the Pentateuch came into existence no earlier than the fifth century BC, many centuries later than previously had been thought. In other words, it was a late invention by later writers and editors. Furthermore, argued Wellhausen and those in his camp, by recognizing these various literary sources of JEDP, one could decipher a development within the Jewish religion. It had evolved from a religion in which the people had an informal, but more personal, relationship with God to a more institutional religion of priests, law, and sacrifices.

By the beginning of the twentieth century, this JEDP documentary hypothesis was widely held among leading scholars in Germany, Britain, France, and the United States. However, due to a number of challenges to it, it is no longer the respected view it once was. Many have now given it up. As one authority in the fray says, "The old historical moorings of the Documentary Hypothesis are in serious trouble."[15] Consider one reason why. In their fine work, *Before Abraham Was*, Isaac Kikawada and Arthur Quinn argue quite persuasively through chiasms* and other structural analyses for thematic unities in the Pentateuch—unities that contradict the documentary hypothesis. For example, they demonstrate not only the thematic unity of Genesis 1–11, but also how such structures shed light on otherwise obscure and troubling stories.[16] These literary unities fly in the face of the documentary hypothesis, for on that view there were multiple authors focusing on different issues over long periods of time; in other words, there should not be a unity to the passage in question. Note, however, the example of the chiastic structure of the flood account described in Genesis 6:10–9:19:

* A chiasm is an intentional arrangement of the elements of a passage in the form of a mirrorlike structure. Examples include the following: ab/ba and abcd/dcba.

Chiastic Structure of the Flood Account[17]

A Noah (6:10a)
  B Shem, Ham, and Japheth (10b)
    C Ark to be built (14–16)
      D Flood announced (17)
        E Covenant with Noah (18–20)
          F Food in the ark (21)
            G Command to enter the ark (7:1–3)
              H 7 days of waiting for the flood (4–5)
                I 7 days of waiting for the flood (7–10)
                  J Entry to ark (11–15)
                    K Yahweh shuts Noah in (16)
                      L 40 days of flooding (17a)
                        M Waters increase (17b–18)
                          N Mountains covered (19–20)
                            O 150 days waters prevail (21–24)
                              P God remembers Noah (8:1)
                            O′ 150 days waters abate (3)
                          N′ Mountaintops visible (4–5)
                        M′ Waters abate (5)
                    L′ 40 days (end of) (6a)
                  K′ Noah opens window of ark (6b)
                J′ Raven and dove leave (7–9)
             I′ 7 days of waiting for waters to subside (10–11)
          H′ 7 days of waiting for waters to subside (12–13)
        G′ Command to leave ark (15–17 [22])
      F′ Food outside ark (9:1–4)
    E′ Covenant with all flesh (8–10)
    D′ No flood in future (11–17)
    C′ Ark (18a)
  B′ Shem, Ham, and Japheth (18b)
A′ Noah (19)

It seems evident that a *single* author of these passages was utilizing a chiastic structure to explain the flood account. After seeing this intentional construction, as well as other textual constructions throughout Genesis 1–11, it is simply no longer very plausible to believe that it was a compilation of works by multiple authors over long periods of time. Nor is it reasonable to believe that a later redactor put them together into one text. As Kikawada and Quinn note, the evidence implies "an author with such complete mastery of his materials . . . that it makes no literary sense to speak of him as an editor." They continue, "The evidence commonly used to show that Genesis 1–11 is a literary patchwork does in our opinion—when closely examined and put in its proper context—support the view that Genesis 1–11 is a literary masterpiece by an extraordinary skill and subtlety."[18]

Such examples, which could be multiplied throughout the Pentateuch, have been at least partially responsible for providing a growing rejection of the original JEDP hypothesis.[19] The Old Testament in general, and the Pentateuch in particular, is a much richer and more unified work than many critical scholars have previously thought. And the discovery of textual structures such as this are causing many of them to rethink their patchwork models. While no theory has at this time replaced JEDP, it is now rarely defended by critical scholars.[20] More unified views are now vying for serious consideration.

What the Old Testament Says about Itself

An important element of the internal test involves considering what the document claims about itself. The Old Testament is filled with references to its containing divinely inspired words. For example, many of the texts are filled with direct quotes from God (e.g., Isaiah 1; Ezekiel 2). Also, the prophets frequently claim that the Lord spoke to them or through them (e.g., 2 Sam. 23:2). As a matter of fact, more than 1,500 times the prophets claim that they received their message directly from God, and these were individuals who were following a very strict moral code in which lying was vehemently renounced (cf. Exod. 20:16).[21] Second, Old Testament prophets and priests made a distinction between false prophets and true ones, and the collected works of the latter were compiled into the Scriptures that make up our Old Testament. These works were understood by both Jews and later Christians—including Jesus himself—as being the authoritative Word of God given through inspired prophets.[22]

A further point that needs to be made regarding the internal test is that no crucial factual contradictions have been established within the texts of the Old Testament. While there are, no doubt, apparent discrepancies, scholars have resolved most of them through historical research, by careful textual analysis, and by giving the text a fair hearing.[23] Regarding a fair hearing, it seems reasonable that the works of antiquity should generally be taken at face value unless and until there is good reason to doubt them.[24]

External Evidence: Archaeological Discoveries

The external test for the reliability of an ancient document involves examining whether material external to the document under review (such as archaeological discoveries—textual or artifactual—or other relevant historical factors) supports or disconfirms the document's reliability. The late nineteenth and mid-twentieth centuries were probably the most significant time periods in history in terms of uncovering evidence for establishing the accuracy and reliability of the Old Testament. But recent new finds and refined archaeological methods, resources, and procedures may surpass even these periods of discovery.[25] Cultures have been un-earthed that were mentioned in the books of the Old Testament but had never been verified by secular sources. Before their verification, certain scholars maintained that this was further evidence for the unreliability of the Old Testament as a historical source. *However, a smattering of archaeological discoveries has confirmed significant parallels between what the Bible says and the known facts from ancient Near Eastern cultures.* This is not to say that there are no questions or concerns about the Bible and archaeological discoveries or even seeming contradictions. But the correlation between what the Bible says and what has been discovered is quite astounding.

One way to divide up biblical history as it relates to archaeological discoveries and their relevance to the Old Testament Jewish community is to separate it into seven periods: pre-patriarchal, patriarchal, slavery in Egypt and the exodus, the entrance into Canaan, the united monarchy, the divided monarchy, and the exile and return. Since the historical reality of each of these periods is denied by most minimalists and other critics, we will examine some of the discoveries that strongly support the existence of these periods in history as described in the biblical documents.[26]

The pre-patriarchal period—the period before the biblical patriarchs Abraham, Isaac, Jacob, and so on—is described in Genesis 1–11. It consists of stories and ideas that, until recently, seemed to many scholars to be mythical, literary constructs and not truly representative of what was occurring during this period of actual Middle Eastern history. Two examples are the very long life spans offered to certain individuals and the flood account mentioned above. However, the discovery of the Sumerian King List, which dates from the third millennium BC, describes kings who lived for thousands of years. While there are various ways to explain why someone was portrayed as living so long, the point here is that the biblical descriptions are in line with other literary structures and stories from that time period.

Similarly, recent literary analysis of the Atrahasis Epic, dating from the early second millennium BC in Mesopotamia, offers a parallel account of Genesis 1–11. It is the oldest near-complete work from the ancient Near East, and it describes creation and flood accounts that are quite similar to those offered in Genesis. What this archaeological evidence demonstrates is that the stories depicted in the pre-patriarchal era are just the kinds of works one should expect to find if they were, in fact, written during that period of history. The cultural, legal, political, military, and literary ambiance of the texts ring true to that era.

The patriarchal accounts described in the book of Genesis are heavily supported. Examples here include the Nuzi and Mari Tablets from

Akkadia (Mesopotamian area located between the Tigris and Euphrates rivers) dating to the twentieth and eighteenth centuries BC.[27] Thousands of tablets have been discovered, and these writings reflect the legal customs (such as adoption and birthright sales), language, gods that are named in the Old Testament, and personal names of the patriarchal age, such as Noah, Abram, and Jacob. These tablets demonstrate that, contrary to the view of the minimalists, the patriarchal narratives give a fair sampling of the cultural practices and conditions of that time and place. Since this information was unknown in later times, it is not necessary to insist that these biblical stories were later literary fictions.[28]

According to the book of Exodus, the Hebrew people were enslaved in Egypt, and God raised up Moses to lead them out of bondage and into the Promised Land. However, the reality of both the Hebrew presence in Egypt as well as the exodus event itself has been seriously questioned by critical scholars. Unfortunately, Egyptian records do not chronicle the event. This should not be surprising, given that the Egyptians typically did not record major defeats and other embarrassing losses. But there are, however, significant supporting evidences that an exodus did occur and that the depictions of this general era match the biblical material.[29] Regarding the latter, two discoveries that are important here are the Mursilis Treaty (a Hittite treaty dating to the second millennium BC) and Hammurabi's Law Code (one of the earliest sets of laws found), a Mesopotamian document dating to 1700 BC. Both of these discoveries have significant parallels with the Sinai covenant as depicted in the biblical books of Exodus, Deuteronomy, and Joshua 24.

The first mention of Israel comes from an Egyptian stele (an inscribed stone slab used for commemorative purposes) from Canaan. It is referred to as the Merneptah Stele, and it dates to the thirteenth century BC. This places Israel in Canaan in the thirteenth century, just as the Bible seems to suggest.

Regarding the united monarchy (the Hebrew tribes united to form the kingdom of Israel), some have claimed that there was no such thing, and even that King David never actually existed as a historical person. For example, one scholar has argued that "The figure of King David is about as historical as King Arthur."[30] However, the discovery of fragments from a ninth-century BC monument, inscribed only two hundred years after his alleged reign, demonstrate that, contrary to the minimalist critics, King David not only existed but ruled a kingdom as well. As *Biblical Archaeology Review* reports:

> Avraham Biran and his team of archaeologists found a remarkable inscription from the 9th century (BC) that refers both to the "House of David"

and to the "King of Israel." This is the first time that the name David has been found in any ancient inscription outside the Bible. That the inscription refers not simply to a "David" but to the House of David, the dynasty of the great Israelite king, is even more remarkable.[31]

Several very interesting archaeological finds also reflect the times of the divided monarchy—the times when Israel was divided into two kingdoms. First, the Mesha Stele dates to the ninth century BC and records the rebellion of the Moabite king Mesha against the Israelite king from "the House of Omri." The biblical book of 1 Kings notes that Israel made Omri their king (16:16).

Second, the Siloam Inscription is a discovery that dates to the late eighth century BC, and it describes the construction of Hezekiah's water channel under the wall of Jerusalem. This channel is mentioned in the Bible in 2 Kings 20:20 and 2 Chronicles 32:30, and its remains can still be seen today.[32]

Third, an Assyrian monument of King Shalmaneser III was raised in 827 BC. This six-foot-tall, black obelisk, currently located in the British Museum, is the most complete Assyrian monument yet discovered. It records Shalmaneser III's military campaigns and other triumphs, including payment of tribute by King Jehu of Israel.

Finally, two discoveries from the biblical period of the exile and return are especially relevant. First is Jehoiachin's Ration Tablets (tablets documenting the food rations allotted to certain special royal individuals). Jehoiachin was the Israelite king who was deported from Jerusalem to Babylon by King Nebuchadnezzar II in 597 BC. Ration tablets were found in a palace in Babylon dating from this time period, and they explicitly name King Jehoiachin.[33]

Second, there is the Elephantine Papyri. In the fifth century BC, a Jewish community in southern Egypt, on an island in the Nile called Elephantine, flourished. These Jews wrote and collected papyri, written in various languages and dating back for centuries. The documents include letters and legal contracts, including divorce documents and business regarding slaves. Written five hundred years before the Dead Sea Scrolls, the largest body of documents is in Aramaic and focuses on the Jewish community. Contrary to some critical views, they describe the high priesthood at this period in a way that is consistent with what is offered in the books of Ezra and Nehemiah.[34] They also present some of the earliest evidences that the Israelites lived in Egypt in ancient times. (Note the chart below for an overview of these archaeological discoveries that reflect full or partial parallels with the biblical materials.[35])

Old Testament Parallels from the Ancient Near East

Biblical Periods	Biblical References[36]	Archaeological and Literary Evidence	Significance
Pre-patriarchs	Gen. 1–11	• Sumerian King List (late 3rd millennium BC)	• The Sumerian King List describes reigns of thousands of years, making the more-than-500-year life spans of the pre-flood patriarchs seem relatively short.
		• Atrahasis Epic (early 2nd millennium BC)	• This Mesopotamian epic gives a parallel account of a worldwide flood complete with an ark.
Patriarchs	Gen. 12–50	• Nuzi Tablets (mid-2nd millennium BC)	• These Akkadian writings reflect the legal customs, like adoptions and birthrights, of the patriarchal age.
		• Mari Tablets (18th century BC)	• These Akkadian writings reflect the customs, language, and names of the patriarchal age.
Slavery, Exodus, and Wilderness	Exodus–Deuteronomy	• Mursilis's Treaty with Duppi-Tessub (mid-2nd millennium BC)	• This Hittite treaty from the time of the exodus closely parallels the form of the Sinai covenant.
		• Hammurabi's Law Code (18th century BC)	• These laws are given in a strikingly similar form as the Israelite covenant, offering a timetable for the original composition of the Sinai covenant.
Entering Canaan	Joshua–Ruth	• Merneptah Stele (early 13th century BC)	• This Egyptian stele from Canaan offers the first mention of the name Israel and places Israel in Canaan in the 13th century BC.
United Monarchy	1 Sam. 1– 1 Kings 11; 1 Chron. 1– 2 Chron. 9	• "House of David" Inscription (9th century BC)	• As the name suggests, this Aramaic inscription mentions King David and his dynasty. Written less than 200 years after King David's reign, it attests to his renown in the land.

Biblical Periods	Biblical References[36]	Archaeological and Literary Evidence	Significance
Divided Monarchy	1 Kings 12–2 Kings 24; 2 Chron. 10–35	• Mesha Stele (mid 9th century BC)	• This Moabite stele records the rebellion of the Moabite king, Mesha, against the Israelite king from "the House of Omri."
		• Siloam Inscription (late 8th century BC)	• This Hebrew inscription describes the construction of Hezekiah's water channel under the wall of Jerusalem. The remains of this channel can still be seen today.
		• Shalmaneser's Black Obelisk (9th century BC)	• This Akkadian stone records the payment of tribute from King Jehu to Assyrian king Shalmaneser III.
Exile and Return	2 Kings 25; 2 Chron. 36–Esther	• Jehoiachin's Ration Tablets (6th century BC)	• This Babylonian document records the rations Nebuchadnezzar II allotted for King Jehoiachin's family.
		• Elephantine Papyri (late 5th century BC)	• These Aramaic documents describe the high priesthood in a way that is consistent with this period, and they also describe the lives of the Israelites who lived in Egypt in ancient times.

These archaeological discoveries are only the tip of the iceberg in terms of historical evidences in support of the authenticity and reliability of the Old Testament texts. They certainly do not prove that what the Old Testament books say is true, nor even that any of the events necessarily happened. However, they do show that the minimalist view, which denies their reliability based on documents that allegedly could not have been written when they claim to have been, is unsubstantiated. Minimalists cannot prove their disclaimers. But the burden of proof lies with them; they need to show falsification. As one Old Testament scholar put it, "Historical documents of high quality deserve tentative acceptance as they are critically examined, not overly suspicious rejection from the start."[37]

While many challenging issues remain, time and time again archaeological discoveries have demonstrated the accuracy of the people, places, and events depicted in the Old Testament. The following statement was written by William F. Albright, widely recognized as one of the most important biblical archaeologists of the twentieth century. While it was penned half a century ago, its truth is not overly exaggerated today: "There can be no doubt that archaeology has confirmed the substantial historicity of Old Testament tradition."[38]

New Testament Reliability

The evidence for the reliability of the New Testament documents is even greater than that of the Old Testament. In examining its reliability, we will continue to utilize the same three basic tests: bibliographical, internal, and external.

Bibliographical Evidence

The bibliographical support for the reliability of the New Testament is really quite staggering. When we compare original documents to the extant manuscript copies of the New Testament on the one hand and other ancient writings on the other hand, their difference is stark. In contrast to other ancient works, such as those of Herodotus, Plato, and Aristotle, of which we have only a handful of copies that are over a thousand years later than the originals, the New Testament is quite unique. We have more than 5,700 ancient Greek manuscripts of New Testament documents containing all or portions of its contents, some of which date back to within less than a hundred years of the originals (see chart below).

Comparison of Ancient Texts[39]

Author	Date Written	Earliest Copy	Time Span	Number of Copies
Homer	9th century BC	NA	NA	643
Herodotus (*History*)	480–425 BC	AD 900	1,300 years	8
Thucydides (*History*)	460–400 BC	AD 900	1,300 years	8
Aristotle	450–385 BC	AD 1100	1,400 years	5*
Plato (*Tetralogies*)	427–347 BC	AD 900	1,200 years	7

Author	Date Written	Earliest Copy	Time Span	Number of Copies
Demosthenes	383–322 BC	AD 1100	1,300 years	200**
Caesar	100–44 BC	AD 900	1,000 years	10
Tacitus (*Annals*)	AD 100	AD 1100	1,000 years	20
New Testament	AD 50–100	2nd century AD (c. AD 130)	fewer than 100 years	5,735

* Of any one work
** All from one copy

The most important early witnesses of the New Testament are the John Ryland's Fragment (dating from the mid-second century) and the Oxyrhynchus, Chester Beatty, and Bodmer Papyri (dating from the mid-second and third centuries). These manuscripts contain portions of the New Testament and, given their early dates, are valuable bibliographical sources. Another important group of early source documents are the Vatican, Sinaitic, and Alexandrian manuscripts, which are each virtually complete texts of the New Testament and date from AD 300–450. In addition to these very early Greek manuscripts, there are also thousands of other ancient translations, most notably the Syriac, Latin, and Coptic versions, of which there are close to ten thousand copies dating back from the third, fourth, and fifth centuries.[40]

Since most historians consider the nonbiblical works noted in the chart above to be textually reliable and accurate, there are no reasonable grounds for rejecting the reliability and accuracy of the New Testament documents. On the contrary, on all bibliographical grounds, the New Testament should be taken to be much more reliable than any extant documents of comparable age. While this does not prove that what is said in the New Testament is true, it does provide good reason to believe that it is an accurate representation of what was originally written. Even though some of this evidence had not been uncovered at the time, Sir Frederic Kenyon—the director of the British Museum in the early twentieth century—had this to say about the New Testament:

> The interval, then, between the dates of the original composition and the earliest extant evidence becomes so small as to be in fact negligible, and the last foundation for any doubt that the Scriptures have come down to us substantially as they were written has now been removed. Both the authenticity and the general integrity of the books of the New Testament may be regarded as finally established.[41]

Internal Evidence

Eyewitness Testimony

Many of the New Testament documents make reference to their author *being* an eyewitness to the events, *mentioning* eyewitnesses to the events, or *interviewing* eyewitnesses to the events. For example, the medical doctor Luke, in his Gospel by the same name, notes that he carefully investigated everything he was writing about and that he gleaned his information from eyewitnesses (Luke 1:1–4). Peter notes that he was himself an eyewitness to the events he writes about and that they are not invented stories (2 Peter 1:16). Paul notes that there are hundreds of witnesses to what he is claiming about Jesus and his resurrection and that many of them are still alive, intimating that should anyone question his claims, he or she can check them out personally (1 Cor. 15:6).

Furthermore, these witnesses are trustworthy. One scholar explains:

> It seems clear that the New Testament writers were able and willing to tell the truth. They had very little to gain and much to lose for their efforts. For one thing, they were mostly Jewish theists. To change the religion of Israel with its observance of the Mosaic law, Sabbath keeping, sacrifices, and clear-cut non-Trinitarian monotheism would be to risk the damnation of their own souls to hell. A modern atheist may not worry about such a thing, but members of the early church surely did. For another thing, the apostles lived lives of great hardship, stress, and affliction (see 2 Cor. 11:23–29) and died martyrs' deaths for their convictions. There is no adequate motive for their labors other than a sincere desire to proclaim what they believed to be the truth.[42]

What the Text Claims about Itself

Some writings are clearly fictional or mythological. Plato's *Republic*, for example, or Homer's *Iliad*, are *not intended* to be read as real history. While they certainly have historical elements in them, they have not been taken by their readers to be works of history. Similarly, the Hindu Bhagavad Gita includes a tale involving the speaking of the sun-god. This isn't meant to be actual history, but rather, as a Hindu colleague once told me, it is poetic language intended to communicate "nonempirical, spiritual truth, not actual history."

In the New Testament, the literary type is clearly not meant by its authors to be either fictional or mythological. As mentioned above, Luke claims that he was careful to investigate what he was writing about. Peter and Paul want to make it known that they checked out the facts with eyewitnesses. These are not the kinds of literary devices used by authors writing fiction or myth. While they were certainly meant to contain theological truth, which goes beyond history, this truth is rooted in history. Without the actual history, the theology wouldn't make sense.[43]

Not only are the texts of the New Testament meant to communicate real history, they are also understood to contain information given by God to their authors. For example, Paul makes it clear that he received his message from God and that no person had made it up (Gal. 1:12). He also makes this claim: "All scripture is inspired by God and is useful for teaching, for reproof, for correction, and for training in righteousness" (2 Tim. 3:16).

While these literary points certainly don't prove that the claims of the New Testament are true, there is no doubt that its authors intended for their readers to take them that way.

External Evidence

Once again, the external test for the reliability of an ancient document involves examining whether material external to it supports or disconfirms its reliability. Next we will examine two kinds of external evidence.

Archaeological Support for the New Testament

Archaeological research takes a different form when it comes to the New Testament than it does the Old Testament. The most important discoveries for the former primarily involve written documents, and since I described this evidence above, there is no need to repeat it here. There are, however, other discoveries that are also relevant to confirming the New Testament record. Here are a few examples:

- *Ossuaries*, stone burial boxes, have been uncovered that support the events described in the New Testament. One example involves the discovery of a man named Yhohnn Yehohanan. He had been crucified in a way similar to the descriptions of crucifixion in the New Testament; nails had been driven through his lower forearms, and there was even a large iron nail that had been driven through both heels and is still lodged in one of them. Also, both his shin bones had been broken. Contrary to some critics who maintain that crucified victims were not buried but were tossed in common graves and eaten by wild animals, this is a clear case of a buried, crucified criminal. A second example involves the discovery of an ossuary with the inscription "Yehosef bar Qayafa" ("Joseph, son of Caiaphas"). Experts are virtually certain that the Caiaphas referred to here is the high priest of Jerusalem—the one who handed Jesus over to Pontius Pilate (cf. John 18).[44] A third example is the James ossuary, recently discovered near Jerusalem. An inscription on this ossuary reads, "James, son of Joseph, brother of Jesus." According to scholar Ben Witherington, "If, as seems probable, the ossuary found in the vicinity of Jerusalem and dated to about AD 63 is indeed the burial box of James, the brother of Jesus, this inscription is the most important extrabiblical evidence of its kind."[45]

- *Israelite cities and other specific sites* have been unearthed that confirm New Testament references to them. For example, it is believed that the city of Capernaum (mentioned in Matt. 11:20–24) is located at Tell Hum; the Pool of Bethesda (mentioned in John 5:1–15) has been discovered just north of the temple mount; an inscription of a letter from Emperor Claudius was discovered at Delphi that reads, "Lucius Junios Gallio, my friend, and the proconsul of Achaia . . ." (in agreement with Acts 18:12).[46]

- *The Gnostic Gospels* are a collection of texts discovered at Nag Hammadi, Egypt, along the west bank of the Nile. Like the Dead Sea Scrolls, and discovered at roughly the same time, these ancient documents consist of forty-six different treatises, most of which were previously unknown. They were written by a group referred to as the Gnostics—an unorthodox sect that believed in secret knowledge for salvation (and therefore the documents were rejected from the biblical canon by the church fathers). These documents are quite early, dating to the second half of the fourth century (although their contents date back to the second century).[47] Their significance here is that they demonstrate that it was not only orthodox Christians who accepted practically the entire collection of New Testament writings as early as the second century, but others—in this case the Gnostics—did as well.[48]

While these are important discoveries, this is only a fraction of the archaeological finds that support the reliability of the New Testament. The evidence continues to confirm its trustworthiness.[49]

Early Writings of the Church Fathers

The early church fathers were Christian clergy who lived between AD 100 and 450. Beginning with Clement of Rome, these Christian leaders followed the teachings of Jesus and the apostles. Many of these church fathers wrote books, and in their writings they regularly cited the various books of the Bible. No other work from antiquity has been quoted as often as the New Testament, and there are literally tens of thousands of New Testament quotations in the works of the church fathers. One scholar has even discovered that, except for eleven verses, the entire New Testament can be found in the quotations of their writings from the second and third centuries.[50]

The archaeological discoveries that relate to the New Testament documents are many, and they are quite confirming of its historical reliability. The words of Sir Isaac Newton (1642–1727) still ring true today, even more so than in his day, thanks to the hard work of archaeologists: "There are more sure marks of authenticity in the Bible than in any profane history." Now, all of these "marks" do not prove that the Bible is a supernatural book, one inspired by God. But they do demonstrate that we have good reason to believe that it is a reliable source of historical information.

Divine Inspiration: Is the Bible God's Word?

So far we have examined evidences for the Bible's reliability. But that leaves unanswered the question of whether or not it is truly God's Word. Its reliability is a necessary, but not a sufficient, condition for establishing its "supra-historical" claims. The Bible claims to be inspired by God (2 Tim. 3:16; 2 Peter 1:20–21). Obviously, on its own merits, this is no good reason for believing that it is so inspired. But there are some significant kinds of evidence for the view that the Bible is, in fact, a supernatural book.

Prophecies of the Messiah

The first type of evidence we will examine for divine inspiration is biblical prophecy. The point of Hebrew prophecy was not merely to foretell events yet to come. Rather, the prophets of ancient Israel were to tell forth the word of God that he had communicated to them, and these prophetic utterances in the Old Testament generally involved one or more of the following four elements: (1) to encourage God's people to trust in his mercy and redemptive power; (2) to remind God's people that their safety was dependent on their completely trusting and following him; (3) to encourage God's people about their destiny—that following judgment for sin would come restoration, a restoration brought about finally through the future Messiah; and (4) to confirm the reality of God's message through the objective verification of fulfilled prophecy.[51] We will consider the third and fourth elements here.

There are 8,352 predictive verses throughout the Bible. That is 27 percent of the entire book. In the Old Testament, many of these passages concern the Messiah to come—prophecies about his lineage, his birth, and his ministry, including his betrayal, trial, death, and resurrection, to name a few.[52] It is unfortunate that these prophecies are not more widely known and studied, for what is remarkable is that they are often quite specific, the kinds of facts and events that would be impossible to predict hundreds of years prior to their occurrence. Consider some of them on the following chart:[53]

Messianic Prophecies Fulfilled by Jesus of Nazareth

Topic	Old Testament Prophecy	New Testament Prophecy Fulfilled in Christ
Line of Abraham	Genesis 12:2	Matthew 1:1
Line of Jacob	Numbers 24:17	Luke 3:23, 34
Line of Judah	Genesis 49:10	Matthew 1:2
Line of Jesse	Isaiah 11:1	Luke 3:23, 32
Line of David	2 Samuel 7:12–16	Matthew 1:1
Virgin Birth	Isaiah 7:14	Matthew 1:23
Birthplace: Bethlehem	Micah 5:2	Matthew 2:6
Forerunner: John	Isaiah 40:3; Malachi 3:1	Matthew 3:3
Escape into Egypt	Hosea 11:1	Matthew 2:14
Herod Kills Children	Jeremiah 31:15	Matthew 2:16–18
King	Psalm 2:6	Matthew 21:5
Prophet	Deuteronomy 18:15–18	Acts 3:22–23
Priest	Psalm 110:4	Hebrews 5:6–10
Judge	Isaiah 33:22	John 5:30
Called "Lord"	Psalm 110:1	Luke 2:11
Called "Immanuel"	Isaiah 7:14	Matthew 1:23
Anointed by Holy Spirit	Isaiah 11:2	Matthew 3:16–17
Zeal for God	Psalm 69:9	John 2:15–17
Ministry in Galilee	Isaiah 9:1–2	Matthew 4:12–16
Ministry of Miracles	Isaiah 35:5–6	Matthew 9:35
Ridiculed	Psalm 22:7–8	Matthew 27:39, 43
Stumbling Stone to Jew	Psalm 118:22	1 Peter 2:7
Rejected by Own People	Isaiah 53:3	John 7:5, 48
Light to Gentiles	Isaiah 60:3	Acts 13:47–48
Taught Parables	Psalm 78:2	Matthew 13:34

Topic	Old Testament Prophecy	New Testament Prophecy Fulfilled in Christ
Cleansed the Temple	Malachi 3:1	Matthew 21:12
Sold for 30 Shekels	Zechariah 11:12	Matthew 26:15
Forsaken by Disciples	Zechariah 13:7	Mark 14:50
Silent before Accusers	Isaiah 53:7	Matthew 27:12–14
Hands and Feet Pierced	Psalm 22:16	John 20:25
Heart Broken	Psalm 22:14	John 19:34
Crucified with Thieves	Isaiah 53:12	Matthew 27:38
No Bones Broken	Psalm 34:20	John 19:33–36
Soldiers Gambled	Psalm 22:18	John 19:24
Suffered Thirst on Cross	Psalm 69:21	John 19:28
Vinegar Offered	Psalm 69:21	Matthew 27:34
Christ's Prayer	Psalm 22:24	Matthew 26:39
Disfigured	Isaiah 52:14	John 19:1
Scourging and Death	Isaiah 53:5	John 19:1, 18
His "Forsaken" Cry	Psalm 22:1	Matthew 27:46
Committed Self to God	Psalm 31:5	Luke 23:46
Rich Man's Tomb	Isaiah 53:9	Matthew 27:57–60
Resurrection	Psalm 16:10	Matthew 28:6
Ascension	Psalm 68:18	Luke 24:50–53
Right Hand of God	Psalm 110:1	Hebrews 1:3

What is so amazing here is the breadth and specificity of many of these prophecies.[54] The passages in Isaiah 53 alone are enough to shock even the most ardent skeptic. So how do skeptics avoid the force of what seems clearly to be fulfilled prophecy, and thus to be profound evidence for their divine inspiration? Scholars critical to the supernatural, or at least to the notion of Jesus being the prophesied Messiah, have offered different responses to them.

Skeptical Responses to Messianic Prophecy

Critics of biblical prophecy usually affirm one or more of the following responses: (1) the alleged prophecies are not prophecies at all. Rather, they were written down after the events occurred. (2) The prophecies are too vague to be of any use. (3) There is no way to verify the alleged fulfillment of the prophecies since they occurred too far in the past. And

(4) they violate the laws of natural science (i.e., there is no scientific verification that people can foretell the future).

Let's briefly look at these one at a time. First, given the Dead Sea Scroll discoveries, there is no doubt that the book of Isaiah was written long before the New Testament. So some of the most important messianic prophecies could not have been made up after the facts (see chart above). Second, many of the prophecies are very specific indeed (as can be seen above). Third, there are ways to examine at least some of these prophecies utilizing widely acknowledged, reliable, historical resources. As the next chapter demonstrates, some of these prophetic claims involving the Messiah can be analyzed using the scientific methods of historical research. We will see that the evidence is quite remarkable. Finally, there is no problem with violating the laws of natural science if, in fact, God exists.

Internal Witness of God's Spirit

The second type of evidence for divine inspiration is the internal witness of God's Spirit. While it is a subjective way of determining the Bible's divine inspiration, Christians do believe that God can, and often does, confirm within them the Bible's being inspired and true. The danger with relying on subjective experience alone is, of course, that one can be mistaken. Even the Bible itself notes that the heart is deceitful above all things (Jer. 17:9). Our spiritual experiences and/or inner feelings, even of what we take to be the presence and communication of God, can no doubt be erroneous. Furthermore, people of all religions have felt as though God has confirmed to them that their holy scriptures were inspired (and many other things as well). But since these scriptures contradict each other, they certainly cannot all be right (unless God is schizophrenic!).

Nonetheless, while subjective experiences can be deceptive, this does not disprove the claim that God can (if he so chooses), and does, witness through his Spirit to the truthfulness of his Word. Protestant Reformer John Calvin put much weight on this kind of evidence, even to the exclusion of other proofs:

> Let this point therefore stand: that those whom the Holy Spirit has inwardly taught truly rest upon Scripture, and that Scripture indeed is self-authenticated; hence, it is not right to subject it to proof and reasoning. And the certainty it deserves with us, it attains by the testimony of the Spirit. For even if it wins reverence for itself by its own majesty, it seriously affects us only when it is sealed upon our hearts through the Spirit. Therefore, illumined by his power, we believe neither by our own nor

by anyone else's judgment that Scripture is from God; but above human judgment we affirm with utter certainty (just as if we were gazing upon the majesty of God himself) that it has flowed to us from the very mouth of God by the ministry of men.[55]

The Transforming Message of the Bible

The third and final type of evidence for divine inspiration that we will examine is its transforming message. Through following the life-changing teachings found within the pages of the Bible, all kinds of people throughout the centuries, from thieves to murderers to regular folks like you and me, have been morally and spiritually transformed in profound ways. The Bible's message transforms individuals, but it also transforms cultures. For example, the emergence of hospitals, ministries of compassion, charity, and outreach, such as World Vision and the Salvation Army, have emerged out of the Christian worldview. Through exhibiting the message of God's love and care for the world, Christian organizations have set the standard for care and concern for those in need.

Prison Fellowship, a ministry devoted to ministering to the incarcerated, has a proven track record of transforming the lives of inmates who become respectable citizens after following the teachings of Jesus as recorded in the Bible. Their documented low recidivism rates (the tendency to relapse into criminal behavior) have even caught the attention of the federal government.[56] The list of individuals who have been transformed through the powerful message of the Bible is virtually endless. (More will be said about this message in chapter 9.)

The Three Theisms: Judaism, Christianity, and Islam

We have examined so far the reliability and divine inspiration of the Bible. We have solid evidence that it is an accurate and inspired book. No doubt this is good evidence for the truth of Christianity. But what about the other major theistic religions, most especially Judaism and Islam? Does this make them false religions?

From the Christian perspective, Judaism is the foundation of Christianity; Christianity is Judaism fulfilled, so to speak. In a sense, then, there is no contradiction between them. It is true that many Jews, both historically and in modern times, reject Jesus as the Messiah. But a thematic unity runs throughout the Old and New Testaments: God is sending a messiah to save people from their sins. Christians would say that Jews who deny that Jesus is the Messiah are wrong. But there are also many Jews who affirm Jesus as the Messiah mentioned in their Hebrew Bible.

As a matter of fact, Jesus himself and his twelve disciples were all Jewish. (The next chapter will focus specifically on the evidence for Jesus as Messiah.) So, from the Christian perspective, there is no contradiction between the Judaism of the Old Testament and the Christianity of the New Testament. There is a spiritual continuity throughout.

Muslims also affirm many things in common with Christians. Here are some of their basic, shared beliefs:

- There is only one, all-powerful God who is the sole creator, sustainer, and ruler of the universe.
- God is holy, just, and merciful.
- God created the world.
- Like God, we are to be just and good.
- God established covenants with Abraham and Moses.
- Jesus was holy and righteous and performed miracles.

Nevertheless, while there are such commonalities, there are also significant disagreements. For example,

- Muslims do not believe in the Trinity; this is the Christian view of God.
- Muslims do not believe that Jesus was crucified or resurrected; these are central teachings of the Christian faith.
- Muslims do not believe that Jesus is the Son of God or Savior of the world; this is the essence of the Christian faith.
- Muslims believe that human beings are naturally good; Christians believe that human beings have a bent toward evil (original sin).
- Muslims believe that the Qur'an, not the Bible, is God's inspired holy book; Christians believe that the Bible, not the Qur'an, is God's inspired holy book.

Clearly, these two religions disagree on some very fundamental issues. More will be noted about their differences in chapter 9. But just given these differences, it is obvious that both religions cannot be true.

Finally, it is important to note that the essence of the Christian faith is love, and while the New Testament affirms that Christianity is exclusively true (as all religions claim about themselves), love must reign supreme. When asked what is the greatest commandment, Jesus responded: "'You shall love the Lord your God with all your heart, and with all your soul, and with all your mind.' This is greatest and first commandment. And a second is like it: 'You shall love your neighbor as yourself.' On these two commandments hang all the law and the prophets" (Matt. 22:37–40). In essence, Jesus is saying that the entire message of God is love—experiential love, not just an abstract principle. If Christians are to reach the world with this central message of the Bible, they need to follow the lead of Jesus and emulate his unconditional love in word and deed. As Mahatma Gandhi noted, "If Christians would really live according to the teachings of Christ, as found in the Bible, all of India would be Christian today."[57]

Summary

In conclusion, I want to make clear that I am not claiming that the reliability and divine inspiration of the Bible are "undeniable" or "proven." There are many thoughtful, intelligent, and well-educated people who do deny both its reliability and its inspiration. But there are also many thoughtful, intelligent, and well-educated people who believe that aliens exist and that American astronauts never really landed on the moon. Perhaps they are right. But what we are after in this book is *plausibility*—what is the most reasonable thing to believe given the evidence we have before us? As with all of the chapters, I encourage you to explore the evidence, both pro and con, for yourself. Given that theism is true—that there really exists a personal, loving, and powerful God, and given the bibliographical, internal, and external evidences for the Bible, I think it is more reasonable to believe in its reliability and inspiration than to deny it.

Questions for Reflection

1. Is the Pentateuch myth? Explain.
2. What relevance are the Dead Sea Scrolls to the reliability of the Old Testament documents?
3. Regarding the New Testament, which of the three tests for reliability is most persuasive? Why?
4. After studying the prophecies of the Messiah, which ones do you find to be most convincing in terms of their having a supernatural origin?
5. How does the evidence offered in this chapter for the reliability and inspiration of the Bible affect the plausibility of other theistic religions? Reflect on specific religions.

For Further Reading in Support of the Reliability of the Bible

Bruce, F. F. *The Canon of Scripture*. Downers Grove, IL: InterVarsity, 1988. The classical evangelical work on how the books of the Bible came to be recognized as Holy Scripture.

Geisler, Norman L., and William E. Nix. *A General Introduction to the Bible*. Rev. ed. Chicago: Moody, 1986. The best book in print detailing the development of the Bible, as well as providing a defense of its authenticity and reliability. Slightly dated in parts but highly recommended. Works well in tandem with Lightfoot's text listed below.

Hoffmeier, James K. *Israel in Egypt: The Evidence for the Authenticity of the Exodus Tradition*. New York: Oxford University Press, 1996. One of the leading archaeologists of our time critiques the minimalist position and defends the historicity of such biblical patriarchs as Joseph and Moses as well as the exodus itself.

Kitchen, K. A. *On the Reliability of the Old Testament*. Grand Rapids: Eerdmans, 2003. This tome is *the* major contemporary work defending the reliability of the Old Testament against the minimalist camp. Detailed and fairly technical.

Lightfoot, Neil R. *How We Got the Bible*. 3rd ed. Grand Rapids: Baker, 2003. An up-to-date and concise exposition of the development of the Bible. Very helpful and readable. Works well in tandem with the Geisler and Nix text listed above.

McDowell, Josh. *The New Evidence That Demands a Verdict*. Nashville: Thomas Nelson, 1999. A classic apologetic for the reliability of the Bible (and other related issues).

Metzger, Bruce, and Bart D. Ehrman. *The Text of the New Testament: Its Transmission, Corruption, and Restoration*. 4th ed. New York: Oxford University Press, 2005. A well-researched and scholarly work on the subject. Fairly technical but well worth a careful read.

For Further Reading against the Reliability of the Bible

Dever, William. *Who Were the Early Israelites and Where Did They Come From?* Grand Rapids: Eerdmans, 2003. Dever holds to a middle-of-the-road position between the minimalists and the conservatives.

Finkelstein, Israel, and Neil Asher Silberman. *The Bible Unearthed*. New York: Touchstone, 2002. A provocative defense of the minimalist camp; probably the leading accessible work against the reliability of the Old Testament.

Friedman, Richard E. *Who Wrote the Bible?* Reprint, San Francisco: HarperSanFrancisco, 1997. A recent defense of the documentary hypothesis.

Mack, Burton L. *Who Wrote the New Testament? The Making of the Christian Myth*. San Francisco: HarperSanFrancisco, 1996. A readable introductory text in which he offers a critical account of the development of Christianity—what he calls "Christian myth."

Thompson, Thomas L. *The Mythic Past: Biblical Archaeology and the Myth of Israel*. New York: Basic Books, 2000. In this important minimalist work, Thompson argues that there never was a united monarchy of Israel in biblical times and that the notion of historical Israel and its history is a literary fiction.

Wells, G. A. *Can We Trust the New Testament? Thoughts on the Reliability of Early Christian Testimony*. La Salle, IL: Open Court, 2004. Wells examines the biblical accounts of Paul, Peter, and the book of Acts and concludes that the events described in Acts and the Gospels cannot be trusted.

Whitelam, Keith. *The Invention of Ancient Israel: The Silencing of Palestinian History*. New York: Routledge, 1997. This is a radical minimalist work. Whitelam argues that the biblical view of ancient Israel as a nation has been invented by scholars—an invention in which Israel has been made in the image of a European nation state.

The Resurrection of Jesus

Fact or Fiction?

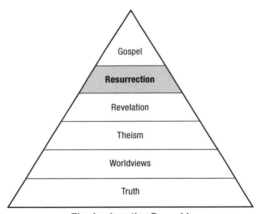

The Apologetics Pyramid

God has paid us the intolerable compliment of loving us, in the deepest, most tragic, most inexorable sense.

C. S. Lewis

Why is it thought incredible by any of you that God raises the dead?

Paul the Apostle (Acts 26:8)

Today, however, historical criticism has made the empty tomb a dubious factor and the conclusions of natural science have rendered it suspect.

Hans Küng

Probably no more important historical questions can be posed than those involving the life and death of Jesus of Nazareth. Worldwide his birth divides time into two parts: BC (before Christ) and AD (Lat., *anno Domini*, "in the year of our Lord"; refers to the approximate birth of Jesus). His death is celebrated as a national holiday in many quarters of the world. The New Testament, a collection of twenty-seven books focused on Jesus and his message and written roughly two thousand years ago, is still the best seller of all time. Who is this man—the most influential person who has ever lived—and why are his life and death so important?

Ever since the first Easter, followers of Jesus have claimed that he rose from the dead in vindication of his messianic claims. He is the Messiah, the Savior of the world, prophesied about in the Old Testament. He would come as the Son of God—one having infinite worth and value—and he would offer himself as the eternal sacrifice for the sins of humankind. He would conquer death, and he would rise up as King of Kings and Lord of Lords. Through him, all the world could be saved.

But are such outrageous assertions believable? In an age of scientific sophistication like our own, can we really be rational in believing that someone literally, bodily, rose from the dead? To believe such radical claims, one needs weighty evidence. The examination of such evidence is the focus of this chapter.

Evidence for the Bodily Resurrection of Jesus of Nazareth

Many claims have been made about the resurrection of Jesus of Nazareth, and we could examine much supporting evidence for his rising from the dead. But rather than spending time investigating questionable and potentially suspect proofs, one is better served by examining the evidences that even many scholarly skeptics of the bodily resurrection agree with. I will present, then, six historical truths and how they support the bodily resurrection of Jesus.[1] I will also present several major objections to them.

Six Historical Truths Supporting the Bodily Resurrection of Jesus

Historical Truth #1: Jesus Died on a Cross and Was Buried in a Tomb

Crucifixion was a brutal, hideous way to die, and ancient Roman authors often referred to it with abhorrence and repulsion. They would use such language as "horrendous torture," "the extreme penalty," and "cruel and disgusting" when mentioning it.[2] Recent medical studies are in agreement that crucifixion is a dreadful method of execution and that what Jesus endured on the cross was more than sufficient to cause his death.[3]

It is almost universally agreed upon by New Testament scholars and critics that Jesus of Nazareth was executed via crucifixion under the Roman governorship of Pontius Pilate. Not only are the events surrounding his crucifixion recorded in all four Gospels, but they are also mentioned in nonbiblical and even non-Christian sources.[4] Consider the words of the ancient Roman historian Cornelius Tacitus (c. AD 55–120), in his book on Roman history called the *Annals*:

> Consequently, to get rid of the report (that he was responsible for the burning of Rome), Nero fastened the guilt and inflicted the most exquisite tortures on a class hated for their abominations, called Christians by the populace. Christus, from whom the name had its origin, suffered the extreme penalty during the reign of Tiberius at the hands of one of the procurators, Pontius Pilate.[5]

New Testament scholars and critics also widely agree that, following his death, Jesus was placed in a tomb in Jerusalem.[6] The reason for the practical unanimity of scholars that Jesus was buried in a tomb is due to several factors. First, it is mentioned in the Gospels, and most especially in the earliest of them: Mark. Second, the apostle Paul mentions the burial in an even earlier work than the Gospel of Mark—1 Corinthians 15 (AD 56–57). These sources are early enough that many eyewitnesses still would have been around to confirm or disconfirm the claim. Third, the details of the tomb listed in the Gospels are consistent with recent archaeological discoveries and thus lend further credibility to the overall account.[7]

Historical Truth #2: Jesus Disappeared from His Tomb[8]

As noted above, Mark's Gospel is the earliest, and it is typically dated to somewhere between AD 60 and 70. The author notes that Mary Magdalene and two other women went to the tomb very early on Sunday morning. When they arrived, they found the tomb empty (cf. Mark 16:1–8). This is an account of the empty tomb written only thirty to forty years after Jesus's death.

Consider, then, the following points. First, as history demonstrates, it takes two or three generations after a historical event occurs for major legend to replace actual history when it is surrounding the same location of the event; often it takes even longer.[9] Thirty to forty years is simply not enough time for an elaborate legendary account of the empty tomb to develop, especially since many of those in the broader community would still be alive to challenge such a claim.

Second, a variety of New Testament sources testify to the tomb being empty.[10] All four Gospels make reference to it, and it is also implied in Paul's writings. This widespread agreement provides independent corroboration of the reality of the event.

Third, even the enemies of the emerging Christian faith admitted that the tomb was empty; they didn't question this claim at all. Their response was to offer hypotheses to explain how the tomb became empty. In Matthew 28:11–15, we see that the chief priests and elders told the soldiers to spread the story that the body was stolen. We will explore this and a few other naturalistic explanations for the missing body below, but for now it is important to note that all of the historical evidence points to the truth that Jesus's body disappeared from his tomb. Even the skeptical historian Michael Grant of Cambridge University notes that the evidence is quite strong: "[Regarding the New Testament Gospels,] if we apply the same sort of criteria that we would apply to any other ancient literary sources, then the evidence is firm and plausible enough to necessitate the conclusion that the tomb was, indeed, found empty."[11]

Finally, all that was necessary to squelch the new religious movement was to produce Jesus's dead body. The fact that this never happened, nor was ever even attempted, is even more proof for the claim that the body was, in fact, missing.[12]

Historical Truth #3: Jesus's Followers Believed He Was Resurrected from the Dead and That He Appeared to and Spoke with Them

The Gospels of the New Testament contain numerous references to the disciples seeing the risen Jesus, talking and eating with him, and even touching his resurrected body. However, rather than examine the appearances of Jesus in the four Gospels, since these are sometimes regarded as legendary by New Testament critics,[13] let us focus on the more historically trusted account offered by the apostle Paul in 1 Corinthians 15:1–8:

> Now I would remind you, brothers and sisters, of the good news that I proclaimed to you, which you in turn received, in which also you stand, through which you are also being saved, if you hold firmly to the message that I proclaimed to you—unless you have come to believe in vain.

> For I handed on to you as of first importance what I in turn had received: that Christ died for our sins in accordance with the scriptures, and that he was buried, and that he was raised on the third day in accordance with the scriptures, and that he appeared to Cephas, then to the twelve. Then he appeared to more than five hundred brothers and sisters at one time, most of whom are still alive, though some have died. Then he appeared to James, then to all the apostles. Last of all, as to one untimely born, he appeared also to me.

Paul is, no doubt, intending to offer a proof here of the veracity of Jesus's resurrection.[14] Two elements of this proof stand out.

First, it is important to note that this letter of Paul's is very early, dating to AD 56 or 57.[15] This puts it very close to the actual death of Jesus—roughly twenty years later. As noted above, twenty years is not much time for legend to develop. Scholar William Lane Craig notes, "Legends do not arise significantly until the generation of eyewitnesses dies off. Hence, legends are given no ground for growth as long as eyewitnesses are alive who remember the facts."[16] (Note: This point is relevant not only for Paul's letters, but for the Gospel accounts as well, since they were written not much more than one generation after Jesus's death even according to the most skeptical, late-dating New Testament critics.)

Beyond this, however, these verses contain formulaic, traditional material. In other words, Paul is passing on something that he "had received." This puts the date even earlier and consequently even closer to the actual event itself. Some have even argued that this passage of Paul's is an early, pre-Pauline formula, or hymn, of the primitive church, and there is certainly strong evidence supporting such a view.[17] But whether or not it was a hymn, formula, or creed, Paul is making it clear for anyone of his time to examine the fact that he has information about Jesus's appearances that date back extremely close to Jesus's actual death. Large numbers of people saw something that led them to believe that he had risen from the dead, and Paul is citing these appearances as evidence for Jesus's resurrection.[18] In its historical and theological context, the rhetorical form of this passage indicates that Paul is presenting here a formal argument to convince the Corinthians that there will be a resurrection of believers. He is grounding this future event in the *fact* of the resurrection of Jesus based on the testimonial witness of himself and many others.[19]

Historical Truth #4: Key Jewish Leaders Were Converted to Belief in, and Worship of, Jesus Shortly after His Death

The apostle Paul. Since we have just looked at the apostle Paul's defense of Jesus's appearances, let's consider his role in the early church.

Paul, also named Saul, was a well-educated Roman citizen and a highly trained Jewish Pharisee. He was trained under the eminent rabbi Gamaliel in Jerusalem and rose to a prominent position among the Pharisees, perhaps even being ranked among the prestigious Sanhedrin.[20]

When early Christianity rose to prominence in Jerusalem, he opposed it strongly, even overseeing the death of some of its adherents. But, while pursuing Christians who had fled to Damascus in Syria, he had a religious experience that changed his life forever. Here is how his biographer and fellow traveler, the medical doctor Luke, described Paul's experience (Acts 9:1–9):

> Meanwhile Saul [Paul], still breathing threats and murder against the disciples of the Lord, went to the high priest and asked him for letters to the synagogues at Damascus, so that if he found any who belonged to the Way, men or women, he might bring them bound to Jerusalem. Now as he was going along and approaching Damascus, suddenly a light from heaven flashed around him. He fell to the ground and heard a voice saying to him, "Saul, Saul, why do you persecute me?" He asked, "Who are you, Lord?" The reply came, "I am Jesus, whom you are persecuting. But get up and enter the city, and you will be told what you are to do." The men who were traveling with him stood speechless because they heard the voice but saw no one. Saul got up from the ground, and though his eyes were open, he could see nothing; so they led him by the hand and brought him into Damascus. For three days he was without sight, and neither ate nor drank.

This experience of seeing Jesus was so dramatic that it caused Paul to completely change his religious convictions. He no longer persecuted Christians, but rather became a follower of Christ himself, and then one of Christianity's most fervent defenders! Unlike other converts to a different religion, Paul's conversion was based entirely on this firsthand experience. Thus, it is not easily explained away as psychological peer pressure (his peers were Jews, not Christians) or as resulting from argumentation by Christian apologists.

What's more, his conviction that he had seen the risen Jesus and had been spoken to by him was so intense that he was willing to be arrested, beaten, flogged, stoned, and finally executed because of it.[21] What would cause such a radical conversion, and such impassioned convictions, if not the reality of the encounter?

James, brother of Jesus. Both within and without the New Testament there are references to James, the brother of Jesus (e.g., Matt. 13:55; Mark 6:3). Before Jesus's crucifixion, neither James nor Jesus's other three brothers mentioned in the New Testament were followers of him (cf. Mark 3:21; John 7:5). After the crucifixion and the alleged resurrection, however, everything changed. All of them are mentioned as later becoming believers in Jesus, and James himself even rose to become the Christian leader in Jerusalem in roughly AD 49.

What caused this brother of Jesus to shift from skeptic to believer? According to Paul, James was visited by Jesus after his resurrection (1 Cor. 15:7). This would certainly explain such a radical conversion, especially since James was willing to die for his convictions, and in fact did die for them.[22]

Historical Truth #5: Many of Jesus's Followers Were Persecuted and Even Executed for Their Belief That He Was Alive as the Risen Messiah

Many of Jesus's followers underwent extreme hardship for their belief in him, including imprisonment and even execution—not only in the earliest days of Christianity, but all through world history to our own day.

Those who have gone to their death because of their belief in the resurrected Jesus do not consist of a few wild-eyed religious fanatics. Quite to the contrary, most of Jesus's twelve disciples were grimly executed. Furthermore, since the birth of Christianity, more than 69.4 million followers of Jesus have been martyred for their faith.[23] Moreover, at least 112 different methods have been used to execute these Christian devotees. Some were crucified; others were boiled in oil, roasted alive, sawed in two, disemboweled, burned at the stake, hanged, strangled, stoned, thrown from airplanes, or thrown to lions, crocodiles, or sharks.[24]

There are at least two intriguing issues here regarding the martyrdom of Christians. First, a number of those martyred were killed claiming that they had seen the risen Jesus. Paul and James were noted above. In the book of Acts, the disciple Stephen sees Jesus standing at the right hand of God (Acts 7:56). He makes this known to his accusers, and they take him out and stone him. All he would have had to do is deny this claim and deny that Jesus is the risen Lord, and he probably would have been let go. But he was willing to die a gruesome death of stoning because of his conviction of Jesus being alive. The same applies for all of the twelve disciples, with the exception of the exiled John. From Jesus onward, countless Christians have followed the example of their Lord to die for, but not kill for, their beliefs.

The second point of intrigue is that so many Christians through the centuries have died for their belief in Jesus. Forty-four million were martyred in the past century alone.[25] What would cause the early disciples, and millions of Christians since them, to go to their deaths in horrific ways for their belief that Jesus is risen from the dead and Lord of the universe? Unlike other religions that have also experienced terrible persecution over the centuries, the central belief of Christianity is the *historical* claim about Jesus's resurrection. It is not a set of general religious claims that they are dying for, but rather the historic, factual claim about a dead body raising to life. What could possibly cause such widespread belief if not the event itself?

Historical Truth #6: Since Jesus's Death, Numerous Rational and Sane People throughout the Centuries Have Had Personal Experiences with One They Claim Is the Risen Jesus

History is inundated with examples of individuals and groups experiencing the risen Jesus. A number of examples during New Testament times were noted above, and throughout the early church, medieval times, and even now in the twenty-first century, countless people have described seeing him, being led by him, and even talking to him and touching him.

There are also numerous documented cases of people having visions and dreams of Jesus visiting them and telling them that he is Savior and Lord. In a recent visit to India, I spoke with a man and his wife who were both from the Brahman caste—the highest caste in the Hindu system—in which conversion to any other religion is quite rare. He told me how he had become a Christian. He was awakened in the middle of the night, and Jesus was there sitting next to him on his bed. He told this young man that he was, in fact, Jesus Christ, Lord of the universe, and invited the man to follow him. The man converted on the spot, and his wife did soon thereafter. Although he has been completely rejected by his family and friends because of his allegiance to Jesus, he stands firmly by his experience and conviction.

These kinds of encounters are now a worldwide phenomenon.[26] For example, over one-fourth of non-Western Muslim converts to Christianity recently surveyed became Christians because of dreams and visions by and about Jesus.[27] What best explains these phenomena if not his real presence?

Evaluating the Evidence for the Resurrection of Jesus: What Are the Options?

I have presented above six historical truths that are widely agreed upon by skeptics and believers alike. The question before us, then, is what best accounts for all of them taken as a whole? Which explanation is most reasonable to believe given this evidence that we have available? There aren't very many options. Let's consider first what seem to be the three most reasonable *naturalistic* possibilities.

Option #1: Stolen or Misplaced Body Theories (But What about the Appearances?)

The oldest recorded nonmiraculous explanation for the missing body of Jesus is that it was stolen from the tomb. However, stolen body accounts are fraught with problems.

The central difficulty involves the question of who would have stolen the body. The book of Matthew records a discussion between the soldiers who were guarding the tomb and the chief priests and elders (Matt. 28:11–15). According to the account, the latter were willing to pay the soldiers for telling the story that Jesus's body was stolen by the disciples, despite the fact that the soldiers knew it wasn't true. But this made-up story doesn't provide a credible scenario, for the same disciples who were accused of stealing the body not only proclaimed his resurrection—and lying was clearly contrary to their Master and message—but they were also willing to suffer the horrendous deaths mentioned above for continuing to assert it. Historically people have been willing to die for what they think is true, even if what they believe turns out to be false. But people are not willing to die torturous deaths for what they know to be a blatant lie.

Another possibility is that either the Jews or the Romans stole the body. But why on earth would they do that? The Jews were desperately trying to squelch the growing Christian religion, so they had no good reason to steal it. The Romans too had no reason to steal Jesus's body, and they certainly didn't want to create further and unnecessary tensions with the Jewish leadership. Furthermore, the Roman government was opposed to new religious movements and considered them to be dangerous sects. Thus, the suggestion that either the Jewish leaders or the Roman authorities would have stolen the body is quite preposterous.

A third possibility is that the body wasn't actually stolen, but rather the disciples and followers of Jesus went to the wrong place when attempting to visit his tomb. But this explanation is more problematic than the stolen body accounts. Consider the following points. First, the Jewish and Roman authorities certainly would have known where the body of this well-known "criminal" was placed. But even if they hadn't known, they would have used this fact as evidence in their favor. On the other hand, if they did know where it was, they simply could have exhumed the dead body, and the early Christian movement would have been over. However, none of this ever happened.

Second, there is no recorded evidence that the body was somehow misplaced or that the disciples were looking in the wrong place. But surely, if this were the case, the critics of the resurrection would have used and documented it. Third, the Gospels point to the bodily resurrection and go into detail about the events surrounding the first discoveries of the empty tomb.

But even if we grant that his body was stolen or misplaced, that does not answer the question of why so many people were claiming to have seen the risen Jesus. So what do we do with the appearance evidence?

Option #2: Hallucination and Vision Theories (But What about the Body?)

One way that skeptics of the bodily resurrection have attempted to explain the appearances of the resurrected Jesus is to suggest that those who claimed to see him were actually having hallucinations or visions. Let's look first at the hallucination hypothesis.

In the last century, hallucination theories were quite popular as attempts to explain the resurrection appearances of Jesus. Spurred on by the helpful work of psychologists and psychiatrists, many unexplainable "visual" appearances and events were explained away as hallucinations. Further psychological research, however, has demonstrated that the appearances of Jesus to the disciples, Paul, and James, as well as the other appearances described in the New Testament, are not the kinds of events that can be classified as hallucinations for a number of reasons. Consider the following:

1. *Hallucinations are individual occurrences*. Psychologist Gary Collins notes:

   Hallucinations are individual occurrences. By their very nature only one person can see any given hallucination at a time. They certainly are not something which can be seen by a group of people. Neither is it possible that one person could somehow induce a hallucination in someone else. Since a hallucination exists only in this objective, personal sense, it is obvious that others cannot witness it.[28]

   However, in the earliest recorded account of the appearances of Jesus by his disciples and others, there are "group appearances" (1 Cor. 15:5–6). We also find such appearances in the Gospel accounts (Luke 24:36–49; John 20:19–29). Thus they could not have been hallucinations.

2. *Hallucinations do not account for the conversion experiences of Paul and James.* As Gary Habermas, one of the leading scholars on the resurrection, has argued, Paul was in no frame of mind to hallucinate a risen Jesus. To the contrary, he believed that he had God's charge to end the Christian movement. Furthermore, James, the brother of Jesus, was a skeptic. He not only didn't believe in Jesus as the Messiah when Jesus was alive, but he seems to have thought that Jesus was deluding himself. James too, then, was in no frame of mind to hallucinate that Jesus was the risen Lord.[29]

3. *Visual hallucinations are rare events.* With the exception of people suffering from schizophrenia, which is not a very common mental illness (and certainly not common enough to account for all of those who saw the risen Jesus), visual hallucinations are quite rare.[30] But in the case of the appearances of Jesus, we have a large number of people being appeared to by him. Despite the claims of some resurrection critics, such as atheist philosopher Michael Martin, collective hallucinations or delusions at this level are not just rare—they are nonexistent.[31]

Regarding visions, New Testament scholar and resurrection critic Gerd Lüdemann puts it this way: "I always talk about *vision*. I think vision is the primary religious experience that led to the whole Christian movement. . . . And a vision can be a force within a person that in many cases leads to a complete reversal and change of one's life."[32]

Surprisingly, Lüdemann and a host of resurrection critics agree that the disciples and followers of Jesus saw *something*, or had some kind of religious experience, yet they deny that these followers saw the actual risen Jesus. What Lüdemann and others in his camp mean when they say that the disciples and early followers of Jesus saw *visions* of him is that they had something in their minds regarding Jesus, not that they were actually seeing a real, historic person. But many of these appearances of Jesus involved his bodily activity, including eating and being touched. How then, if not for the reality of the risen Jesus, does one explain these kinds of appearances? While they could call these specific examples "literary fictions," the testimony of the early church is based on these literal types of encounters, not vague, generic visions of something they knew not what.

Finally, if one is going to consider hallucination or vision theories, he or she is also going to have to hold to some version of the stolen body theory, since there would be little point in having a hallucination or vision of a person who claims to have risen from the dead when the body is still lying in the grave. But perhaps there is another way of explaining the missing body.

Option #3: Resuscitation Theories (The Body Problem All Over Again)

While there is no doubt that Jesus was crucified, another way of explaining the empty tomb and the appearances of Jesus is to suggest that he didn't actually die on the cross, but rather he only appeared to be dead. The technical term is *swoon*, which means to lose consciousness. On this account, Jesus swooned due to the beatings, the loss of blood, and exhaustion, and those tending to him thought that he had died. But after a good rest in the tomb, he resuscitated and came to his senses. He then realized what had happened and made up the story to his followers that he had actually risen from the dead.

As with the other two, however, this hypothesis is also loaded with difficulties. First, this puts Jesus's character in quite a bad light and contradicts all of the depictions of him from friend and foe. His teachings always embodied the highest moral virtues. His Sermon on the Mount (Matthew 5–7), for example, is one of the most profound treatises on ethics ever spoken or penned. Not only did he preach righteousness and holiness, but all accounts indicate that he lived it as well. One thing Jesus was not was a grand liar.

Second, would the disciples really have believed that a beaten, bruised, and bloody Jesus was the resurrected Son of God? Imagine just what such a man would look like—nails through the hands and feet, thorns punched through the skull, a spear through the side, and stretched muscles and ligaments due to the actual crucifixion itself. Could any human being bounce back from such an ordeal to make his closest comrades believe that he was now a new, resurrected creation? This is clearly an unreasonable explanation.

Third, there is the problem of what crucifixion actually does to a person and what Jesus would have experienced. As is quite accurately depicted in the blockbuster movie *The Passion of the Christ*, there is simply no way Jesus would have survived this grueling experience. Many physicians have studied crucifixion in recent years and have demonstrated that asphyxiation was a common cause of death for those who were crucified. Asphyxiation especially would have been a problem for Jesus given his severe beating before being crucified. Added to this is the spear that was thrust into his side and the attending blood and water that flowed out. As a major medical journal explains the account, there is simply no way Jesus could have survived this ordeal.[33]

Finally, there is the problem with resuscitation theories of what happened to Jesus's body when he did eventually die—whenever that may have been. Surely his followers would have venerated his tomb. But the historical evidence demonstrates that no such thing actually happened;

the tomb was, and is, empty. So, once again, we are left with a missing body, and we have just gone full circle.

Option #4: Divine Miracle

The other option, of course, is that we have here a divine miracle: God raised Jesus from the dead. But some rule out such a possibility even before examining the evidence. Former atheist philosopher Antony Flew makes the following point regarding such miraculous events:

> Confronted with testimonial evidence for the occurrence of a miracle, the secular historian must recognize that however unlikely it may seem that all the witnesses were in error, the occurrence of a genuine miracle is, by definition, naturally impossible. Yet this should not be the end of the affair. For historians, like everyone else, ought to be ever ready, for sufficient reason, to correct their assumptions about what is probable or improbable, possible or impossible. And this readiness should allow that even the qualification *secular* may, for sufficient reason, have to be abandoned.[34]

These words reflect an open mind, for unlike many skeptics of miracles, Flew is at least open to their possibility; he doesn't rule them out a priori. So, taking his cue, we should be ready to abandon a naturalistic explanation if we have sufficient reason.

But do we have sufficient reason? In addition to the testimonial evidence we have available, we must also remember that we are examining it having already seen, from previous chapters, that the proofs for God's existence are staggering. If, therefore, we believe that a personal God exists, this lends incredible support to the view that such a miraculous event as Jesus's resurrection could occur. Given this previous evidence for God's existence, then, it surely should cause one to question the assumption that miracles cannot happen. After all, if God created the heavens and the earth, he certainly could raise his Son from the dead.[35]

Considering everything we have examined in each of the previous chapters and the historical evidence offered in this chapter, the case for Christ's resurrection is overwhelming.

Who Is This Jesus, and What Does His Resurrection Mean for You and Me?

Now that we have examined some of the hard evidence for Jesus's resurrection, suppose that, like me, you too believe that he rose from the dead. What does that mean for us? Who is this death-defying person, and how is his resurrection relevant to my life and yours?

Liar, Lunatic, or Lord?

One of the great Christian thinkers and writers of the twentieth century was the Cambridge University medieval scholar C. S. Lewis. In his classic work *Mere Christianity*, he presents the following trilemma:

> I am trying here to prevent anyone from saying the really foolish thing that people often say about Him: "I'm ready to accept Jesus as a great moral teacher, but I don't accept His claim to be God." That is one thing we must not say. A man who was merely a man and said the sort of things Jesus said would not be a great moral teacher. He would either be a lunatic—on a level with the man who says he is a poached egg—or else he would be the Devil of Hell. You must make your choice. Either this man was, and is, the Son of God: or else a madman or something worse. You can shut Him up for a fool, or you can spit at Him and kill Him as a demon; or you can fall at His feet and call Him Lord and God. But let us not come with any patronizing nonsense about His being a great human teacher. He has not left that open to us. He did not intend to.[36]

Those who hold to Jesus as a great moral teacher—a mere man with solid ethical principles—are not taking Jesus's words and teachings seriously. Consider a few of his radical claims about himself:[37]

- Thomas answered him, *"My Lord and my God!"* Jesus said to him, "Have you believed because you have seen me? Blessed are those who have not seen and yet have come to believe." (John 20:28–29)
- "For those who want to save their life will lose it, and those who lose their life for my sake will find it." (Matt. 16:25)
- "The Father and I are one." (John 10:30)
- "Those who are ashamed of me and my words in this adulterous and sinful generation, of them the Son of Man will also be ashamed when he comes in the glory of his Father with the holy angels." (Mark 8:38)
- Jesus said to them, "Very truly, I tell you, before Abraham was, I am." (John 8:58; the "I am" claim is a direct quote of God describing himself in Exod. 3:14)
- "I do not judge anyone who hears my words and does not keep them, for I came not to judge the world, but to save the world." (John 12:47)

These words are not the words of a mere moral teacher. If that is all Jesus was, then he was undoubtedly either insane or a lying devil.[38] But given both the evidence for the resurrection that we have examined above and the descriptions of his character by his closest disciples—including their willingness to follow him to their death—it seems that the best explanation for Jesus's identity is that he is the divine Son of God.[39] As Dallas Willard once quipped, "The best indirect evidence for Jesus's divinity is the fact that twelve men spent three years on a camping trip with him, and when it was over, all but one of them still worshiped him as the divine Son of God."[40]

Why a Sacrifice?

But why did Jesus die on the cross, anyway? If he were truly the Son of God, couldn't he have easily escaped such a horrible death?

On a recent trip to India, I was hiking up a mountain in the state of West Bengal on the coast. About halfway up, I came across a shrine to the god Kali. Blood covered the ground next to the shrine, and several Indian men were there working on the small building that housed sculptures and statues depicting the Hindu god. I asked them, through a translator, what the blood was from. They informed me that an animal sacrifice had been offered the night before. A goat had been offered to Kali.

In both ancient and present times, sacrifice is and has been a common phenomenon among the world's religions. Even the great philosopher Socrates, shortly after he drank the poisonous hemlock as his mode of execution, insisted that his student Crito make the appropriate animal sacrifice to the god for him.[41] But what's the point? Why a sacrifice?

A common theme running through the religions, including ancient Judaism, is that sacrifice is a ritual act in which an offering is made to appease and venerate the deity. It is widely recognized by human beings that something is wrong with the human condition: we are not morally perfect and holy people. God *is* morally perfect and holy, however, and so there is a wide chasm, a significant moral and spiritual gap, between us and him. The Old Testament puts it this way: "Your iniquities have been barriers between you and your God, and your sins have hidden his face from you so that he does not hear" (Isa. 59:2). The New Testament continues the same theme: "All have sinned and fall short of the glory of God" (Rom. 3:23). Yet we long to be with God, to seek affinity and relationship with him. We search for a way to make things right with our God. Sacrifice—whether food, animal, or human—is our way of attempting to accomplish this.

God, however, being infinitely wise and good, has made a way for us to cross over the gulf of separation. Jesus, as divine Son of God, has offered himself as the infinite sacrifice for sins. The apostle Peter describes this in his first book: "Christ suffered for sins once for all, the righteous for the unrighteous, in order to bring you to God" (1 Peter 3:18). And the apostle John says that God has given us an opportunity to "pass over from death to life" through the sacrifice of Jesus (John 5:24). The following Bridge Illustration helps to make the significance of Jesus's sacrifice on the cross clear:[42]

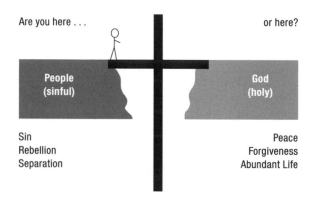

It is really quite simple. Jesus died so that we might have peace, forgiveness, and abundant life forever. All we have to do is believe and repent, that is, simply turn over our lives to him as Lord and Savior.[43]

So we are left with a question: liar, lunatic, or Lord? These are the only options Jesus left open to us about himself. Having examined the evidence, which of the three do you take him to be?

Summary

In this chapter I have presented several evidences for the resurrection of Jesus. I offered six historical truths—events that honest skeptics and critics typically agree upon—and considered the answers that best explain them. The potentially reasonable options are few: the disciples stole or misplaced the body and lied about it (but they were executed for their convictions), they hallucinated or had visions about it (but we still have a missing body), or Jesus didn't really die from his crucifixion but recovered a few days later and lied to his disciples about that (and again we are still left with a missing body). If atheism is true, one of these options would most likely have to be true. But, considering all of the available evidence, and given theism, the best explanation seems clearly to be that Jesus really did rise from the dead.

The two questions that naturally follow, then, are these: (1) Who is this man, and (2) What does his resurrection mean for me? We saw that here, too, the options are few. He was who he said he was—the Messiah prophesied about in the Old Testament—or he was a liar, or he was insane. Jesus claimed that he was the Son of God—divinity becoming humanity—and that he came to save the world. His descending from heaven to earth was for a purpose, and that was to offer himself as the infinite sacrifice for sins. Because he died and rose again, we can have eternal life with him.

It is this eternal life—a wonderful new life that can begin now and never ends—that the next chapter is all about.

Questions for Reflection

1. Is the case for the resurrection of Jesus more plausible given the foundation already built in previous chapters? Most especially, do the arguments for theism make the resurrection more reasonable to believe? Explain.
2. Which of the six historical truths do you believe most supports the resurrection?
3. What appears to be an underlying assumption of many critical scholars who deny all of the miraculous claims of the New Testament? What would warrant this assumption?
4. Why is the bodily resurrection of Jesus so crucial for Christian faith?
5. Does *hard evidence* for the resurrection disallow *faith* in Jesus? Does evidence contradict faith?

For Further Reading Supporting the Literal Bodily Resurrection of Jesus

Craig, William Lane. *The Son Rises: The Historical Evidence for the Resurrection of Jesus*. Eugene, OR: Wipf & Stock, 1981. A well-researched and highly readable work by a leading defender of the bodily resurrection of Jesus.

Habermas, Gary R., and Michael R. Licona. *The Case for the Resurrection of Jesus*. Grand Rapids: Kregel, 2004. A user-friendly text (with a CD included) on the resurrection evidence. Solid, accessible research.

Pannenberg, Wolfhart. *Jesus—God and Man*. 2nd ed. Translated by Lewis L. Wilkins and Duane A. Priebe. Philadelphia: Westminster, 1977. A scholarly and profound work on the resurrection.

Strobel, Lee. *The Case for Christ*. Grand Rapids: Zondervan, 1998. Like Socrates of old, Strobel is "keen, like a Spartan hound, at chasing and running down arguments" (Plato) as he interviews leading scholars on a variety of evidences for Jesus's life, death, and resurrection. A tremendously engaging book; highly recommended.

Swinburne, Richard. *The Resurrection of God Incarnate*. New York: Oxford University Press, 2003. A philosophical work on the resurrection.

Wilkins, Michael J., and J. P. Moreland. *Jesus Under Fire: Modern Scholarship Reinvents the Historical Jesus*. Grand Rapids: Zondervan, 1995. A critique of and response to the work of the Jesus Seminar—a liberal group of scholars who deny the literal resurrection of Jesus—by a number of evangelical scholars; scholarly but quite readable.

Wright, N. T. *The Resurrection of the Son of God*. Minneapolis: Fortress, 2003. A massive tome (817 pages) on the resurrection by one of the leading New Testament scholars in the world. He first surveys ancient conceptions of the afterlife in contrast to Jewish concepts of resurrection before investigating the New Testament claims of Jesus's resurrection and its significance.

For Further Reading against the Literal Bodily Resurrection of Jesus

Crossan, John Dominic. *The Historical Jesus: The Life of a Mediterranean Jewish Peasant*. San Francisco: HarperSanFrancisco, 1993. A scholarly but readable work by a leading liberal biblical scholar on Jesus's life and ministry as well as his death and cultural and religious influence.

Funk, Robert W. *Honest to Jesus: Jesus for a New Millennium*. San Francisco: HarperSanFrancisco, 1997. A "demythologized" description of Jesus by the founder of the Jesus Seminar.

Lüdemann, Gerd. *The Resurrection of Christ: A Historical Inquiry*. Amherst, NY: Prometheus, 2004. Lüdemann argues that early belief in the resurrection was based on the self-deceptions of Peter and Paul. Probably the leading work against the bodily resurrection of Jesus.

Martin, Michael. *The Case against Christianity*. Philadelphia: Temple University Press, 1991. A critique of various aspects of the Christian faith, including the resurrection of Jesus, by a leading atheist philosopher.

Price, Robert M., and Jeffery Jay Lowder, eds. *The Empty Tomb: Jesus Beyond the Grave*. Amherst, NY: Prometheus, 2005. A collection of works by scholars, historians, and philosophers responding to William Lane Craig and other Christian apologists who defend the bodily resurrection of Jesus.

Spong, John Shelby. *Resurrection: Myth or Reality?* San Francisco: HarperSanFrancisco, 1994. Bishop Spong was the Episcopal bishop of Newark, New Jersey, for many years and has written widely on Jesus and the Bible. His work is well researched and articulate. In this book, Spong questions the literal narrative concerning the resurrection of Jesus and presents a nonliteral understanding of it.

Thompson, Thomas L. *The Messiah Myth: The Near Eastern Roots of Jesus and David*. New York: Basic Books, 2005. Thompson argues that the view of Jesus as Messiah, like King David before him, is an amalgamation of themes and traditions from Near Eastern mythology.

For Further Reading Pro and Con

Borg, Marcus, and N. T. Wright. *The Meaning of Jesus: Two Visions*. San Francisco: HarperSanFrancisco, 1999. A brilliant dialogue between two leading scholars from radically differing perspectives on the meaning of Jesus and his resurrection. Parts 3 and 4 focus specifically on Jesus's death and resurrection.

Copan, Paul, ed. *Will the Real Jesus Please Stand Up?* Grand Rapids: Baker, 1998. An exciting debate on the resurrection of Jesus by John Dominic Crossan, former cochair of the Jesus Seminar, and philosopher William Lane Craig. I had the opportunity to watch this exchange live; it is well worth a careful read.

Miethe, Terry L., ed. *Did Jesus Rise from the Dead? The Resurrection Debate*. San Francisco: Harper & Row, 1987. A formal debate between Christian philosopher and apologist Gary Habermas and (former) atheist philosopher Antony Flew.

9

Reaching the Peak

The Good News of the Kingdom of God

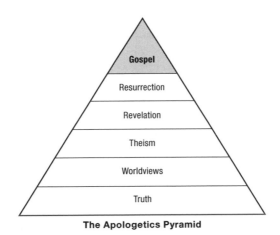

The Apologetics Pyramid

There comes a time when one asks even of Shakespeare, even of Beethoven, is this all?

Aldous Huxley

I came that they may have life, and have it abundantly.

Jesus

We started our journey at the very beginning—presupposing nothing. We asked one of the most fundamental questions of all: What is truth?

Once we discovered that truth is absolute and involves a correspondence with reality rather than coherence or pragmatics, and that this nonrelative view of truth can be demonstrated through the most basic law of logic, the law of noncontradiction, we were then able to begin constructing faith from the ground up as we climbed the levels of the Apologetics Pyramid. We moved from truth to worldviews, up through arguments for and against the existence of God, through an analysis of divine revelation, and finally we examined evidences for the life, death, and resurrection of Jesus of Nazareth. I argued that an objective, rational assessment of the historical truths leads one to the conclusion that it is more reasonable to believe that Jesus rose from the dead in vindication of his being Messiah than not to believe it.

However, *believing* that Jesus is the Messiah and *being a follower* of Jesus are two very different matters. While I would never judge whether someone else is a true Christian or not—that is God's job, not mine—the Bible makes it clear that a person can believe *that*, without believing *in*. In the book of James, for example, the author notes that the demons "believe" and shudder (James 2:19). In other words, they know all the facts *about* God, Jesus, salvation, and so on, but they have not put their trust *in* him; they have not committed their lives to him. Simply put, they have no faith.

The point of this chapter is to spell out the essence of Christian faith (in contrast to other faiths) and to explain why the Bible refers to it as "good news"—why it is that Jesus compares it to hidden treasure and to a pearl of great price (Matthew 13)—and to invite you not merely to believe *that*, but to believe *in*. For as we will see, it is not only good news, it is the best news imaginable.[1]

The Gospels of the World and Religious Fatalism

Wherever we look in world history, we find people attempting to answer a central question of humanity: "What is wrong with us, and how can we fix it?" Things are not as they should be. As a global community we are constantly at war, constantly judging others, ever hoping for a future time in which there will be no more tears and terror. As individuals we are constantly missing our own mark, rarely living up to our own standards of morality, justice, and accomplishment. We are ever hoping for a time in which we will be better. We are always wanting more. The essence of religion involves an attempt to solve this very real human predicament.[2]

Every world religion offers hope. In a major strain of Buddhism, for example, the answer to our dilemma is to eliminate all desires and cravings—this is nirvana. In Hinduism there are a number of solutions, but they all center around *moksha*—release from the terrible cycle of reincarnation (unlike typical Western views of reincarnation, for Hindus and Buddhists it is something to be freed from) and finally entering into union with Ultimate Reality. Islam, too, has its answer to the human condition, as do Judaism and all of the enduring faith traditions.[3]

The Christian response is radically different from all of the world religions, however, for at its core is relationship—relationship with a personal God. This is the gospel,* or "good news," the New Testament speaks about. It involves knowing God personally and by grace, through faith, entering into his wonderful and eternal kingdom. The connotation of the biblical gospel, though, is not always as clear as it could be, and in some cases it has been transformed or even distorted beyond recognition.

In a profoundly insightful book by educator/philosopher/pastor Dallas Willard titled *The Divine Conspiracy*, he describes what he calls "gospels of sin management."[4] These two "gospels" come from the left and the right in Christian circles, and they both involve trying to manage a central aspect of the human predicament: sin. On the liberal side, the emphasis is on social concerns and the eradication of evils in the world. But no real connection is made between these efforts and eternal life. On the conservative side, the emphasis is on getting into heaven when we die, but there is no real correlation between heaven and life in the here and now.

I think Willard is right on target here. But his insights extend beyond where he takes them, it seems to me; they extend to virtually every human system of religion. Building on Willard's work, then, I will argue that on one end of the spectrum is the gospel of the world—a system of good deeds that involves working our way to a better life, a gospel of human achievement.

On the other end of the spectrum is a version of the religious gospel—a fatalistic view in which everything is taken care of by God (or the Fates) and is completely and absolutely controlled, and even determined, by him (or them). The emphasis here is primarily about the afterlife, and it is a gospel in which human choice plays no significant role, if any role at all, in our world and future state. We can glean many insights from both of these "gospels," but the good news that Jesus taught goes far beyond each of them.

* The English word *gospel* comes from the Anglo-Saxon term *god-spell*, which means "God-story," and it is the usual translation of the Greek term *euangelion*, which occurs more than seventy-five times in the New Testament.

The Gospel of the World

What I am referring to as the gospel of the world is reflected in all of the major non-Christian religions, in versions of Christianity itself, and even among irreligious people. Let's look at each of these three groups individually.

The Gospel of the World in the World Religions

As noted above, virtually everyone is unsatisfied with the human condition. Something is amiss, and we are not content with life as it is. We want more. Huston Smith, one of the most eloquent authorities on the history of religions, summarizes this longing:

> The world's offerings are not bad. By and large they are good. Some of them are good enough to command our enthusiasm for many lifetimes. Eventually, however, every human being comes to realize with Simone Weil that "there is no true good here below, that everything that appears to be good in this world is finite, limited, wears out, and once worn out, leaves necessity exposed in all its nakedness." When this point is reached, one finds oneself asking even of the best this world can offer, "Is this all?"[5]

The different religions, then, respond in unique ways to this yearning for liberation and fulfillment. Each has its own "gospel" solution. But one common theme among them all is that we ourselves can do something about our plot. We are not merely actors in a cosmic play; we are in charge of our destiny.

Consider the following paths to eternal salvation/liberation among some of the major world religions:

- *Hinduism.* The ultimate goal is *moksha*, release from the cycle of death and rebirth (*samsara*), and absorption into Brahman. This can be accomplished through following one of the three paths (*margas*): (1) The Path of Knowledge (*jnanamarga*), (2) The Path of Devotion (*bhaktimarga*), and (3) The Path of Action (*karmamarga*). In each of these paths, human effort is central for accomplishing *moksha.*[6]
- *Buddhism.* The ultimate goal is *nirvana*, liberation from the wheel of *samsara* and extinction of all desires, cravings, and suffering. This is accomplished by understanding the four noble truths and practicing the final one: (1) All existence is suffering (*dukkha*). (2) All suffering is caused by craving (*trishna*). (3) All suffering can be ended (*nirvana*). (4) The way to end suffering and achieve *nirvana* is by practicing the noble eightfold path of right views, right reso-

lution or aspiration, right speech, right behavior, right livelihood, right effort, right thoughts, and right concentration.

- *Judaism.* The ultimate goal is blessedness with God in the hereafter. This may be accomplished by fulfilling the divine commandments (*mitzvot*), which include the following practices: (1) observance of the Sabbath, (2) regular attendance at synagogue, (3) celebration of the annual festivals, and (4) strict obedience to Jewish Law.[7]
- *Islam.* The ultimate goal is blessedness in paradise through divine submission. This may be accomplished by following the five pillars: (1) faith in Allah and his prophet Muhammad (*shahada*), (2) five daily prayers (*salah*), (3) almsgiving (*zakah*), (4) fasting (*sawm*), and (5) pilgrimage to Mecca (the *hajj*).

Of course, for each of these religions, broadly speaking, there is more to salvation than good deeds accomplished through human effort. As we will see below, there is also an element of divine sovereignty, or fate, in each of them. But the point here is that for a significant number of religious devotees in the history of the world, one primary way of salvation or liberation is centered around human effort—we can fix the problem on our own.

The Gospel of the World in Christianity

In the words of Marcus Borg, a contemporary leading liberal Christian scholar, one of the main elements of Jesus's ministry and teaching involved being a "social prophet." This prophetic vocation of Jesus focused on "engaging in a radical critique of the domination system of his day."[8] Whether it was political and religious oppression or economic exploitation, says Borg, Jesus was about freeing the captives from subjugation and manipulation. He is not alone in this understanding of Jesus's ministry focus.

Another leading Christian scholar, this one of the last century, had this to say: "[He, Jesus, is] the one who identified with and loved oppressed people and those who are different."[9] Indeed, there is no denying that Jesus did place emphasis on "loving thy neighbor," on "freeing the captives," and on "providing justice for the oppressed." Fortunately, this social emphasis of ministry has influenced a number of the mainline denominations of Protestant Christianity on the left as well as many Roman Catholics, and through its different manifestations this emphasis has sometimes evolved into notable social activism.

Unfortunately, the response by many on the Christian right to this cultural engagement on the left has often been an absence of social concern. If the goal of Christians is to get to heaven when we die, they wonder, then why be concerned with physical and material needs here on this earth? After all, if the Christian mandate is to go into all the world and preach the good news about eternal life, why focus on things of this world?

The following anecdote is all too common of the way this understanding of the Christian gospel gets worked out in real life. A few years ago, while I was volunteering at an evangelical church in a large midwestern city, the leadership decided to buck the trend and get involved in inner-city missions work—an endeavor focused on helping the physical needs of those less materially blessed. In one large suburb close to our church, where the "poorest of the poor" dwelt, we found that there existed only one food pantry. As we probed into who was providing the food and supplies—considerable amounts of it, I might add—we discovered that only two churches were involved, and they were both liberal mainline churches. None of the many evangelical, fundamentalist churches and groups in the surrounding area were lifting a hand to help. This makes sense if souls are important and bodies are not.[10]

This is not to say that conservative Christians are never involved in social action. Far from it. There are many very fine examples of those on the Christian right placing heavy emphasis on the "down and out." *The point here, though, is that often there is no connection made between such generous deeds and the gospel message itself.*

The emphasis on "this-worldly" needs rather than "otherworldly" hopes has been typical, as a part of the gospel message, for those on the liberal side of Christianity. This doesn't imply that they deny an afterlife, though. For many on the left, the afterlife is a real experience awaiting those who live as they should, for there will be compensatory rewards for one's good deeds and perhaps even recompense for bad ones. But the urgency is placed *here* on earth rather than *there* in heaven, whereas the gospel of the right has it the other way around.

To summarize, the gospel on the Christian left is one of social action; the good news is that if we work hard, we can remove social evils and perhaps live a blessed life here on earth. To do this is to live the life Jesus himself lived and called us to.[11]

The Gospel of the World among the Irreligious

The religions of the world are not alone in emphasizing the role of good deeds and social concern as being the primary answer to the human predicament. The eighteenth-century humanist Thomas Paine once said, "The world is my country, and to do good my religion." Paine is just one of many historical and contemporary humanists who, devoid of strong (traditional) religious beliefs, still maintain that human effort is primary in accomplishing the central goal of life—improving the human condition.

But even beyond formal groups and societies of nonreligious people, the good news of human potential for advancing humanity, both individually and collectively, is now a common humanist ideology around the globe.[12] As we will soon see, however, while this is an important part of Jesus's gospel, it is only a part.

The Gospel of Religious Fatalism

What I am referring to as the gospel of religious fatalism, like the gospel of the world, is also reflected in all of the major non-Christian religions, in versions of Christianity itself, and even among irreligious people. Let's look at each of these three groups individually.

The Gospel of Religious Fatalism in the World Religions

Throughout the centuries there has been an enduring tension in the various religions between human freedom and divine providence. On the one hand, there is a common theme that human beings are responsible moral agents, and while there is not always a moral component to religious practice, there is a widespread notion among the religions that God, or the gods, are moral exemplars and that they have an expectation that human beings emulate their moral nature.

Whether referring to the Persian god Ahura Mazda, the Egyptian god Osiris, the Hindu Brahman, Allah of Islam, the God of the Jews, or the teachings of the Buddha, there is reward for right action and recompense for wrong action. This responsibility imposed on human beings presupposes a kind of freedom of the will in which there is a choice to be made—we can choose to go either in the right direction or the wrong direction; it is up to us. For many of the Eastern religions, it is primarily through karma that our future reflects our present choices. In Judaism, Islam, and Christianity as well, our future state also has much to do with the choices we make here in our present lives. This emphasis on human choice to do right or wrong, as already noted, bodes well with the gospel of the world.

On the other hand there is also the pervasive religious belief that God (or the gods) is in direct control of the universe—that he (or she or they) is governing all of the events of world history, including human affairs.[13] Sometimes providence takes a radically strong form, so strong in fact that it is better described as *religious fatalism* than as providence. What I mean by the term *fatalism* in this context is the belief that whatever happens—including all of our actions and choices—is determined by God in such a way that human effort is ultimately irrelevant.[14]

Consider the following examples. In Islam the term *qadar*, which appears in the Islamic holy book called the Qur'an, is the decree of Allah that determines all eventualities. There is debate in Islam over the meaning of this word, but one of the historic definitions entails absolute determinism whereby humans have no free will whatsoever; all is completely predestined by Allah.[15] As the Qur'an states, "Nothing will happen to us except what God has decreed for us" (9.51).

In Hinduism the term *daiva* came to mean, at least in certain Hindu sects, divine fatalism, which was included as a part of the very essence of Hindu religion. Even the meaning of the more commonly used term *karma* (the consequences of meritorious and demeritorious actions) is sometimes construed fatalistically by Hindus, since the very meaning of the word is that the actions of a previous life—whether good or bad—totally determine one's present condition. But even here, God is the one controlling fate.[16] The classic Hindu work the Bhagavad Gita puts it this way:

> Whatever you do not wish to do
>   because of your delusions,
> You will do even against your will,
>   bound by your natural duty karma
> The Lord, Arjuna, is present
>   inside all beings,
> Moving them like puppets
>   by his magic power. (18.60–61)

Such examples of (what appears to be, at least) religious fatalism could be cited from all of the major religious writings. The point here is this: God has determined everything, so what will be will be. In terms of our present life and destiny, then, human effort is pointless. Whether we finally achieve *nirvana*, *moksha*, or some other future state is clearly in the cards, and the deck has been stacked.

The Gospel of Religious Fatalism in Christianity

Within Christianity there also exists a strand of fatalism. One of the most influential Christians in church history is the Protestant Reformer John Calvin (1509–1564). His *Institutes of the Christian Religion* is a monumental work in Christian theology. Probably no one in the history of Christianity has been more influential in expounding on the nature of God than John Calvin. And probably no one in the history of Christianity has been more influential in promoting the theological doctrine of predestination, either. Some theologians regard predestination as a fatalistic doctrine, and Calvin's writings do contain strong language that some think supports a fatalistic interpretation. For example, consider these words: "But of all the things which happen, the first cause is to be understood to be His will, because He so governs the natures created by Him as *to determine all the counsels and the actions of men to the end decreed by Him.*"[17]

I would argue that Calvin himself was not a fatalist. And neither have most Calvinists since his time been fatalists in the sense defined earlier. But, as with any theological treatise, there are various ways of interpreting what is written. And "armchair theologians" have occasionally gone to work with the writings of the Reformers—especially Calvin's—turning them into theological heresies. The problem is that when an author is no longer around to clarify issues he or she wrote about, and these issues have been debated and discussed for centuries, misunderstanding abounds.

One reason why I believe that Calvin was not a fatalist is that both in his own writings and in the writings of many of his later followers, there is a clear affirmation of indeterminism and human choice.[18] But the tendency for a fatalistic interpretation of his work is there, for if God has predestined all human events (and we need to understand what he means by predestination), both good and evil, there seems to be no room left for human choice and action. Following this tendency, Ulrich Zwingli (1484–1531), a leader of the early Protestant Reformation in Switzerland, went so far as to imply that God is the cause of all events, even sinful ones:

> What God brings about through man's agency is imputed a crime to man but not also to God. For the one is under law, the other is the free spirit and mind of the law. . . . What God does, he does freely, uninfluenced by any evil emotion, therefore also without sin. David's adultery, *so far as it concerns God as the author of it* is no more a sin to God, than a steer [that] covers and impregnates a whole herd.[19]

If God brings about all things, and he even brought about King David's adulterous affair, then one may ask what choices in life are left up to the individual. If God is the underlying cause of how we will act in this life and where we will go in the next life, then what actions or decisions are left up to us? The answer seems to be none. This is the essence of fatalism, for no matter what actions one performs or what decisions one makes, they have already been predetermined to occur.

One needs to be careful not to lay blame on our predecessors, including Calvin and Zwingli, for how their works are interpreted centuries later.

185

The Reformers are to be treasured for their valiant efforts to reform the church, efforts that have produced tremendous fruit over the centuries. And while I don't agree with all of their theological positions in every detail, their writings do offer us a rich heritage of Christian teaching. Their emphasis on God's sovereignty, for example, is to be commended, and I have grown in my own understanding of the glory, power, and majesty of God through works such as the *Institutes*. But we must also be careful in our understanding and presentation of the work and nature of God. In conversations with a number of Christians over the years, for example, I have seen a fatalistic mind-set even affect the way some view prayer. As one friend recently inquired, "Why pray if God already knows and has totally predetermined what will happen?" That is a good question and one well worth pondering.[20]

The Gospel of Religious Fatalism among the Irreligious

Fatalism isn't limited to the religious, however. Throughout intellectual history, both in the East and the West, numerous philosophical systems have emerged that also contain fatalistic strains. In the West, Stoicism, for example, a philosophical school founded in roughly 300 BC in Greece, was an unusual combination of materialism and pantheism. It stressed human cognitive ability and argued that the highest human good is a life lived in accord with right reason.

Among the central beliefs of Stoic reason was the view that there exists no human free will. Everything that happens occurs by necessity, and thus there is no way for one to alter his or her future; fate is set for each of us. The Stoics even used the terms *fate*, *destiny*, and *providence* to describe the divine reality. They claimed that real virtue, then, could only be found in coming to the realization that life will be the way it will be. Thus, one should live a detached life, devoid of passions and emotional struggles, and submit one's will to that of the fates.[21]

Another philosophical system, this one from the East, is Confucianism. Founded in the sixth century BC by Confucius (551–479), it generally focuses on the question, What are the ultimate human values and virtues necessary to create a good society? Reflecting on the nature of the Tao (undifferentiated unity) and the role of *yin* and *yang* forces (complimentary principles), one of its central teachings involves the idea of *ming*, a Chinese word for fate or destiny in which all events are totally beyond human control. As with other major belief systems throughout history, Confucianism contains within it different understandings of the role of fate in the lives of individuals, both deterministic and nondeterministic ones. And while the Confucian perspective has always emphasized moral cultivation, how such practices combine with the fatalism of *ming* is not clearly articulated.

Beyond these more well-established philosophical traditions, a number of irreligious, or nonreligious, people also held and continue to hold to some form of fate. One example of this in recent times is the rise of astrology in both the East and West. Millions of people from all over the world take quite seriously the view that the positions of the sun, moon, and planets determine everything from personality traits to every event that happens in one's daily and future life. While not all teachers and practitioners of astrology would hold to fatalism strictly speaking, many do believe that our lives are completely in the hands of the celestial bodies, and therefore, what we do to try to change things makes no difference.

While Jesus and the early disciples and apostles did place much weight on God's sovereignty in worldly affairs, including human salvation, this too is only a part of that gospel. For as we will see below, we have a significant role to play as well.

The Gospel of the Kingdom of God

In contrast to the gospels of the world and fatalism stands the gospel of Jesus—the good news of the kingdom of God. But what, exactly, is this gospel? For many Christians, the gospel is understood to be the death, burial, and resurrection of Jesus Christ for the remission of sins and the future hope of heaven. They point to the Bible for support:

> Now I would remind you, brothers and sisters, of the *good news* that I proclaimed to you. . . . For I handed on to you as of first importance what I in turn had received: that Christ died for our sins in accordance with the scriptures, and that he was buried, and that he was raised on the third day.
>
> 1 Corinthians 15:1–4

> But *our citizenship is in heaven*, and it is from there that we are expecting a Savior, the Lord Jesus Christ.
>
> Philippians 3:20

Paul explains elsewhere that all people have sinned against God, and therefore all are in need of spiritual cleansing.[22] Since God is perfectly holy, righteous, and just and we are imperfect and unholy, we need his saving grace to be made right. Jesus's death on the cross, given his infinite sacrificial worth as Son of God, covers our sins and allows us to enter into a right relationship with God. As theologian John Stott succinctly describes it, "Christianity is a rescue religion. It declares that God has taken the initiative in Jesus Christ to deliver us from our sins. This is the main theme of the Bible."[23]

It is indeed wonderful news that Jesus has given us the opportunity to be made right with God so that after death we can enter into heaven with him forever. What is surprising to discover, however, is that this is not exactly the gospel that Jesus himself proclaimed and taught. Nor is it the gospel that Paul and the other apostles and disciples preached. It is a *part* of their gospel, no doubt, and a significant part. But it is clearly not the whole of it.[24]

The Threefold Ministry of Jesus

As a careful study of the New Testament Gospels reveals, Jesus's ministry involved three fundamental aspects each focused on one central theme: the kingdom of God. These three aspects were:

1. preaching (or proclaiming) the kingdom of God
2. teaching about the kingdom of God
3. manifesting the kingdom reality through healing, exorcism, and other miracles

This emphasis of Jesus's ministry on the kingdom of God was not only his emphasis but was also the focal teaching of the early disciples. Here is a sampling of relevant New Testament passages:

Jesus went throughout Galilee, teaching in their synagogues and proclaiming the good news of the kingdom and curing every disease and every sickness among the people.

Matthew 4:23 (note all three aspects listed here)

Then Jesus called the twelve together and gave them power and authority over all demons and to cure diseases, and he sent them out to proclaim the kingdom of God and to heal.

Luke 9:1–2

After his suffering he presented himself alive to them by many convincing proofs, appearing to them during forty days and speaking about the kingdom of God.

Acts 1:3

But when they believed Philip, who was proclaiming the good news about the kingdom of God and the name of Jesus Christ, they were baptized, both men and women.

Acts 8:12

He [Paul] lived there two whole years at his own expense and welcomed all who came to him, proclaiming the kingdom of God and teaching about the Lord Jesus Christ with all boldness and without hindrance.

Acts 28:30

For the kingdom of God is not food and drink but righteousness and peace and joy in the Holy Spirit.

Romans 14:17

He has rescued us from the power of darkness and transferred us into the kingdom of his beloved Son, in whom we have redemption, the forgiveness of sins.

Colossians 1:13

The New Testament is filled with "kingdom" language, and there are a number of ways of interpreting what such language actually means. For some, the kingdom is understood to be the supernatural reality of God breaking into the present order of things and refers to a time in the future when history will change and a new world order will be put in place.[25] For others, it is only a present inward reality—a subjective realm where God and the individual meet.[26]

While both of these understandings are indeed biblical and each one captures an important element of the kingdom teaching, it seems that both are incomplete. For to make sense of *all* of the relevant passages of the Bible having to do with the kingdom of God, the best and most comprehensive interpretation is that it is his "kingship, His rule, His authority."[27] It is God ruling, both now and on into the future, in the lives of those who will allow him to be their King. In other words, Jesus and the disciples were teaching the good news that a kingdom exists—a present reality where God is King and Ruler—and we are invited to enter into that domain. The New Testament gospel, then, is the *good news* of the reality and availability of the presence of God's kingdom in the lives of all who will enter into it.

We are not, today, very familiar with kings and kingdoms and the way they work. Unfortunately, history is filled with bad examples of kings and queens who took advantage of their subjects, and so this clouds our understanding of the wonderful kingdom arrangement Jesus was proclaiming. A good kingdom is one in which a king (or queen) governs the people of that kingdom. The king loves his subjects, and he cares for, protects, and provides for them. In turn, the subjects of the kingdom love their king. They have deep admiration and respect for him, and they work hard to advance the kingdom and make it what it should be. This may require sacrifice of one sort or another, but the people of the kingdom are willing to do this because they know full well that the king (or queen) has their best interests in mind.

To better understand what Jesus was intending us to grasp here and why his kingdom news is so good, perhaps it is best to reflect on the legendary King Arthur and his kingdom of Camelot. In this legendary tale, King Arthur creates a kingdom, Camelot. It is a kingdom of beauty—a land where peace, unity, and love reign supreme. It is a kingdom of plenty—a land where desires are granted because none are selfish. It is a kingdom of dreams—a land where everyone has his or her place, because all are heirs of the king. Camelot is heaven on earth.[28]

What an incredible place to dwell! Amazingly, this is what the kingdom of God is really like. Eventually this kingdom reality will fill the earth (Dan. 2:44; Rev. 11:15). But the good news is that we don't have to wait for this eventuality, for as noted in chapter 8, God is inviting us to enter now through the redemptive work of Jesus.[29] Many people have entered in, and it is here that the transforming power of God and his rule in our lives can be manifest.

Jesus's Parabolic Teachings on the Kingdom

Jesus spent much time not only proclaiming the good news of the kingdom of God, but also teaching about it. As a matter of fact, most of his parables were focused on this very issue. We don't have space here to delve into an explication of the various kingdom parables, but perhaps the following brief overview of several of them will provide a clearer picture of their meaning as well as demonstrate their importance in Jesus's teaching ministry.[30]

As a master teacher, Jesus adapted his teaching to the needs of his learners, and many of them had a serious "learning disability." Jesus explains their problem in Matthew 13:15:

> For this people's heart has grown dull,
>   and their ears are hard of hearing,
>   and *they have shut their eyes*;
>   so that they might not look with their eyes,
>   and listen with their ears,
>   and understand with their heart and turn.

Jesus realized that many of his listeners had become hard-hearted and could not hear his message if he spoke to them straightforwardly. Parables were thus a way of reaching into his listeners' cold hearts and, if they were open to the parables' messages at all, eventually transforming them.[31]

Let's look briefly at four kingdom parables: the mustard seed, the yeast, the treasure, and the pearls. Consider the first two first:

> He [Jesus] put before them another parable: "The kingdom of heaven is like a mustard seed that someone took and sowed in his field; it is the smallest of all the seeds, but when it has grown it is the greatest of shrubs and becomes a tree, so that the birds of the air come and make nests in its branches."
>
> He told them another parable: "The kingdom of heaven is like yeast that a woman took and mixed in with three measures of flour until all of it was leavened."
>
> Matthew 13:31–33

The kingdom of heaven is like a mustard seed, says Jesus. In rabbinical teaching in Jesus's day, the mustard seed was used proverbially to designate smallness. Mustard seeds are indeed quite small seeds. But once they get planted in the ground, they begin to grow and expand significantly. Mustard plants become so large, in fact, that birds can perch in their branches.

The kingdom of heaven is also like yeast in that it spreads into its surroundings and finally ends up consuming them. In reference to this leaven parable, New Testament scholar D. A. Carson says: "The general thrust of this parable is the same as that of the mustard seed. The kingdom produces ultimate consequences out of all proportion to its insignificant beginnings."[32]

The advancing kingdom of God was no mere pipe dream of Jesus. God's kingly role in the hearts and minds of human beings has been growing exponentially over the past two thousand years, and this growth can, in a certain sense, be scientifically and statistically verified. Examine the bar chart that follows, which reflects just how expansive the rule of God is on the earth.[33]

In the next two parables, Jesus describes how wonderful this kingdom really is:

> The kingdom of heaven is like treasure hidden in a field, which someone found and hid; then in his joy he goes and sells all that he has and buys that field.
>
> Again, the kingdom of heaven is like a merchant in search of fine pearls; on finding one pearl of great value, he went and sold all that he had and bought it.
>
> Matthew 13:44–45

The language Jesus uses here is intended to be very descriptive and inviting. It is the strongest language of his day that Jesus could use to entice people

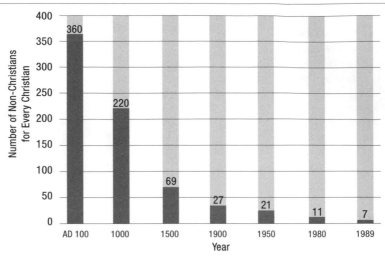

The Advancing Kingdom of God

The bold portion of the columns represents the dwindling numbers of non-Christians to Christians (committed adherents) in the world; or, to put it differently, the lightly shaded portion represents the advancing kingdom of God.

to enter into the kingship or government of God. To use modern parables to make the same point, we might say that the kingdom of heaven is like winning the Powerball lottery; or the kingdom of heaven is like finding a twenty-carat diamond in your backyard. It is riches beyond belief.

It is here, in the kingdom, that we find the blessed life. Jesus emphasizes this point in the Sermon on the Mount, for he begins the beatitudes in Matthew 5 with these words: "Blessed are the poor in spirit, for theirs is the kingdom of heaven." As Dallas Willard points out, the people Jesus was speaking to, the poor and the meek and so on, are blessed not because they are poor and meek, but because they too can enter into the kingdom of God. One's station in life makes no difference whatsoever.[34]

When we dwell in the kingdom of God, we are no longer controlled by our fleshly nature, but rather we are controlled by the Spirit of God, and we then receive the "fruit" of that relationship. The apostle Paul gives a depiction of what a blessed life in the kingdom of God can look like: "The fruit of the Spirit is love, joy, peace, patience, kindness, generosity, faithfulness, gentleness, and self-control" (Gal. 5:22–23). Imagine a life filled with these attitudes! Paul goes on to note that there is no law against such things, for everyone recognizes that they are simply so good that any law against them would be ridiculous. This is the kind of life humanity is longing for; this is the "fix" of the human condition we are seeking; this is life in the kingdom of God.

How to Enter and Dwell in the Kingdom of God

There is no doubt that God's kingdom is a present reality and is moving forward. The question before us, then, is, how does a person enter into this advancing and marvelous kingdom?

Entering the Kingdom

Jesus had strong words for certain religious leaders of his time who were actually hindering people from entering God's kingdom: "Woe to you, scribes and Pharisees, hypocrites! For you lock people out of the kingdom of heaven. For you do not go in yourselves, and when others are going in, you stop them" (Matt. 23:13–14). So how do we enter in?

The answer is surprisingly simple, but we are to make it our primary goal. Jesus puts it this way, "Strive first for the kingdom of God and his righteousness, and all these things will be given to you as well" (Matt. 6:33). We must seek the kingdom with everything we have, and this is impossible without turning from a life of sin against God. Time and time again Jesus proclaimed the importance of first turning from our worldly ways. To use his words: "Repent, for the kingdom of heaven has come near" (Matt. 4:17).[35]

The term *repentance* in the original Greek language means a change of mind. In the sense Jesus is using the word, it involves a change of mind from doing wrong against God to following him wholeheartedly. It also involves a confession of what we have done: "If we confess our sins, he who is faithful and just will forgive us our sins and cleanse us from all unrighteousness" (1 John 1:9). This kind of confession and change involves an element of faith, or trust, in God, and he is so kind and gracious that all we need is the faith of a mustard seed to be forgiven. As one early seeker (and semi-doubter) of God exclaimed when Jesus asked him about his faith, "I believe; help my unbelief!" (Mark 9:24). This small step of trust is all we need to enter into God's glorious kingdom, and he will even help us with that if we will simply ask him.

The following prayer, offered by Richard Foster, is one that can guide us in this matter:

> Today, O Lord, I yield myself to you.
>> May your will be my delight today.
>> May your way have perfect sway in me.
>> May your love be the pattern of my living.
>
> I surrender to you
>> my hopes,

my dreams,
my ambitions.
Do with me what you will, when you will, as you will.
I place into your loving care
my family,
my friends,
my future.
Care for them with a care that I can never give.

I release into your hands
my need to control,
my craving for status,
my fear of obscurity.
Eradicate the evil, purify the good, and establish your
kingdom [in my life].

For Jesus' sake,
Amen.[36]

Dwelling in the Kingdom

We have seen that the Good News involves the real presence of the kingdom of God—we can enter in by faith through God's goodness and grace. One final issue needs to be addressed. Once we enter into the kingdom of God, into his kingly rule in our lives, how do we dwell there? How do we live daily in his presence? This is where God's grace and our effort work together.

Works versus Grace

Some theologians have struggled with the apparent tension in the New Testament between God's grace and our good works. For example, Paul says that it is by *grace* that we are saved through faith, and not by our works (Eph. 2:8–9). On the other hand, the Bible also says that if we don't have good works, our faith is dead (James 2:17). So which is it, grace or works?

The solution to the seeming dilemma is that God's grace saves us as we actively respond in faith. And once we have entered his kingdom by grace, we have yet another active role—living out the life he calls us to. If we aren't doing the works of God, we have lost faith, or trust, in him. Consider the analogy of trusting one's dentist. If we say we trust our dentist but then don't do what he says we should do with our teeth, we aren't really trusting him.[37] So it is with Jesus. If we say we trust in him for salvation but then don't do what he tells us—don't strive to live the life he invites us into—we simply aren't trusting him. We don't really have faith in him after all.[38]

Thus, there is no contradiction between works and grace. We enter God's kingdom by grace through faith, and we dwell there richly by grace through living for him.

The Joy of Spiritual Exercises

What kind of effort, then, is involved in dwelling in the kingdom of God? Again, the apostle Paul gives us direction: "Train yourself in godliness, for, while physical training is of some value, godliness is valuable in every way, holding promise for both the present life and the life to come" (1 Tim. 4:7–8). He and the other disciples and apostles were involved in intensive spiritual training, or exercises, for the explicit purpose of richly living in the kingdom.

The Bible is full of such training exercises, or spiritual disciplines, and as I have experienced in my own life, one simply cannot advance in the spiritual life, let alone experience God's presence to the fullest, without exercising one's spiritual muscles. This principle is just as true in the spiritual realm as it is in the physical realm. A true story makes the point.

Several years ago my wife gave me an acoustic guitar for Christmas. I had been wanting one for some time, and I was quite excited to begin playing. A friend of mine is an outstanding guitarist, and I wanted to play like him. So, after getting this guitar, along with a guidebook for beginners, I sat down to practice one evening. After an hour or two, my fingers were hurting and I wasn't getting anywhere but frustrated. My fingers just didn't do what they were supposed to do.

I haven't taken my guitar out of the closet (except to move it when cleaning and to use it as an illustration in class) since that horrible evening. As you may guess, even though to this day I really want to play the guitar, I cannot play even a single chord. I can wish for the ability to play, and I can even pray for it. But if I'm truly going to be able to play the guitar, I'm going to have to practice.

This principle is just as true in the spiritual realm. If I plan to dwell richly in God's kingdom—growing in godliness and righteousness and faith—then I must exercise for that very purpose. I must fast, pray, spend time in solitude with God, and do many other things as well. The good news here, as spiritual teacher Richard Foster notes, is that these exercises need not be daunting; there can, and should, be a "celebration" in the disciplines.[39]

Summary

We have now reached the peak; the apex of the Apologetics Pyramid. The Good News is the gospel of the kingdom of God—and it really is good news! We can enter into new life with the risen Jesus in such a way that he is King; that is, he comes into our lives, cleanses us, and offers us love and peace and joy. Since he not only knows what is best for us but desires that we have life to the full (John 10:10), this is where life *now* truly begins—forgiveness of sins, a transformed life, and the blessings of the fruit of his Spirit. This is indeed better than finding a diamond or winning the lottery. It is the life for which we all are searching.

Questions for Reflection

1. What is the gospel that you have believed? Is it a worldly or fatalistic one? Is it biblical?
2. How would you define the kingdom of God in your own words?
3. Have you ever considered the possibility of really, constantly, experiencing the fruit of the Spirit mentioned in Galatians 5:22–23? Do you believe it can be your life?
4. Why is the gospel good news *now*? And who can truly receive such news?
5. Read Psalm 145, noting especially verses 10–13. How does this apply to your life?

For Further Reading on the Gospel of the Kingdom and Spiritual Growth

Bright, John. *The Kingdom of God*. Rev. ed. New York: Abingdon, 1957. A clear exposition of the meaning of the kingdom of God as described in the Old and New Testaments.

Capon, Robert Farrer. *Kingdom, Grace, and Judgment: Paradox, Outrage, and Vindication in the Parables of Jesus*. Grand Rapids: Eerdmans, 2002. A fresh and insightful analysis of many of Jesus's parables.

Foster, Richard *Celebration of Discipline: The Path to Spiritual Growth*. Special 20th anniversary ed. San Francisco: HarperSanFrancisco, 1998. This book set me on the path to spiritual growth. Highly recommended.

Kelly, Thomas. *A Testament of Devotion*. San Francisco: HarperSanFrancisco, 1992. An enduring spiritual classic written in 1941 by a Quaker missionary and philosophy professor.

Ladd, George Eldon. *The Gospel of the Kingdom: Scriptural Studies in the Kingdom of God*. Grand Rapids: Eerdmans, 1959. This book, originally delivered as sermons and lectures, is the classic work for a general audience on the gospel of the kingdom.

————. *The Presence of the Future: The Eschatology of Biblical Realism*. Grand Rapids: Eerdmans, 1974. This is the scholarly version of *The Gospel of the Kingdom* mentioned above.

Morgan, G. Campbell. *The Parables of the Kingdom*. Eugene, OR: Wipf & Stock, 1998. A very helpful and concise study of the kingdom parables.

Ortberg, John. *The Life You've Always Wanted: Spiritual Disciplines for Ordinary People*. Expanded ed. Grand Rapids: Zondervan, 2002. A very readable and practical book. Ortberg jokingly calls it "Dallas Willard for dummies." Reading it along with *Celebration of Discipline* by Foster would be an invaluable experience.

Willard, Dallas. *The Divine Conspiracy: Rediscovering Our Hidden Life in God*. San Francisco: HarperSanFrancisco, 1998. The best book I have ever read. To quote Richard Foster, it is "a masterpiece and a wonder."

For Further Reading on Liberation in Other World Religions

Hopfe, Lewis M., and Mark R. Woodward. *Religions of the World*. 9th ed. Englewood Cliffs, NJ: Prentice Hall, 2003. A best-selling introduction to world religions and their central beliefs. It includes some of the lesser-known religions, such as Native American and African religions, Jainism, Sikhism, Zoroastrianism, and the Baha'i faith.

Noss, David S. *A History of the World's Religions*. 11th ed. Englewood Cliffs, NJ: Prentice Hall, 2002. Highly regarded as the standard of fairness and accuracy in the field of religion. It is the most comprehensive history of world religions in a single volume in print.

Sharma, Arvind. *Our Religions*. San Francisco: HarperSanFrancisco, 1993. A fine set of essays offering an overview and the central message of the major world religions by experts from each of the traditions. Highly recommended.

Smith, Huston. *The World's Religions*. San Francisco: HarperSanFrancisco, 1991. This classic on the world religions, which includes an emphasis on their solutions to the human condition, has now sold over two million copies.

Van Voorst, Robert E., ed. *Anthology of World Scriptures*. 3rd ed. New York: Wadsworth, 2000. A collection of some of the major teachings of the different religions from their own scriptures.

Conclusion

It is not the facts which divide people but the interpretation of those facts.

Aristotle

This book has focused on building belief. From the first page to the last, I have attempted to offer an objective strategy for finding truth about God—a strategy any open-minded seeker can follow. We began with the broadest kind of question one can ask—"What is truth?"—and systematically worked up through the various levels of the Apologetics Pyramid, continually narrowing the options at each level along the way. In the final chapter we finally reached the peak of the pyramid, the good news of the kingdom of God.

The arguments and evidences provide a cumulative case for the Christian faith. That is, *taken together*, they offer powerful reasons for believing that Christianity is true. Nevertheless, I am not claiming that they provide 100 percent proof. Although very few really important matters in life give us this kind of undeniable certainty, the issue here is not undeniability, but reasonability. And it seems to me that Christianity is more reasonable to believe than not.

But as the last chapter intimated, belief is not only about reasons; it also involves the will. A few years ago I was talking to an agnostic friend of mine about God's existence, and after working up the first few levels of the pyramid, I presented the kalam argument to her. She was following along, point by point, and even agreeing along the way. And then, all of a sudden, she said, "I'm not sure I'm ready to believe in God." She had all the evidence, all the facts, but what she did with those facts was another matter.

As I pointed out in the final chapter, God is not primarily concerned with our merely believing that he exists. He wants us to believe *in* him; to put our trust in him and to surrender our lives to his loving care. He wants us to enter into his wonderful kingdom, and he provides abundant evidence for us to believe that he exists if we are honestly interested in looking for him. But we can remain closed to this evidence if we want; he gives us that choice. God won't force himself on us, and that is why he hides. He could appear before the world as a thousand-foot giant if he wanted to. But that wouldn't accomplish what he is after.

In the introduction I mentioned that I had an opportunity to talk with an atheist named Bill about God. He and I went through many of the arguments presented in this book, both pro and con. As we worked through the different topics, methodically working up each level, I could tell that he was struggling on the inside. A battle was raging within him—a battle I had fought myself a number of years before—a battle with truth.

Bill was a real truth seeker, and in the end he came to believe that God exists and that Jesus is Lord. Furthermore, he surrendered his life to God and entered into the eternal kingdom of life. Bill reached the peak. By working up the Apologetics Pyramid, many others have done so as well.

There is no more important quest than an open-minded search for truth about God and how that truth is relevant to life. Wherever you are in your spiritual pilgrimage, I encourage you to continue that quest. I trust that if you do, you too will find life in the kingdom of God.

Notes

Introduction

1. The term *apologetics* is derived from the Greek and refers to a defense of a point of view, not saying that one is sorry or apologizing for one's beliefs.

Chapter 1 Your Truth and My Truth

1. For recent statistics on this issue, see Barna Research Online at www.barna.org.

2. According to the Barna research, for those thirty-six years old and younger, only 14 percent embrace absolute moral truth. See The Barna Update, "Americans Are Most Likely to Base Truth on Feelings," The Barna Group, February 12, 2002, www.barna. org/FlexPage.aspx?Page=BarnaUpdate&BarnaUpdateID=106.

3. Allan Bloom, *The Closing of the American Mind: How Higher Education Has Failed Democracy and Impoverished the Souls of Today's Students* (New York: Simon & Schuster, 1987), 25.

4. The question of moral truth is examined in chapter 3.

5. *Sophist*, in *The Collected Dialogues of Plato*, ed. Edith Hamilton and Huntington Cairns (Princeton, NJ: Princeton University Press, 1989), 262E–263D.

6. *Metaphysics*, in *The Complete Works of Aristotle*, revised Oxford translation, ed. Jonathan Barnes (Princeton, NJ: Princeton Unversity Press, 1984), 4.1011b25–27. Richard Kirkham notes that Plato, in the *Sophist*, is presenting a correspondence theory of truth—possibly correspondence as congruence—and that Aristotle is here presenting the earliest correspondence as correlation theory. See Kirkham, *Theories of Truth: A Critical Introduction* (Cambridge, MA: MIT Press, 1992), chap. 4.

7. Exploration of this theoretical jungle is no easy task. As Kirkham puts it, "What we have here is a conceptual mess that one should venture into only with a patient mind and a wary eye" (Kirkham, *Theories of Truth*, 55). For a helpful but technical explanation of the difficulties, see Kirkham's text as well as Richard Lynch, ed., *The Nature of Truth: Classic and Contemporary Perspectives* (Cambridge, MA: MIT Press, 2001).

8. For an influential critique of this "verificationist" theory of truth and meaning, see Carl Hempel, "Problems and Changes in the Empiricist Criterion of Meaning," *Revue internationale de philosophie* 4 (1950): 41–63, repr. in L. Linsky, ed., *Semantics and the Philosophy of Language* (Urbana: University of Illinois Press, 1952). For a helpful and

very readable defense of the correspondence view of truth as well as a rebuttal to post-modern relativism in general, see Douglas Groothuis, *Truth Decay* (Downers Grove, IL: InterVarsity, 2000).

9. Peter Kreeft puts it this way: "Two propositions contradict each other only when the truth of either one necessarily means the falsity of the other, *and* the falsity of either one necessarily means the truth of the other" (Peter Kreeft, *Socratic Logic* [South Bend, IN: St. Augustine's Press, 2004], 174).

10. I first discovered this general approach as a college student by hearing a lecture of Christian apologist Ravi Zacharias. I later read a description of the denial of the law from Greek philosopher Aristotle, of the fourth century BC, in his work *Metaphysics*, 4.4.1006a5–22; 11.5.1061b33–1062a19. A more recent presentation is offered in Ronald Nash's wonderful little book *Worldviews in Conflict* (Grand Rapids: Zondervan, 1992), 73–88.

11. A thoughtful relativist may attempt to respond to this argument by saying that *both* the law of relativism and the law of noncontradiction are true, not just the one. But a similar problem follows here. For if both the law of relativism and the law of noncontradiction are true, then this is contrary to just the law of relativism being true. In other words, *either* both the law of relativism and the law of noncontradiction *or* just the law of relativism is true, not just the one. Once again, then, the "either/or" element of the law of noncontradiction emerges. It is simply impossible to deny the law without using it.

The law of noncontradiction, along with the two other laws of thought (law of identity and law of excluded middle), are often held to be *cognitively necessary* (you cannot think consistently without using them), *ontologically real* (they describe the true features of reality), and *uninferred knowledge* (they are basic and timeless principles that are grasped directly and immediately through rational reflection). Cf. Peter A. Angeles, ed., *The Harper Collins Dictionary of Philosophy*, 2nd ed. (New York: HarperPerennial, 1992), s.v. "laws of thought."

12. William James, *Essays on Pragmatism* (New York: Hafner, 1948), 170.

13. For a recent interesting and radical (and quite technical) version of pragmatism regarding truth, see Michael Dummett, "Truth," in Lynch, *Nature of Truth*, 229–49. See also many of the works by Richard Rorty. Both Dummett and Rorty appear to give up the central laws of logic. But as I note, to do so is self-stultifying.

14. A number of current truth theorists are attempting to develop new noncorrespondence theories—most of which are called "deflationary accounts." For a helpful overview of the history of the various theories of truth, including the most recent ones, see Lynch, *Nature of Truth*. One of the leading deflationist works is Paul Horwich, *Truth*, 2nd ed. (Oxford: Clarendon, 1998).

15. Mortimer Adler, *Truth in Religion: The Plurality of Religions and the Unity of Truth* (New York: Macmillan, 1990), 75.

16. The form of religious pluralism presented here is that offered by John Hick, the leading religious pluralist of our day. It is obviously simplified and condensed here. For his complete defense of pluralism, see his book *An Interpretation of Religion: Human Responses to the Transcendent*, 2nd ed. (New Haven: Yale University Press, 2004).

17. For a cogent response to religious pluralism, see Harold Netland, *Encountering Religious Pluralism* (Downers Grove, IL: InterVarsity, 2001). For another helpful critique of pluralism, see Keith Yandell, *Philosophy of Religion* (New York: Routledge, 1999), chap. 6.

18. See Francis A. Schaeffer, *The God Who Is There*, vol. 1 of *The Complete Works of Francis A. Schaeffer*, 2nd ed. (Westchester, IL: Crossway, 1982).

19. Wilfred Cantwell Smith, *Questions of Religious Truth* (London: Victor Gollancz, 1967), 67–68, as quoted in Harold Netland, *Dissonant Voices* (Grand Rapids: Eerdmans, 1991), 119.

20. For more on this, see Wilfred Cantwell Smith's "Conflicting Truth Claims: A Rejoinder," in John Hick, ed., *Truth and Dialogue in World Religions* (Philadelphia: Westminster, 1974), 159ff. Adler, *Truth in Religion* (p. 12), refers to this kind of truth in religion as "poetical truth," a term used "to signify the kind of truth that is not subject to contradiction, the kind of truth that belongs to narratives that, though differing, are in no way incompatible with one another."

21. Yandell, *Philosophy of Religion*, 56.

22. Joseph Runzo, "God, Commitment, and Other Faiths," *Faith and Philosophy* 5 (October 1988): 350.

23. John G. Stackhouse, *Humble Apologetics* (New York: Oxford University Press, 2002), 95.

Chapter 2 Clashing Worldviews

1. Several excellent resources on worldviews include Nash, *Worldviews in Conflict*; Francis Schaeffer, *He Is There and He Is Not Silent*, vol. 1 of *The Complete Works of Francis A. Schaeffer*, 2nd ed. (Westchester, IL: Crossway, 1982); Norman Geisler and William D. Watkins, *Worlds Apart*, 2nd ed. (Grand Rapids: Baker, 1989); James Sire, *The Universe Next Door*, 4th ed. (Downers Grove, IL: InterVarsity, 2004); and David K. Naugle, *Worldview: The History of a Concept* (Grand Rapids: Eerdmans, 2002).

2. For more on this, see Schaeffer, *He Is There and He Is Not Silent*.

3. Technically, there are other logical possibilities besides the three as I define them, and one could even mix and match these three to develop others. In lectures on worldviews, my colleague and friend Timothy Erdel notes that there may be an indefinite number of them. But historically these are the central three that continue to reappear century after century under different guises. By defining a worldview broadly enough, one could actually limit the options to only two logical possibilities: atheism and theism (for either there is a God or there is not). But the three developed here have been historically prominent.

4. See Nash, *Worldviews in Conflict*, 26–33.

5. James Sire has written two very good books on worldviews: *The Universe Next Door* and *Naming the Elephant: Worldview as a Concept* (Downers Grove, IL: InterVarsity, 2004). In both books he lists seven central questions that a worldview must answer, and they are very similar to the five offered here. He also notes the significance of their sequence in *Naming the Elephant*, chap. 3.

6. A solid critique of the Mormon religion is offered by Norman Geisler et al., *The Counterfeit Gospel of Mormonism: The Great Divide between Mormonism and Christianity* (Eugene, OR: Harvest House, 1998). For a response to deism, see chapters 4–8.

7. For an excellent overview of the Greek and Roman religions, as well as other religions of the ancient world, see Jack Finegan, *Myth and Mystery: An Introduction to the Pagan Religions of the Biblical World* (Grand Rapids: Baker, 1989).

8. For an example of this, see the account of Saul of Tarsus, who became Paul the apostle, and the Christian he met after his divine encounter as described in Acts 9.

9. For an insightful work on God speaking, see Dallas Willard, *Hearing God* (Downers Grove, IL: InterVarsity, 1999). Willard makes the case that God speaks to us often, but we need to learn to hear his voice.

10. For several different theistic explanations for basing morality in God's nature, see C. S. Lewis, *Mere Christianity* (New York: Macmillan, 1952); Richard Swinburne, *The Existence of God* (New York: Oxford University Press, 1991); and John Hick, *Evil and the God of Love*, rev. ed. (San Francisco: HarperSanFrancisco, 1977).

11. Among Christians there is an array of possibilities concerning the creation of humankind. For a cursory overview of three of them—special creationism, progressive

creationism, and theistic evolution—see J. P. Moreland, ed., *Three Views on Creation and Evolution* (Grand Rapids: Zondervan, 1999).

12. Blaise Pascal (1623–62), *Penseés* (New York: Penguin, 1995).

13. Agnosticism and skepticism can be found in a variety of forms. For more on this, see J. P. Moreland and William Lane Craig, *Philosophical Foundations for a Christian Worldview* (Downers Grove, IL: InterVarsity, 2003), chap. 4. Some may consider agnosticism or skepticism to be a worldview itself. But since it makes no positive claims (except the claim that one cannot be certain about this or that), I do not consider it to be a worldview. Nor do I think people actually see the world in this way. While most everyone has doubts about this or that aspect of the world, we still generally make decisions from within one of the three worldviews, or at least a combination thereof.

14. For an analysis of the demise of belief in God from the nineteenth century and into the twentieth, see A. N. Wilson, *God's Funeral: The Decline of Faith in Western Civilization* (New York: W. W. Norton, 1999).

15. *Scientism* and *naturalism* have different meanings, and I am not intending to conflate them here.

16. Carl Sagan, from the *Cosmos* television series on PBS, 1980.

17. For a lively but somewhat technical discussion by a theist and an atheist on this topic, see William Lane Craig and Quentin Smith, *Theism, Atheism, and Big Bang Cosmology* (New York: Oxford University Press, 1993).

18. However, such a view of knowledge does seem to lead to deep philosophical problems, for on this view there can be no knowledge of necessary truths. But since we do have knowledge of necessary truths (such as the law of noncontradiction), this view of knowledge must be false. Furthermore, we seem to have knowledge of truths, such as moral truths, which necessarily cannot be grasped through physical means (see chap. 6). For more on the knowledge of necessary truths and what has come to be called the "knowledge argument," see "The Anti-Materialist Strategy and the 'Knowledge Argument'" in *Objections to Physicalism*, ed. Howard Robinson (New York: Oxford University Press, 1993), 159–83. This article by Robinson is somewhat advanced and philosophically technical.

19. William Lane Craig and Walter Sinnott-Armstrong, *God? A Debate between a Christian and an Atheist* (New York: Oxford University Press, 2004), 32–36.

20. George Gaylord Simpson, *The Meaning of Evolution* (New Haven: Yale University Press, 1967), 345.

21. Richard Dawkins, *The Selfish Gene*, new ed. (New York: Oxford University Press, 1989), preface to 1976 edition.

22. See, e.g., Daniel C. Dennett, *Consciousness Explained* (New York: Back Bay, 1991), 33–39. It should be noted that some theists, even Christian theists, don't believe in a soul.

23. In many ways, the views of the Jesus Seminar could be classified as such. While most, if not all, of the members would not classify themselves as atheists, nonetheless, their general conclusions about religion, God, and Jesus are more naturalistic than supernaturalistic. See, e.g., Robert Funk, R. Hoover, and the Jesus Seminar, *The Five Gospels: What Did Jesus Really Say?* (New York: Macmillan, 1994). For a defense of religious naturalism, see Jerome Stone, *The Minimalist Vision of Transcendence: A Naturalist Philosophy of Religion* (New York: State University of New York Press, 1992).

24. Michael Levine, *Pantheism: A Non-theistic Concept of Deity* (New York: Routledge, 1994), 14.

25. For an overview of Spinoza's pantheism, see ibid. See also Norman Geisler and David Clark, *Apologetics in the New Age: A Christian Critique of Pantheism* (Grand Rapids: Baker, 1990), chap. 5.

26. For more on Parmenides and his philosophy, see William K. C. Guthrie, *The Greek Philosophers from Thales to Aristotle* (New York: Harper & Row, 1975), and A. A. Long, ed., *The Cambridge Companion to Early Greek Philosophy* (New York: Cambridge University Press, 1999), chap. 6. One of Zeno's paradoxes will be discussed in chapter 5.

27. Bansi Pandit, a Hindu himself, has written a fine overview of Hindu thought in his book *The Hindu Mind* (Glen Ellyn, IL: B & V Enterprises, 1996).

28. For a very concise analysis of various types of pantheism, see Geisler and Clark, *Apologetics in the New Age*.

29. Geisler and Watkins, *Worlds Apart*, 98.

30. This is to speak loosely, for technically there are no "parts" of the universe. All is one intrinsically and extrinsically.

31. Seng-ts'an, *Hsin-hsin Ming*, as quoted in Alan W. Watts, *The Way of Zen* (New York: Pantheon, 1957), 116.

32. Mary Baker Eddy, *Science and Health with Key to the Scriptures* (Boston: First Church of Christ, Scientist, 1934), 480.

33. For a helpful overview of karma and reincarnation and Hindu thought in general by a Hindu thinker, see Pandit, *Hindu Mind*.

34. Three insightful works on the rise of the New Age in the West, along with its critique, are Russell Chandler, *Understanding the New Age* (Dallas: Word, 1991); Douglas R. Groothuis, *Unmasking the New Age* (Downers Grove, IL: InterVarsity, 1986); and Vishal Mangalwadi, *When the New Age Gets Old* (Downers Grove, IL: InterVarsity, 1992).

Chapter 3 Theism, Atheism, and Pantheism

1. John Stackhouse puts it this way: "Most apologetics throughout Christian history have been directed at the issue of credibility: 'Is it true?' Nowadays, however, we are faced with the prior question, the question of plausibility: '*Might* it be true? Is Christian argument something I should seriously entertain even for a moment?' Without dealing with this prior question of plausibility, apologetics cannot proceed to the traditional task of offering good reasons to believe" (*Humble Apologetics*, 38).

2. For several helpful works on worldview analysis, see Keith Yandell, *Christianity and Philosophy* (Grand Rapids: Eerdmans, 1984), chap. 8; Netland, *Dissonant Voices*; Schaeffer, *He Is There and He Is Not Silent*; and Nash, *Worldviews in Conflict*.

3. For two powerful works against theism, see Robin Le Poidevin, *Arguing for Atheism: An Introduction to the Philosophy of Religion* (New York: Routledge, 1996); and Michael Martin, *Atheism: A Philosophical Justification* (Philadelphia: Temple University Press, 1990).

4. David Hume, *Dialogues Concerning Natural Religion*, 2nd ed., ed. Richard H. Popkin (Indianapolis: Hackett, 1998), part X, 63.

5. See Augustine, *On the Free Choice of the Will*, trans. Thomas Williams (Indianapolis: Hackett, 1993). Interestingly, Augustine derived this argument from the *Enneads*, written by the neoplatonic philosopher Plotinus (c. 205–270 BC).

6. For a powerful response to the problem of evil by one of the leading philosophers of the twentieth century, see Alvin Plantinga, *God, Freedom, and Evil* (Grand Rapids: Eerdmans, 1991).

7. C. S. Lewis, *The Problem of Pain* (New York: Macmillan, 1962), 93.

8. Two very different approaches to the problem of evil are offered in the following: R. Douglas Geivett, *Evil and the Evidence for God* (Philadelphia: Temple University Press, 1993); and John Hick, *Evil and the God of Love*. William Lane Craig also responds to evil and suffering in a very readable book entitled *Hard Questions, Real Answers* (Wheaton, IL: Crossway, 2003).

9. David Hume, *An Enquiry Concerning Human Understanding* (Indianapolis: Hackett, 1977), 76–77.

10. Ironically, this view has not only been held by atheists, but even some Christians agree with it. For more on this, see J. P. Moreland, "Theistic Science and Methodological Naturalism," in *The Creation Hypothesis: Scientific Evidence for an Intelligent Designer*, ed. J. P. Moreland (Downers Grove, IL: InterVarsity, 1994), 41–66. For various theistic attempts to explain the integration of science and theology, see Chad V. Meister, "Science and Theology: On Formulating a Critical Realist Model of Integration" (master's thesis, Trinity Evangelical Divinity School, 1993).

11. This is the way my good friend Donald McLaughlin likes to pose the question. It really gets to the heart of the matter.

12. Alvin Plantinga has argued for belief in God as being properly basic in a number of works. For his most recent defense of Christian theism, see *Warranted Christian Belief* (New York: Oxford University Press, 2000).

13. For more on this important issue of methodological naturalism and the presumption of atheism, especially as it relates to the human person, see James Stump, "Christians and the Philosophy of Mind," *Philosophia Christi* 5, no. 2 (2003): 589–99.

14. R. Douglas Geivett and Gary R. Habermas, eds., *In Defense of Miracles: A Comprehensive Case for God's Actions in History* (Downers Grove, IL: InterVarsity, 1997).

15. For an argument defending moral relativism, see Gilbert Harman, "Moral Relativism Defended," in *Relativism: Cognitive and Moral*, ed. Michael Krausz and Jack W. Meiland (Notre Dame: University of Notre Dame Press, 1982), 189–204. John Arthur, in his article "Religion, Morality, and Conscience," in *Morality and Moral Controversies*, ed. John Arthur, 4th ed. (Upper Saddle River, NJ: Prentice Hall, 1996), 21–29, argues that morality is a social convention and need not be based in religion.

16. Michael Ruse and Edward O. Wilson, "The Evolution of Ethics," in *Philosophy of Biology*, ed. Michael Ruse (New York: Macmillan, 1989), 316.

17. Norman Geisler, *The Roots of Evil* (Grand Rapids: Zondervan, 1978), 38.

18. Lewis, *Mere Christianity*, 19–20. For an updated and sophisticated defense of Lewis's argument for God from reason, see Victor Reppert, *C. S. Lewis's Dangerous Idea* (Downers Grove, IL: InterVarsity, 2003).

19. Charles Templeton, *Farewell to God* (Toronto: McClelland & Stewart, 1996), 232.

20. This idea was not my own. I remembered it from a story told by Francis Schaeffer in *The God Who Is There*, 110.

21. See, e.g., the work of Zen expert Alan W. Watts, in which he quotes a Zen master claiming that he came to the realization of his oneness with the cosmos, *The Way of Zen*, 122.

22. For a description of these kinds of practices and their importance in Zen Buddhism, see Alan W. Watts, *The Spirit of Zen* (New York: Grove Press, 1958), 65–81.

23. To deny one of these contradictions, one could also hold that God is impersonal but also changes. However, this raises another philosophical problem: what is causing this impersonal God to change? It seems that for me to change and realize my impersonal divine self, there is a self involved in the process. Of course, this could all be an illusion, but then why worry about changing?

24. Geisler and Watkins offer positive contributions of each of the worldviews in *Worlds Apart*.

Chapter 4 The Fingerprints of God

1. William A. Dembski, "Explaining Specified Complexity," first appeared in *Metanexus: The Online Forum on Religion and Science* (www.metanexus.net); it can also be found at www.leaderu.com/offices/dembski/docs/bd-specified.html.

2. Ibid.

3. For more on SETI and intelligent design, see William A. Dembski, "Reinstating Design within Science," *Rhetoric and Public Affairs* 1, no. 2 (1998): 507–9.

4. For an in-depth explanation of a filter for detecting design, see William A. Dembski, *The Design Inference: Eliminating Chance through Small Probabilities* (Cambridge: Cambridge University Press, 1998), chap. 2.

5. See Walter Bradley, "The 'Just So' Universe," in *Signs of Intelligence: Understanding Intelligent Design*, ed. William A. Dembski and James M. Kushiner (Grand Rapids: Brazos, 2001), 160–63.

6. Paul Davies, *Superforce: The Search for a Grand Unified Theory of Nature* (New York: Simon & Schuster, 1984), 68.

7. Ibid., 243.

8. This data on cosmic constants is drawn from the following sources: John Leslie, "The Prerequisites of Life in Our Universe," in *Philosophy of Religion: A Reader and Guide*, ed. William Lane Craig (New Brunswick, NJ: Rutgers University Press, 2002); John Leslie, *Universes* (New York: Routledge, 1989), 114–29; Paul Davies, *God and the New Physics* (New York: Simon & Schuster, 1983), chap. 13; Davies, *Superforce*; Paul Davies, *The Accidental Universe* (Cambridge: Cambridge University Press, 1982); Hugh Ross, "Astronomical Evidences for a Personal Transcendent God," in Moreland, *Creation Hypothesis*, 160–69; Robin Collins, "The Teleological Argument," in *The Rationality of Theism*, ed. Paul Copan and Paul K. Moser (New York: Routledge, 2003), 132–48; Robin Collins, "A Scientific Argument for the Existence of God: The Fine-Tuning Design Argument," in *Reason for the Hope Within*, ed. Michael J. Murray (Grand Rapids: Eerdmans, 1999), 47–75; and John D. Barrow and Frank J. Tipler, *The Anthropic Cosmological Principle* (New York: Oxford University Press, 1988), 123–575.

9. For a readable and interesting overview of the current state of cosmological theories and various hypotheses on which they depend, see Brian Greene, *The Elegant Universe* (New York: Vintage, 2003). See also John Gribbin, *The Search for Superstrings, Symmetry, and the Theory of Everything* (New York: Little, Brown, 1998).

10. For an insightful analysis of the many-worlds hypothesis, see Robin Collins, "Design and the Many-Worlds Hypothesis," in Craig, *Philosophy of Religion*, 130–48.

11. See Collins, "Teleological Argument," 143–44. Regarding the many-universes hypothesis, philosopher Alvin Plantinga writes: "Well, perhaps all this is logically possible (and then again perhaps not). As a response to a probabilistic argument, however, it's pretty anemic. How would this kind of reply play in Tombstone, or Dodge City? 'Waal, shore, Tex, I *know* it's a leetle mite suspicious that every time I deal I git four aces and a wild card, but have you considered the following? Possibly there is an infinite succession of universes, so that for any possible distribution of possible poker hands, there is a universe in which that possibility is realized; we just happen to find ourselves in one where someone like me always deals himself only aces and wild cards without ever cheating. So put up that shootin' arn and set down 'n shet yore yap, ya dumb galoot'" ("Darwin, Mind and Meaning," originally published in *Books & Culture*, May/June 1996; also at http://id-www.ucsb.edu/fscf/library/plantinga/dennett.html.

12. Collins makes this insightful point in "Design and the Many-Worlds Hypothesis," 137.

13. This comment was offered by my friend and colleague Donald McLaughlin in private conversation.

14. Barrow and Tipler, *Anthropic Cosmological Principle*, 15.

15. Ibid., 1–2.

16. John Leslie, "Anthropic Principle, World Ensemble, Design," *American Philosophical Quarterly* 19 (1982): 150; and "How to Draw Conclusions from a Finely-Tuned Cosmos,"

in *Physics, Philosophy, and Theology: A Common Quest for Understanding*, ed. Robert Russell, Nancey Murphy, and C. J. Isham (Vatican City State: Vatican Observatory Press, 1988), 300.

17. For an excellent analysis of the anthropic principle, see William Lane Craig, "The Teleological Argument and the Anthropic Principle," in William Lane Craig and Mark S. McLeod, eds., *The Logic of Rational Theism* (Lewiston, NY: Mellen, 1990), 127–53.

18. David Hume, *Dialogues Concerning Natural Religion*, pt. 4, 31.

19. Atheist philosopher J. L. Mackie expounds on Hume's critiques of the design argument in *The Miracle of Theism: Arguments for and against the Existence of God* (New York: Oxford University Press, 1982), 133–45. Richard Dawkins makes a similar point as it applies to biological systems in his *Blind Watchmaker: Why the Evidence of Evolution Reveals a Universe without Design* (New York: W. W. Norton, 1987), 141.

20. For a similar argument, see Collins, "Teleological Argument." Many theologians historically have held to God's simplicity, in which God is not divisible into parts of any sort—he lacks all metaphysical composition. For a readable overview of divine simplicity by Thomas Aquinas, see Brian Davies, *The Thought of Thomas Aquinas* (New York: Oxford University Press, 1993), chap. 3.

21. The book that led the way is Phillip Johnson's *Darwin on Trial*, 2nd ed. (Downers Grove, IL: InterVarsity, 1993).

22. Michael Behe, *Darwin's Black Box: The Biochemical Challenge to Evolution* (New York: Free Press, 1996), 39.

23. For an up-to-date overview of bacterial flagella in a standard microbiology textbook, see Lansing M. Prescott, John P. Harley, and Donald A. Klein, *Microbiology*, 6th ed. (New York: McGraw-Hill, 2004).

24. Diagram used by permission of Access Research Network (www.arn.org). For the web image, see http://www.arn.org/docs/mm/flag_labels.jpg.

25. Charles Darwin, *Origin of Species*, 6th ed. (New York: New York University Press, 1988), 154, as quoted in Behe, *Darwin's Black Box*, 39.

26. For an updated version of Behe's argument involving irreducible complexity, see his "Irreducible Complexity: Obstacle to Darwinian Evolution," in *Debating Design: From Darwin to DNA*, ed. William A. Dembski and Michael Ruse (Cambridge: Cambridge University Press, 2004), 352–70; and "The Challenge of Irreducible Complexity," *Natural History* 111 (April 2002): 74. For a critique of the irreducible complexity argument, see Kenneth R. Miller, "The Flagellum Unspin: The Collapse of 'Irreducible Complexity,'" in *Debating Design*, ed. Dembski and Ruse, 81–97; and "The Flaw in the Mousetrap," *Natural History* 111 (April 2002): 75, http://www.naturalhistorymag.com. For further critique, see Niall Shanks, *God, the Devil, and Darwin: A Critique of the Intelligent Design Theory* (New York: Oxford University Press, 2004), esp. chap. 5; and Paul Draper, "Irreducible Complexity and Darwinian Gradualism: A Reply to Michael J. Behe," *Faith and Philosophy* 19 (2002): 3–21.

27. Ernst Mayr, *What Evolution Is* (New York: Basic Books, 2001), 8.

28. As the research of Jonathan Wells indicates (Jonathan Wells, *Icons of Evolution: Science or Myth?* [Washington, DC: Regnery, 2000], 249–58), the following textbooks utilize the peppered moth case as a clear demonstration of natural selection: Burton S. Guttman, *Biology* (Boston: WCB/McGraw-Hill, 1999); Sylvia Mader, *Biology*, 6th ed. (Boston: WCB/McGraw-Hill, 1998); Kenneth R. Miller and Joseph Levine, *Biology*, 5th ed. (Upper Saddle River, NJ: Prentice-Hall, 2000); William D. Shraer and Herbert J. Stoltze, *Biology: The Study of Life*, 7th ed. (Upper Saddle River, NJ: Prentice-Hall, 1999); and Cecie Starr and Ralph Taggart, *Biology: The Unity and Diversity of Life*, 8th ed. (Belmont, CA: Wadsworth, 1998).

29. For an overview of the evidence, see Jonathan Wells, *Icons of Evolution*, chap. 7. Wells is a well-published and recognized scholar who holds Ph.D.s from Yale University and the University of California at Berkeley. See also Judith Hooper, *Of Moths and Men: The Untold Story of Science and the Peppered Moth* (New York: W. W. Norton, 2003).

30. Johnson, *Darwin on Trial*, 69.

31. See, for example, Michael Denton, *Evolution: A Theory in Crisis* (Bethesda, MD: Adler and Adler, 1986).

32. Miller, "Flaw in the Mousetrap," 75.

33. Ibid. For a more comprehensive critique, see his "The Flagellum Unspin."

34. Behe responds to some of Miller's criticisms in his "Irreducible Complexity." For an advanced philosophical critique of the design argument, see Elliott Sober, "The Design Argument," in *Debating Design*, ed. Dembski and Ruse, 98–129. See also Martin, *Atheism*, chap. 5, and Mackie, *The Miracle of Theism*, chap. 8.

35. This information is based on the research of microbiologist Scott Minnich, University of Idaho.

36. Paul Davies, *The Fifth Miracle: The Search for the Origin and Meaning of Life* (New York: Simon & Schuster, 2000), 112. While Davies does not support ID, he admits that scientific laws capable of explaining how life originated are going to have to be significantly different from any laws which are currently known.

37. A. G. Cairns-Smith, *Seven Clues to the Origins of Life: A Scientific Detective Story* (Cambridge: Cambridge University Press, 1986), 6, as quoted in Shanks, *God, the Devil, and Darwin*, 163.

38. Email correspondence. For various reasons, I shall keep the name of my colleague confidential.

39. Cairns-Smith, *Seven Clues*, 6, as quoted in Shanks, *God, the Devil, and Darwin*, 163. Italics added by Shanks.

40. For an excellent critique of methodological naturalism, see J. P. Moreland, "Theistic Science and Methodological Naturalism," in Moreland, *Creation Hypothesis*, 41–66. For a readable explanation of how to develop a scientific research program for investigating the effects of intelligent causes, see William A. Dembski, *Intelligent Design: The Bridge between Science and Theology* (Downers Grove, IL: InterVarsity, 1999).

41. See Flew's interview with Gary Habermas in *Philosophia Christi* 6, no. 2 (2004): 197–211.

Chapter 5 In the Beginning . . . Bang!

1. For a very helpful overview of the wide variety of cosmological arguments, see William Lane Craig, *The Cosmological Argument from Plato to Leibniz* (Eugene, OR: Wipf & Stock, 2001).

2. This argument was developed by the Dominican monk Thomas Aquinas (AD 1224–74) and is referred to as the "Third Way." See his *Summa Theologica*, Benzinger Bros. ed. (Notre Dame, IN: Ave Maria, 1989), 1a2.3.

3. Davies, *God and the New Physics*, 199.

4. For an elaboration of the empirical evidence for the second law, see William Lane Craig, *The Kalam Cosmological Argument* (Eugene, OR: Wipf & Stock, 1979), 130–40.

5. See, e.g., John Gribbin, "Oscillating Universe Bounces Back," in *Nature*, 259 (1976).

6. See Stephen Hawking and George Ellis, eds., *The Large-Scale Structure of Space-Time*, (Cambridge: Cambridge University Press, 1975).

7. See William Lane Craig, "The Ultimate Question of Origins: God and the Beginning of the Universe," *Astrophysics and Space Science*, no. 0 (1999): 723–40; Joseph Silk, *The Big Bang*, 3rd ed. (New York: Times Books, 2000), 269–70.

8. See, e.g., Stephen Hawking, *A Brief History of Time* (New York: Bantam, 1988), 45. See also William Lane Craig, "Philosophical and Scientific Pointers to Creatio ex Nihilo," in *Contemporary Perspectives on Religious Epistemology*, ed. R. Douglas Geivett and Brendan Sweetman (New York: Oxford University Press, 1992), 185–200.

9. For more on points 4 and 5, see especially William Lane Craig, "The Kalam Cosmological Argument," in Craig, *Philosophy of Religion*; and Ross, "Astronomical Evidences for a Personal, Transcendent God," in Moreland, *Creation Hypothesis*, 148–51. See also Alan Guth and Marc Sher, "The Impossibility of a Bouncing Universe," *Nature* 302 (1983), 505–7.

10. For examples of the evidence, see Craig and Smith, *Theism, Atheism, and Big Bang Cosmology*; see also Hugh Ross, *The Fingerprint of God*, 2nd ed. (Orange, CA: Promise, 1991), chap. 9.

11. See, e.g., Paul J. Steinhardt and Neil Turok, "A Cyclical Model of the Universe," *Science* 296, (2002): 1436–39; see also Paul Steinhardt's introductory essay at http://wwwphy.princeton.edu/~steinh/cyclintro.pdf.

12. Stephen Hawking and Roger Penrose, *The Nature of Space and Time*, The Isaac Newton Institute Series of Lectures (Princeton, NJ: Princeton University Press, 1996), 20, as quoted in Craig and Sinnott-Armstrong, *God?* 8.

13. This is a slightly modified version of William Lane Craig's argument spelled out in his book *The Kalam Cosmological Argument*, 103.

14. This argument is presupposing what is referred to as an A-theory of time, in which there is a real flow to time. But this view of time is debated. For a strong defense of it, see William Lane Craig, *Time and Eternity: Exploring God's Relationship to Time* (Wheaton: Crossway, 2001). For several defenses of the B-theory of time, see Nathan Oaklander and Quentin Smith, eds., *The New Theory of Time* (New Haven: Yale University Press, 1994).

15. The field of mathematics that deals with actual infinites is called set theory, and there is lively debate about whether actual infinite sets exist in reality or are mere ideas in the mind. For more on set theory, see Patrick Suppes, *Axiomatic Set Theory* (Mineola, NY: Dover, 1972).

16. William Lane Craig, "The Existence of God and the Beginning of the Universe," *Truth: A Journal of Modern Thought* 3 (1991), 88–89, http://www.leaderu.com/truth/3truth11.html.

17. Nicholas Everitt, *The Nonexistence of God* (New York: Routledge, 2004), 63–65. A similar argument is offered by J. L. Mackie in his *Miracle of Theism*, 93. See also Martin, *Atheism*, 103–6; and William Wainwright, review of Craig, *Kalam Cosmological Argument*, in *Nous* 16 (1982): 328–34.

18. See Aristotle *Physics*, 263a.4–264a.6 in *The Complete Words of Aristotle*, ed. Jonathan Barnes (Princeton, NJ: Princeton University Press, 1984), 1:439–40.

19. For a helpful analysis of Zeno's paradoxes, see Craig, *Kalam Cosmological Argument*, app. 1, "The Kalam Cosmological Argument and Zeno's Paradoxes." See also Max Black, "Achilles and the Tortoise," *Analysis* 15 (1950–51): 91–101.

20. For one interesting exception, see the chapter by atheist philosopher Quentin Smith, "The Uncaused Beginning of the Universe," in Craig and Smith, *Theism, Atheism, and Big Bang Cosmology*, 108–40 (note: this essay is rather technical).

21. For some of this evidence, see the chapter by theistic philosopher William Lane Craig, "The Caused Beginning of the Universe," in Craig and Smith, *Theism, Atheism, and Big Bang Cosmology*, 141–60 (note: this essay is rather technical). For a less technical work on this topic, see Craig, *Kalam Cosmological Argument*, 141–48.

22. Some particle physicists have recently claimed that something can come into existence without a cause, namely, virtual particles. On this view, these theoretical entities pop

into existence in a quantum vacuum, a vacuum that is subject to quantum uncertainties. Given this fact, it is argued, the universe, too, could have popped into existence in such a quantum vacuum. However, this argument is faulty since quantum vacuums are not absolute nothing—they are full of fluctuating energy that can be described by the laws of physics. Furthermore, virtual particles are only "theoretical" entities, and their actual existence is yet to be proved. For more on this, see William Lane Craig, "The Caused Beginning of the Universe: A Reply to Quentin Smith," *British Journal for the Philosophy of Science* 44 (1993), 623–39.

23. Sometime in the past I heard philosopher Norman Geisler give this parable, or at least something close to it.

24. For more on this notion of freedom of the will, see Richard Taylor, *Metaphysics*, 4th ed. (Englewood Cliffs, NJ: Prentice Hall, 1992), chap. 5. For an advanced defense of free will, see Peter Van Inwagen, *An Essay on Free Will* (Oxford: Clarendon, 1983).

Chapter 6 Morality, Evil, and Religion

1. See, e.g., Ruth Benedict, "Anthropology and the Abnormal," *The Journal of General Psychology* 10 (1934): 59–82, reprinted as "A Defense of Ethical Relativism" in *Right and Wrong: Basic Readings in Ethics*, ed. Christina Hoff Sommers (New York: Harcourt Brace Jovanovich, 1986), 133–41.

2. These examples are taken from ethicist James Rachels, *The Elements of Moral Philosophy*, 3rd ed. (New York: McGraw-Hill, 1999), 23–24.

3. From Walter T. Stace, *The Concept of Morals* (New York: Macmillan, 1937), reprinted as "Ethical Relativism: A Critique," in *Right and Wrong*, ed. Sommers, 146.

4. For more on this point, see Bimal Krishna Matilal, "Ethical Relativism and Confrontation of Cultures," in Michael Krausz, *Relativism: Interpretation and Confrontation* (Notre Dame, IN: University of Notre Dame Press, 1989), 339–62.

5. For an interesting collection of a universal set of moral standards, see C. S. Lewis, *The Abolition of Man* (San Francisco: HarperSanFrancisco, 2001), app.

6. Rachels spells out a version of this argument in *Elements of Moral Philosophy*, 47.

7. A statement by Ted Bundy, paraphrased and rewritten by Harry V. Jaffa, *Homosexuality and the Natural Law* (Montclair, CA: Claremont Institute of the Study of Statesmanship and Political Philosophy, 1990), 3–4; Louis P. Pojman, *Ethics: Discovering Right and Wrong*, 5th ed. (Belmont, CA: Thompson Wadsworth, 2006), 30.

8. For a concise introductory assessment of moral relativism, see Pojman, *Ethics*, chap. 2.

9. For a very helpful overview and critique of scientism, see Moreland, *Creation Hypothesis*, intro. and chap. 1.

10. Again, note Lewis, *Abolition of Man*, app.

11. For a philosophical definition and analysis of transworld depravity, see Plantinga, *God, Freedom, and Evil*, 45–53.

12. Dawkins, *Selfish Gene*, v.

13. Ruse and Wilson, "Evolution of Ethics," 316.

14. For more on how we know such truths, see Moreland and Craig, *Philosophical Foundations*, 71–129. For rebutting the skeptic, see also Roderick Chisholm, *The Problem of the Criterion* (Milwaukee: Marquette University Press, 1973).

15. Charles Darwin, letter to William Graham Down, July 3, 1881, in *The Life and Letters of Charles Darwin, Including an Autobiographical Chapter*, ed. Francis Darwin (London: John Murray, 1887), 1:315–16, as quoted in Alvin Plantinga, *Warrant and Proper Function* (New York: Oxford University Press, 1993), 219.

16. Plantinga, *Warrant and Proper Function*, 219.

17. Craig and Sinnott-Armstrong, *God?* 33.

18. For an insightful overview of this point, see George Mavrodes, "Religion and the Queerness of Morality," in *Rationality, Religious Belief, and Moral Commitment*, ed. Robert Audi and William Wainwright (Ithaca, NY: Cornell University Press, 1986).

19. Cf. Schaeffer, *He Is There and He Is Not Silent*. On page 20 Schaeffer offers these insightful words: "If one starts with an impersonal beginning, the answer to morals eventually turns out to be the assertion that there are no morals (in however a sophisticated way this may be expressed). This is true whether one begins with the Eastern pantheism . . . or with the energy particle. With an impersonal beginning, everything is finally equal in the area of morals. With an impersonal beginning, eventually morals are just another form of metaphysics, of being."

20. Hume, *Dialogues Concerning Natural Religion*, 63.

21. Sinnott-Armstrong offers this argument in Craig and Sinnott-Armstrong, *God?* 85.

22. Some of these examples come from the insightful article by Marilyn McCord Adams, "Horrendous Evils and the Goodness of God," in *The Problem of Evil*, ed. Marilyn McCord Adams and Robert Merrihew Adams (New York: Oxford University Press, 1990), 211–12. Marilyn McCord Adams coined the phrase "horrendous evil."

23. Plantinga, *God, Freedom, and Evil*, 30.

24. See Julian of Norwich, *Revelations of Divine Love* in *The Treasury of Christian Spiritual Classics* (Nashville: Thomas Nelson, 1994), 352–53. Any edition is fine. I am indebted to Marilyn McCord Adams for noting this point. For more on this response to horrendous evils, see her "Horrendous Evils."

25. As quoted by Peter Kreeft in Lee Strobel, *The Case for Faith* (Grand Rapids: Zondervan, 2000), 47.

Chapter 7 Divine Revelation

1. However, a recent discovery in China may bring the earliest writing to 6000 BC. Archaeologists at Jiahu in Henan Province, western China, have identified eleven separate symbols inscribed on tortoise shells. The shells were found buried along with human remains in twenty-four Neolithic graves. Radiocarbon dating has them dated somewhere between 6600 and 6200 BC. The verdict is still out on this one. Paul Rincon, "'Earliest Writing' Found in China," BBC News, April 17, 2003, http://news.bbc.co.uk/1/hi/sci/tech/2956925.htm.

2. Critics have claimed that Moses could not have written the first five books of the Bible, as it has historically been believed, since, they argue, writing had not yet been developed. But now the archaeological evidence confirms that not only one, but five different systems of writing existed around the time and place of Moses. For a fascinating overview of the most recent evidence for the historical basis of ancient written treaties (such as the Sinai covenant in the book of Deuteronomy) being written in the late second millennium BC, see K. A. Kitchen, *On the Reliability of the Old Testament* (Grand Rapids: Eerdmans, 2003), 299–312.

3. The Jewish historian Josephus noted that no new book was added to the collection after the time of the Persian king Artaxerxes (c. 465–425 BC) in his *Against Apion*, in *Josephus: The Life against Apion*, trans. H. St. J. Thackeray, Loeb Classical Library (Cambridge, MA: Harvard University Press, 1926), 1.8.

4. For recent and helpful discussions on these issues, see Iain Provan, V. Philips Long, and Tremper Longman III, *A Biblical History of Israel* (Louisville: Westminster John Knox, 2003); and David M. Howard Jr. and Michael A. Grisanti, eds., *Giving the Sense: Understanding and Using Old Testament Historical Texts* (Grand Rapids: Kregel, 2003).

5. These three basic tests of historiography regarding historical writings (primarily aimed at Shakespeare and others), were first developed by Chauncey Sanders in his *In-*

troduction to Research in English Literary History (New York: Macmillan, 1952). They have proven to be invaluable aids in determining the veracity of ancient writings, and they have been utilized by a number of Christian apologists in determining the reliability of the Bible. See, e.g., Josh McDowell, *The New Evidence That Demands a Verdict* (Nashville: Thomas Nelson, 1999), and J. P. Moreland, *Scaling the Secular City* (Grand Rapids: Baker, 1987), 133–57.

6. Neil R. Lightfoot, *How We Got the Bible*, 3rd ed. (Grand Rapids: Baker, 2003), 132.

7. This information is noted by Bill T. Arnold and Bryan E. Beyer in their helpful and concise text, *Encountering the Old Testament* (Grand Rapids: Baker, 1999), 27.

8. Gleason L. Archer, *A Survey of Old Testament Introduction* (Chicago: Moody, 1994), 72–73.

9. Ibid., 44.

10. For more on the transmission of the Old Testament from a well-respected scholar in the field (and a leading expert on the Dead Sea Scrolls), see Emmanuel Tov, *Textual Criticism of the Hebrew Bible*, 2nd rev. ed. (Minneapolis: Augsburg Fortress, 2001).

11. Thomas L. Thompson, *The Historicity of the Patriarchal Narratives* (Berlin: de Gruyter, 1974); and John Van Seters, *Abraham in History and Tradition* (New Haven: Yale University Press, 1975).

12. James Hoffmeier, "The North Sinai Archaeological Project's Excavations at Tell el-Borg (Sinai): An Example of the 'New' Biblical Archaeology?" in *The Future of Biblical Archaeology: Reassessing Methodologies and Assumptions*, ed. James Hoffmeier and Alan Millard (Grand Rapids: Eerdmans, 2004), 53. This excellent collection of essays is a compendium of the proceedings of a symposium, August 12–14, 2001, at Trinity International University.

13. Wellhausen published his thesis in 1886 in a book titled *Prolegomena zur Geschichte Israels* [Prolegomena to the History of Israel] (repr.; Whitefish, MT: Kessiger, 2004).

14. For a full but concise discussion of the documentary hypothesis, see E. E. Carpenter, "Pentateuch," in *The International Standard Bible Encyclopedia*, ed. Geoffrey W. Bromiley (Grand Rapids: Eerdmans, 1986), 3:740–53.

15. James K. Hoffmeier, *Israel in Egypt: The Evidence for the Authenticity of the Exodus Tradition* (New York: Oxford University Press, 1996).

16. Isaac M. Kikawada and Arthur Quinn, *Before Abraham Was* (Nashville: Abingdon, 1985). For a thorough work on the *linguistic* unity of Genesis from beginning to end, see Gary A. Rendsburg, *The Redaction of Genesis* (Winona Lake, IN: Eisenbrauns, 1986).

17. The flood account chiasm is taken from Kikawada and Quinn, *Before Abraham Was*, 104.

18. Ibid., 83.

19. For a concise overview of the demise of the documentary hypothesis, see Hoffmeier, *Israel in Egypt*, chap. 1.

20. However, for a recent defense of the documentarty hypothesis, see Richard E. Friedman, *Who Wrote the Bible?* reprint ed. (San Francisco: HarperSanFrancisco, 1997).

21. I am indebted to Paul Little and Norman Geisler for noting these important points. For more on them, see Norman Geisler and William E. Nix, *A General Introduction to the Bible*, rev. ed. (Chicago: Moody, 1986); and Paul E. Little, *Know Why You Believe*, 4th ed. (Downers Grove, IL: InterVarsity, 2000).

22. Norman L. Geisler and William E. Nix make this point in their book *From God to Us: How We Got Our Bible* (Chicago: Moody, 1974), 54–55.

23. Norman Geisler and Thomas Howe, *When Critics Ask* (Wheaton: Victor, 1992), provide responses to many of the apparent discrepancies in the Bible. For more on difficult or troubling passages, see Walter C. Kaiser Jr., Peter H. Davids, F. F. Bruce, and Manfred T. Brauch, *Hard Sayings of the Bible* (Downers Grove, IL: InterVarsity, 1996).

24. For more on this, see Iain W. Provan, "In the Stable with Dwarves: Testimony, Interpretation, Faith, and the History of Israel," in *Windows into Old Testament History: Evidence, Argument, and the Crisis of "Biblical Israel*," ed. V. Philips Long, David W. Baker, and Gordon J. Wehham (Grand Rapids: Eerdmans, 2002), 161–97. For an excellent work on how to avoid the fallacies that historians often make, see David Hackett Fischer, *Historian's Fallacies: Toward Logic of Historical Thought* (New York: Harper Torchbooks, 1970).

25. For an overview of exciting developments in this arena, see David W. Baker and Bill T. Arnold, eds., *The Face of Old Testament Studies: A Survey of Contemporary Approaches* (Grand Rapids: Baker, 1999), esp. 19–115 and 145–75.

26. Much of the following information is derived from Kitchen, *On the Reliability of the Old Testament*.

27. For an interesting visual experience of some of these finds, visit the Online Semitic Museum at http://www.fas.harvard.edu/~semitic/hsm/NFNuziTablets.htm.

28. For a concise and readable overview of archaeological discoveries and other historical issues relevant to the Bible, see the journal *Bible and Spade*. 18, no. 1 (Winter 2005), which has a short essay on the Mari and Nuzi Tablets.

29. For a well-researched text dealing with the exodus account, see Hoffmeier, *Israel in Egypt*.

30. Philip R. Davies, professor of religious studies at the University of Sheffield in England, as quoted in John Noble Wilford, "A New Armageddon Erupts over Ancient Battlefield," *New York Times*, January 4, 2000, http://home.gwu.edu/~ehcline/NYTarticle2.html.

31. Aureham Biran, "David Found at Dan" *Biblical Archaeology Review* 20, no. 2 (March/April 1994): 26.

32. To view pictures of Hezekiah's water channel, visit http://holylandphotos.org/whats_new.asp?d=m1.

33. For more on the ration dockets, see J. B. Pritchard, ed., *Ancient Near Eastern Texts Relating to the Old Testament*, 3rd ed. (Princeton, NJ: Princeton University Press, 1969), 308.

34. For more on this, see Deborah W. Rooke, *Zadok's Heirs: The Role and Development of the High Priesthood in Ancient Israel* (New York: Oxford University Press, 2000).

35. Special thanks to David Cramer for his helpful research assistance for this section and for the formation of this chart.

36. These references are from the historical books of the Bible only. Wisdom literature and prophets could also be included.

37. This quote is from Old Testament scholar Eugene Carpenter in private conversation. See also Provan, Long, and Longman, *Biblical History of Israel*, 43–56.

38. William F. Albright, *Archaeology and the Religions of Israel* (Baltimore: Johns Hopkins University Press, 1956), 176.

39. This chart is adapted from Norman L. Geisler, *Christian Apologetics* (Grand Rapids: Baker, 1976), 307; and Moreland, *Scaling the Secular City*, 135.

40. For an up-to-date overview of the early manuscripts, see Lightfoot, *How We Got the Bible*, chaps. 3–6, 11.

41. Sir Frederic Kenyon, *The Bible and Archaeology* (New York: Harper & Brothers, 1940), 288.

42. Moreland, *Scaling the Secular City*, 138.

43. For more on this point, see Francis A. Schaeffer, *A Christian View of the Bible as Truth*, vol. 2 of *The Complete Works of Francis A. Schaeffer*, 2nd ed. (Westchester, IL: Crossway, 1982).

44. These examples are cited in Jeffery L. Sheler, *Is the Bible True? How Modern Debates and Discoveries Affirm the Essence of the Scriptures* (San Francisco: HarperSanFrancisco,

1999), 110–13. See also John J. Rousseau and Rami Arav, *Jesus and His World* (Minneapolis: Fortress Press, 1995).

45. As quoted on Beliefnet.com, http://www.beliefnet.com/story/115/story_11561_html. For more on the James ossuary, see Hershel Shanks and Ben Witherington, *The Brother of Jesus: The Dramatic Story and Meaning of the First Archaeological Link to Jesus and His Family* (San Francisco: HarperSanFrancisco, 2003).

46. For more on archaeological finds relating to the New Testament, see John McRay, *Archaeology and the New Testament* (Grand Rapids: Baker, 1991).

47. See Wilhelm Schneemelcher, ed., and R. McL. Wilson, trans., *New Testament Apocrypha*, vols. 1 and 2 (Louisville: Westminster John Knox, 1991). See also Bart D. Ehrman, *Lost Scriptures: Books That Did Not Make It into the New Testament* (New York: Oxford University Press, 2003).

48. This point is noted by F. F. Bruce in his book *The New Testament Documents: Are They Reliable?* rev. 5th ed. (Downers Grove, IL: InterVarsity, 1960), 98–99.

49. For more on archaeology and the New Testament, see Edwin M. Yamauchi, "Archaeology and the New Testament," in *The Expositor's Bible Commentary*, vol. 1, ed. Frank E. Gaebelein (Grand Rapids: Zondervan, 1979), 647–69.

50. The scholar is Sir David Dalrymple, and his quote can be found in Geisler and Nix, *From God to Us*, 157.

51. These four elements are described by Archer, *Survey of Old Testament Introduction*, 331–32.

52. For a helpful collection of many of the messianic prophecies, see Abram K. Abraham, *New Testament Fulfillment of Old Testament Prophecies* (Westwood, NJ: Barbour, 1987).

53. This chart is adapted from Ron Rhodes, *Christ before the Manger* (Grand Rapids: Baker, 1992), 235–36, and is used courtesy of his kind permission.

54. For an interesting attempt to specify the probabilities of various prophecies, see Hugh Ross, "Fulfilled Prophecy: Evidence for the Reliability of the Bible," http://www.reasons.org/resources/apologetics/prophecy.shtml.

55. John Calvin, *Institutes of the Christian Religion* (repr.; Philadelphia: Westminster, 1960), 1.7.80. For the role of the witness of God's Spirit to the inerrancy of Scripture, see R. C. Sproul, "The Internal Witness of the Holy Spirit," in *Inerrancy*, ed. Norman L. Geisler (Grand Rapids: Zondervan, 1980), 337–54.

56. For a careful study of the recidivism rates among inmates who were involved in Prison Fellowship, see Byron R. Johnson, David B. Larson, and Timothy C. Pitts, "Religious Programs, Institutional Adjustment, and Recidivism among Former Inmates in Prison Fellowship Programs," *Justice Quarterly* 14, no. 1 (March 1997), http://www.leaderu.com/humanities/johnson.html.

57. Mahatma Gandhi (1869–1948) was an Indian nationalist and spiritual leader. This is a widely referenced quote, but its original source is unobtainable.

Chapter 8 The Resurrection of Jesus

1. For helpful sources on these alleged facts from a wide variety of perspectives, see the following sources.

Pro bodily resurrection: William Lane Craig, *The Son Rises: The Historical Evidence for the Resurrection of Jesus* (Eugene, OR: Wipf & Stock, 1981); idem, *Assessing the New Testament Evidence for the Historicity of the Resurrection of Jesus* (Lewiston, NY: Mellen, 1989); Robert E. Van Voorst, *Jesus Outside the New Testament: An Introduction to the Ancient Evidences* (Grand Rapids: Eerdmans, 2000); Gary R. Habermas, *The Historical Jesus: Ancient Evidence for the Life of Christ* (Joplin, MO: College Press, 1996); Stephen T. Davis, *Risen Indeed: Making Sense of the Resurrection* (Grand Rapids: Eerdmans, 1993).

Against bodily resurrection: Gerd Lüdemann, *The Resurrection of Christ: A Historical Inquiry* (Amherst, NY: Prometheus, 2004); Robert M. Price and Jeffery Jay Lowder, eds., *The Empty Tomb: Jesus Beyond the Grave* (Amherst, NY: Prometheus, 2005); John Dominick Crossan, *Jesus: A Revolutionary Biography* (San Francisco: HarperSanFrancisco, 1995); John Shelby Spong, *Resurrection: Myth or Reality?* (San Francisco: HarperSanFrancisco, 1994); Michael Martin, *The Case against Christianity* (Philadelphia: Temple University Press, 1991).

2. For some examples, see Gary R. Habermas and Michael R. Licona, *The Case for the Resurrection of Jesus* (Grand Rapids: Kregel, 2004), 48–49; and Gerard S. Sloyan, *The Crucifixion of Jesus: History, Myth, Faith* (Philadelphia: Fortress, 1977).

3. William D. Edwards, Wesley J. Gabel, and Floyd E. Hosmer, "On the Physical Death of Jesus Christ," *Journal of the American Medical Association* 225, no. 11 (March 21, 1986): 1455–63.

4. For an excellent overview of these sources, see Habermas, *Historical Jesus*, 143–255.

5. *Annals*, 15.44, as quoted in ibid., 188.

6. It should be noted, however, that one scholar, John Dominic Crossan, believes that, while Jesus was crucified, he was not buried in a tomb but rather was probably buried in a common shallow grave and eaten by wild dogs after his crucifixion. See his *Jesus: A Revolutionary Biography* as well as Richard N. Ostling, "Jesus Christ, Plain and Simple" *Time*, January 10, 1994. For a response to Crossan's views about Jesus's burial and alleged resurrection, see Gregory Boyd, *Cynic, Sage, or Son of God?* (Wheaton: Bridgepoint, 1995), chap. 13. For a debate between Crossan and Craig, see *Will the Real Jesus Please Stand Up? A Debate between William Lane Craig and John Dominic Crossan*, ed. Paul Copan (Grand Rapids: Baker, 1998).

7. For an elaboration of these points, as well as other supporting evidence for Jesus being placed in a tomb, see Craig, *Son Rises*, 46–67.

8. While not as firmly held by skeptical scholars as the other historical truths mentioned, scholar Gary Habermas notes that roughly 75 percent of scholars who have written on the subject hold to the view that the tomb was empty based on the evidence. See Habermas and Licona, *Case for the Resurrection of Jesus*, 69–70.

9. For an analysis of how there was insufficient time for these accounts to be legend, see Craig, *Son Rises*, 100–108.

10. See Murray J. Harris, *Raised Immortal: Resurrection and Immortality in the New Testament* (Grand Rapids: Eerdmans, 1985).

11. Michael Grant, *Jesus: An Historian's Review of the Gospels* (New York: Charles Scribner's Sons, 1977), 176, as quoted in Strobel, *Case for Christ*, 215.

12. For more on the empty tomb, see Davis, *Risen Indeed*, chap. 4; and Craig, *Son Rises*, chap. 3.

13. For an overview of the historical value of the Gospel evidence for Jesus, see R. T. France, *The Evidence for Jesus* (Downers Grove, IL: InterVarsity, 1986), 93–139.

14. New Testament scholar Wolfhart Pannenberg demonstrates this point in his fine work *Jesus—God and Man*, 2nd ed., trans. Lewis L. Wilkins and Duane A. Priebe (Philadelphia: Westminster, 1977), 88–106.

15. See, e.g., Pannenberg, *Jesus—God and Man*, 90.

16. Craig, *Son Rises*, 107. For an overview of this point, see 100–107.

17. For an advanced discussion of this point, see Craig, *Assessing the New Testament Evidence*, 1–49.

18. For a helpful analysis of these appearances and their relation to the empty tomb, see Pannenberg, *Jesus—God and Man*, 88–106.

19. Colleague and New Testament scholar Fred Long first made me aware of this significant point.

20. For a concise overview of the apostle Paul, see John W. Drane, "Paul," in *The Oxford Guide to People and Places of the Bible*, ed. Bruce M. Metzger and Michael D. Coogan (New York: Oxford University Press, 2001), 228–32. For an in-depth overview of the life, ministry, and theology of Paul, see F. F. Bruce, *Paul: Apostle of the Heart Set Free* (Grand Rapids: Eerdmans, 1977).

21. For a listing of some of these events, see Acts 14:19; 16:19–24; 21:27–36; 2 Corinthians 11:23–28. For an overview of nonbiblical sources regarding these events in the life of Paul, see Habermas and Licona, *Case for the Resurrection of Jesus*, 57–59.

22. For more on James from a variety of perspectives, see Bruce Chilton and Jacob Neusner, *The Brother of Jesus: James the Just and His Mission* (Philadelphia: Westminster John Knox, 2001).

23. For solid documentation of these numbers, see David B. Barrett and Todd M. Johnson, *World Christian Trends AD 30–AD 2200: Interpreting the Annual Christian Megacensus* (Pasadena, CA: William Carey Library, 2001), 227–64. For early Christian and non-Christian sources on the execution of the disciples, see Habermas and Licona, *Case for the Resurrection of Jesus*, 56–62.

24. Barrett and Johnson, *World Christian Trends*, 230. For more on the persecution of Christians, see the classic by John Foxe (AD 1517–87), *Foxe's Book of Martyrs: A History of the Lives, Sufferings, and Deaths of the Early Christian and Protestant Martyrs*, ed. William Byron Forbush (repr.; Grand Rapids: Zondervan, 1978).

25. Barrett and Johnson, *World Christian Trends*, 227–31.

26. For documentation of many of these experiences from all around the world, see Jane Rumph, *Stories from the Front Lines* (Longwood, FL: Xulon Press, 2001).

27. See the research of J. Dudley Woodberry and Russell G. Shubin at http://www.missionfrontiers.org/2001/01/muslim.htm.

28. Gary R. Collins, in a personal conversation with Gary R. Habermas and J. P. Moreland, as quoted in Gary R. Habermas and J. P. Moreland, *Beyond Death* (Wheaton, IL: Crossway, 1998), 119–20.

29. For more on the work of Habermas regarding hallucinations and delusions of Jesus, see Habermas and Licona, *Case for the Resurrection of Jesus*, 104–10.

30. For more on the frequency of visual hallucinations, see the more than five hundred citations at the National Center for Biotechnology Information at http://www.ncbi.nlm.nih.gov/entrez/query.fcgi?cmd=Search&db=PubMed&term=frequency+of+visual+hallucinations&tool=QuerySuggestion.

31. See Martin, *Case against Christianity*, 91–95.

32. Paul Copan and Ronald K. Tacelli, eds., *Jesus' Resurrection: Fact or Figment?* (Downers Grove, IL: InterVarsity, 2000), 53.

33. Edwards, Gabel, and Hosmer, "On the Physical Death of Jesus Christ," 1458ff.

34. Gary Habermas and Antony Flew, *Did Jesus Rise from the Dead? The Resurrection Debate*, ed. Terry L. Miethe (New York: Harper & Row, 1987), 6.

35. Oxford philosopher Richard Swinburne argues that the character of God is such that it supports the probability of Jesus's resurrection. See his *The Resurrection of God Incarnate* (New York: Oxford University Press, 2003).

36. C. S. Lewis, *Mere Christianity*, 55–56.

37. For more on Jesus's claims to divinity and the Trinity in general, see James R. White, *The Forgotten Trinity* (Minneapolis: Bethany House, 1998).

38. Josh McDowell develops Lewis's trilemma in his classic work *Evidence That Demands a Verdict*, 103–7.

39. For an insightful overview of a discussion with psychologist Gary Collins on Jesus's character and sanity, see "The Psychological Evidence: Was Jesus Crazy When He Claimed to Be the Son of God?" in Strobel, *Case for Christ*, 144–54.

40. This is not a direct quote but is close to something Dr. Willard stated in a sermon several years ago. For more on the risen Jesus as the Son of God, see N. T. Wright, *The Resurrection of the Son of God* (Minneapolis: Fortress, 2003), 719–38.

41. See the last few lines of Plato's *Phaedo*.

42. Used by the kind permission of the Navigators. For more on the Bridge Illustration, see http://home.navigators.org/us.

43. See John 3:16–18; 5:24; Romans 10:13; Ephesians 2:8–9; 1 John 5:12–13.

Chapter 9 Reaching the Peak

1. I am indebted to Dallas Willard for his invaluable insights on the theme of this chapter. My understanding of the Christian faith has been immeasurably transformed because of his writings, teachings, and sermons. He is, in my opinion, God's prophet for our day.

2. In *The World's Religions*, an enlightening work by Huston Smith (San Francisco: HarperSanFrancisco, 1991), Smith claims that the three major things people want in life are (1) being—no healthy person wants to die, (2) knowledge—we are insatiably curious, and (3) joy—the opposite of frustration and boredom. And we want each of these infinitely! For more on this, see esp. pp. 19–22.

3. For more on the world's religions and their answer to the human condition from experts within each of the traditions, see Arvind Sharma, ed., *Our Religions* (San Francisco: HarperSanFrancisco, 1993).

4. Dallas Willard, *The Divine Conspiracy: Rediscovering Our Hidden Life in God* (San Francisco: HarperSanFrancisco, 1998), chap. 2.

5. Smith, *World's Religions*, 20.

6. For an interesting work on the Hindu gospel, see Sri Ramakrishna, *The Gospel of Sri Ramakrishna*, trans. Swami Nikhilananda (New York: Ramakrishna-Vivekananda Center, 1980).

7. There are different strains of Judaism, and not all of them would adhere to these practices.

8. Marcus Borg makes this point in his work with N. T. Wright, *The Meaning of Jesus: Two Visions* (New York: HarperSanFrancisco, 1999), 72.

9. A. T. Robinson, *But That I Can't Believe* (London: Collins-Fontana, 1967), 52. I am indebted to Dallas Willard for noting this reference.

10. This has not always been the case, however. There are also a number of conservative organizations that are heavily focused on the physical needs of the "down and out." The Salvation Army, World Vision, and Prison Fellowship are three prime examples.

11. For an overview of the history of the social gospel movement in the United States, see Ronald C. White and C. Howard Hopkins, *Social Gospel: Religion and Reform in Changing America* (Philadelphia: Temple University Press, 1975). For a unique call to reach a broken world, see Bruce Rauschenbusch, *A Theology for the Social Gospel* (Louisville: Westminster John Knox, 1997).

12. For more on the human potential movement globally, see *Encyclopedia of World Problems and Human Potential*, http://www.uia.org/encyclopedia/volall.php#potential.

13. In Greek and Roman mythology, there even existed the Fates—three goddesses who determined human destiny. For a concise overview of divine providence, especially as reflected in Christianity, see the *Catholic Encyclopedia*, "Divine Providence," http://www. newadvent.org/cathen/12510a.htm.

14. For a very readable philosophical analysis of the distinction between determinism and fatalism, see Taylor, *Metaphysics*, chap. 6.

15. For more on the historic meaning of *qadar*, see "Qadar" in *The Oxford Dictionary of World Religions*, ed. John Bowker (New York: Oxford University Press, 1997).

16. For more on the meaning of *daiva* and *karma*, see *The Oxford Dictionary of World Religions*; and Satguru Sivaya Subramuniyaswami, *Dancing with Siva: Hinduism's Contemporary Catechism*, 6th ed. (India; Kapaa, HI: Himalayan Academy Publications, 1997).

17. John Calvin, *Concerning the Eternal Predestination of God*, trans. J. K. S. Reid (London: James Clarke, 1961), 10.12, as quoted in Robert Shank, *Elect in the Son: A Study of the Doctrine of Election* (Minneapolis: Bethany House, 1989), 139, italics mine.

18. For a concise listing of some of Calvin's own comments in support of indeterminism, see Shank, *Elect in the Son*, 135–43.

19. Ulrich Zwingli, *On Providence and Other Essays* (repr.; Durham, NC: Labyrinth, 1983), 18182, italics mine.

20. For helpful examples of both sides of the Calvinism-Arminianism debate (which tends to focus on free will, determinism, and fate), see *The Grace of God, the Bondage of the Will*, vol. 2 of *Historical and Theological Perspectives on Calvinism*, ed. Thomas R. Schreiner and Bruce A. Ware (Grand Rapids: Baker, 1995); and Paul Marston and Roger Forster, *God's Strategy in Human History* (Eugene, OR: Wipf & Stock, 2000). Millard J. Erickson does a fine job of navigating these theological waters in his magisterial work *Christian Theology*, 2nd ed. (Grand Rapids: Baker, 1998), esp. chaps. 19, 44.

21. For an overview of the main elements of Stoicism, see *The Cambridge Companion to the Stoics*, ed. Brad Inwood (Cambridge: Cambridge University Press, 2003).

22. See, e.g., Romans 3:20–23; 6:23; 1 Corinthians 15:56. Other biblical references include John 16:7–11; James 1:14–15; 1 John 1:8; 3:6–9.

23. John R. W. Stott, *Basic Christianity* (Downers Grove, IL: InterVarsity, 1971), 81.

24. For a comprehensive overview of early Christian thought in the context of the history, worldview, and social makeup of Palestinian Judaism and its place in Greco-Roman culture, see N. T. Wright, *The New Testament and the People of God* (Minneapolis: Fortress, 1992). See also James S. Jeffers, *The Greco-Roman World of the New Testament Era: Exploring the Background of Early Christianity* (Downers Grove, IL: InterVarsity, 1999).

25. See, e.g., Albert Schweitzer, *The Mystery of the Kingdom of God: The Secret of Jesus' Messiahship and Passion* (repr.; New York: Prometheus, 1985).

26. See, e.g., Adolf von Harnack, *What Is Christianity?* trans. Thomas Bailey Sanders (New York: Harper & Row, 1957).

27. George Eldon Ladd, *The Gospel of the Kingdom: Scriptural Studies in the Kingdom of God* (repr.; Grand Rapids: Eerdmans, 1959, repr. 2002), 21. Ladd's work on the kingdom of God is renowned. His most well-known scholarly work on the topic is *The Presence of the Future: The Eschatology of Biblical Realism* (Grand Rapids: Eerdmans, 1974).

28. This is my brief summary of Camelot. For many interesting tales about King Arthur and Camelot, see Sir Thomas Malory, *Le Morte d'Arthur*, reissue ed. (New York: Modern Library, 1994).

29. For an appealing Hollywood adaptation of King Arthur and Camelot that captures much of what I am referring to here in terms of a good kingdom, see the movie *First Knight*, starring Sean Connery, Richard Gere, and Julia Ormond.

30. For an insightful work on Jesus's kingdom parables, see G. Campbell Morgan, *Parables of the Kingdom* (Eugene, OR: Wipf & Stock, 1998). For more on Jesus's parables, see Robert Farrer Capon, *Kingdom, Grace, Judgment: Paradox, Outrage, and Vindication in the Parables of Jesus* (Grand Rapids: Eerdmans, 2002).

31. There is another interpretation of this passage in which Jesus is understood to be intentionally hiding the truth so that people will not find it. In other words, Jesus does not want people to be saved, so he hides the truth from them. This interpretation makes no sense in the light of the love for the world by Jesus and God the Father. See, e.g., John

3:16–17; Ephesians 3:18–19; Romans 5:18–19; 1 Timothy 4:10; Hebrews 2:9; 1 John 2:2; 4:7–19. This is not to deny that sometimes Jesus used parables as a pronouncement of judgment against those opposed to God, as he does in Mark 12:1–12.

32. As New Testament scholar D. A. Carson explains in his commentary on Matthew in *The Expositor's Bible Commentary*, vol. 8, ed. Frank E. Gaebelein (Grand Rapids: Zondervan, 1984), 317–19, there is more going on in this parable than mere size.

33. I was made aware of this research through William Lane Craig's debate with Walter Sinnott-Armstrong in *God?* 122. It is based on the excellent research of *Mission Frontiers* magazine (November 1990) and www.missionfrontiers.org. Special thanks to my research assistant David Wright for his invaluable research and graphics work on this diagram and to my colleague Robert Myers for his helpful data analysis.

34. See Willard, *Divine Conspiracy*, chap. 4.

35. For a sampling of Jesus's proclamations on repentance, see Matthew 3:2; 4:17; Mark 1:15; Luke 13:3, 5; Revelation 2:5, 16.

36. This prayer, offered by Richard Foster in his *Prayers from the Heart* (New York: HarperCollins, 1994), 24, is slightly modified as indicated by the brackets.

37. I heard Dallas Willard offer an analogy similar to this one in a sermon he once gave. Unfortunately, I do not remember where or when.

38. It should be noted here that faith is not a work deserving of recompense (cf. Rom. 4:3–5). It may take effort, but it involves no earnings. If I tell someone to hold out his hand because I have a gift for him, and he trusts me enough to hold out his hand to receive what I promise, he certainly has not earned the twenty-dollar bill I give him!

39. Richard Foster's book, *Celebration of Discipline: The Path to Spiritual Growth*, 20th anniversary ed. (SanFrancisco: HarperSanFrancisco, 1998), changed my spiritual life. I read it nearly every year with unending benefit.

Index

221

Chad V. Meister (Ph.D., Marquette University) is the former head of Defenders (now called Truthquest), an apologetics ministry at Willow Creek Community Church. While pursuing his Ph.D. in philosophy, Chad developed the Apologetics Pyramid method highlighted in this book. It is based on his own journey from a spiritually seeking engineer to a convinced Christian philosopher. He is currently an assistant professor of philosophy at Bethel College in Indiana.